Property Investing

3rd Australian Edition

by Nicola McDougall and Bruce Brammall

A Wiley Brand

T0324629

Property Investing For Dummies®, 3rd Australian Edition

Published by

John Wiley & Sons Australia, Ltd

Level 1, 155 Cremorne Street

Richmond, Vic 3121

www.dummies.com

Copyright © 2023 John Wiley & Sons Australia, Ltd

The moral rights of the authors have been asserted.

ISBN: 978-1-394-17048-7

A catalogue record for this book is available from the National Library of Australia

Cover image: © Shuang Li/Shutterstock

Typeset by Straive

Contents at a Glance

Table of Contents

Introduction

Welcome to *Property Investing For Dummies*, 3rd Australian Edition! We're delighted to be your tour guides. Throughout this book, we emphasise three fundamental cornerstones that we believe to be true:

» Property is one of the three time-tested ways for people of varied economic means to build wealth (the others are shares and small business). Over the long term, you should be able to make an annual total return of around 7 to 9 per cent per year investing in real estate.

» Investing in real estate isn't rocket science but does require doing your homework. If you're sloppy with your legwork, you're more likely to end up with inferior properties or to overpay for a property. Our book clearly explains how to buy the best properties at a fair (even below-market) price. (Although we cover all types of properties, our book concentrates on residential investment opportunities, which are more accessible and appropriate for non-experts.)

» Although you should make money over the long term investing in good real estate properties, you can lose money, especially in the short term. Don't unrealistically expect real estate values to increase every year. When you invest in real estate for the long term, which is what we advocate and practise ourselves, the occasional price declines should be merely bumps on an otherwise fruitful journey.

About This Book

To say that much has changed since the 2nd edition was published would be an understatement of significant proportions. Back then, the lingering effects of the global financial crisis (GFC) permeated property and financial markets both in Australia and overseas. Fast-forward to late 2022, and the world is re-emerging from the COVID-19 pandemic — a health (and economic) emergency that no-one could have predicted all those years ago.

Since the last edition, we have seen property values rise and fall in various markets around the nation, including one almighty boom in 2021, when record low interest rates as well as bumper buyer demand pushed property prices to eye-watering levels around the nation. Those heady days are thankfully behind us at the time of writing, but ahead lies increasing interest rates as well as a generational undersupply of rental properties in most markets.

The property investment profession has also evolved over the past decade, with a higher calibre of people generally working in the sector — however, investors still need to be mindful of spruikers who, alas, are as present as ever.

The property investment sector is one that is festooned with ever-changing rules and regulations, as well as monetary policy, so it is nigh-on-impossible to update a book as detailed as this one without some recognition that prices and policies may well be different even by the time it hits the shelves. That said, this updated edition is one that reflects the market as it was in 2022, which was one of moderating market conditions.

One thing that has not changed over the years is the potential financial and life-style benefits for anyone who wants to consider using property investment as a wealth creation vehicle.

History continues to show us that real estate is one of the most low-risk investments you can make — as long as you educate yourself on the pros and the cons, and tap into expert advice when needed to assist you along the way. A great place to begin your education is reading this book — and re-reading it, too — to ensure that you are as informed as possible before you set out on your very own property investment journey.

If you expect us (in property spruiker fashion) to tell you how to become an overnight multi-millionaire, this is definitely not the book for you. And please allow us to save you money, disappointment and heartache by telling you that such shysters are only enriching themselves through their grossly overpriced seminars or online courses, or are likely urging you into their property developments with funding from their related-party loans.

Property Investing For Dummies, 3rd Australian Edition, covers tried and proven real estate investing strategies that real people, just like you, use to build wealth. Specifically, this book explains how to invest in houses, units, apartments, small apartment blocks, commercial properties (including office, industrial and retail) and raw (undeveloped) land.

Unlike so many property investment book authors, we don't have an alternative agenda in writing this book. Some real estate investing books are little more than promotional materials for high-priced seminars or developments the author is selling. The objective of our book is to give you the best crash course in property investing, so that, if you choose to make investments in properties, you may do so wisely and confidently.

Foolish Assumptions

Whenever authors sit down to write books, they have particular audiences in mind. Because of this, they must make some assumptions about who the reader is and what that reader is looking for. Here are a few assumptions we've made about you:

>> You're looking for a way to invest in real estate but don't know what types of properties and strategies are best. (We'll show you.)

>> You're considering buying an investment property, be it a house, a unit, an apartment or flat, a small apartment or unit complex or an office building, but your real estate experience is largely limited to renting an apartment or owning your own home.

>> You may have a small amount of money already invested in real estate, but you're ready to go after more or bigger properties.

>> You're looking for a way to diversify your investment portfolio.

If any of these descriptions hits home for you, you've come to the right place.

Icons Used in This Book

Throughout this book, you can find friendly and useful icons to enhance your reading pleasure and to note specific types of information. Here's what each icon means:

REMEMBER

This icon flags concepts and facts that we want to ensure you remember as you make your real estate investments.

TECHNICAL STUFF

Included with this icon are complex examples and interesting technical stuff that you may want to read to become even more familiar with the topic.

TIP

This icon points out something that can save you time, headaches, money or all of the above!

WARNING

Here we're trying to direct you away from blunders and errors that others have made when investing in property. We're also alerting you to those who may have conflicts of interest or offer biased advice, as well as other concerns that could really cost you big bucks.

Where to Go from Here

If you have the time and desire, we encourage you to read this book in its entirety. It provides you with a detailed picture of how to maximise your returns while minimising your risks in the property market. But you may also choose to read selected portions. That's one of the great things (among many) about *For Dummies* books. You can readily pick and choose the information you read based on your individual needs.

1

Understanding Real Estate as an Investment

Compare real estate investing with alternatives you may consider and understand how to fit real estate into your overall wealth creation plans.

Uncover the different types of properties you can buy and the different methods of buying them, and consider other property strategies — such as buying and flipping, and property development.

Find out how to assemble a team of competent property investment professionals to help ensure your long-term property investment dreams can be realised.

IN THIS CHAPTER

» **Getting started**

» **Contrasting real estate with other investment options**

» **Deciding whether real estate works for you**

» **Arranging your overall financial plans to include real estate**

» **Watching out for performance statistics**

Chapter **1**

Comparing Real Estate to Other Investments

The vast array of choices available to Australians can be both a privilege and a burden. Go to the supermarket in search of something as simple as bread and you'll know exactly what we mean. Choice is even more widespread when it comes to the world of investment. You have thousands of choices among property, managed funds, shares, bonds . . . the list is seemingly endless.

Allow us to help you through a portion of the cluttered world of investment. In this chapter, we start to explain how, why, when and where to invest successfully in real estate. And, even though we're advocates for property investing, we also take you through some issues to weigh up if you're wondering whether you have what it takes to make money and be comfortable investing in real estate. We share our experiences, insights and thoughts on the long-term strategy for building wealth through real estate that, at its core, is a fundamentally simple and low-risk investment strategy that virtually everyone with a long-term time frame and determination can understand and achieve.

Finding Your Motivation

It's never too early or too late to formulate your own plan into a comprehensive wealth-building strategy. Such a strategy can help with improving your financial future and ensuring a comfortable retirement.

One of the challenges involved with real estate is that it takes some real planning to get started. Without doubt, calling a stockbroker and purchasing a few shares in your favourite company is a lot easier than purchasing your first rental property. But buying good property can be more time-consuming than difficult. You just need a financial and real estate investment plan, a lot of patience, and the willingness to do some research and legwork, and you're on your way to building your own real estate portfolio — and you can even hire an expert team to do the heavy lifting for you.

REMEMBER

The vast majority of people who don't make money in real estate made easily avoidable mistakes, which we help you steer clear of.

In this chapter, we give you some information that can help you decide whether you have what it takes to make money and be comfortable with investing in real estate. Unlike almost any other type of investment, real estate is hands-on. When you own shares in a company, you can't personally dictate how that company operates, or influence how profitable it is. Direct investment in property is the opposite. You're in control. Major decisions are in your hands. You can determine how to lift your income and how to raise your profits (or capital gains or equity). We compare real estate investments with other investments you may be considering. We provide some questions you need to ask yourself before making decisions. And, finally, we offer guidance on how real estate investments can fit into your overall personal financial plans.

Throughout history, some of the wealthiest people — regardless of their industry — have also increased their net worth via property investment in both residential and commercial assets. They have done so because they understand the profit potential of strategic real estate holdings. They invest in property not only for diversification and capital growth reasons, but also to supercharge their income streams.

Stacking Up Real Estate Against Other Investments

You've surely heard about or even considered many different investments over the years. To help you appreciate and understand the unique attributes of real estate, in the following sections we compare it with other wealth-building investments such as shares and running your own business, using key economic attributes.

Returns

Clearly, a major reason many people invest in real estate is for the healthy *total returns* (which can include both ongoing income and the capital appreciation of the property). Real estate can generate robust long-term returns because, like shares and small business, it's an ownership investment. By that, we mean that real estate is an asset that has the ability to produce income and capital growth.

Our research and experience suggest that total real estate investment returns are comparable to those from shares (about 7 to 10 per cent annually, measured over decades). And you can earn returns better than 10 per cent per year if you select excellent properties in the best areas and manage them well. That said, investing in real estate is accompanied by the following:

>> **Few knockout wins:** Your returns from real estate probably won't approach the knockout wins that can be achieved by the most accomplished entrepreneurs in the business world or by picking penny-dreadful shares on the stock market and doubling your return in a month, but that is speculation rather than investment strategy. Real estate profits take time — profits are gained through hard work, good judgement, plenty of research, and tapping into expert advice and guidance when needed.

>> **Ups and downs:** You're not going to earn a 7 to 10 per cent return every year. Although you have the potential for significant capital growth, owning real estate isn't like owning a licence to print money. Like stocks and other types of ownership investments, real estate goes through down as well as up periods. Most people who make money investing in real estate do so because they buy and hold property over a number of market cycles.

>> **High transaction costs:** If you buy a property and then want out a year or two later, you may find that, even though the property has appreciated in value, much of your profit has been wiped away by the high transaction costs. Typically, the costs of buying and selling — which include stamp duty, real estate agent commissions, loan fees, property taxes, and other settlement costs — can amount to up to 10 per cent of the purchase (or selling) price of a

property. So, although you may be elated if your property appreciates 10 per cent in value in a short time, you may not be so thrilled to realise that most of the capital growth disappears in selling costs.

>> **Tax implications:** Last, but not least, when you make a profit on your real estate investment, the Australian Taxation Office (ATO) is waiting with open hands for their share. So, throughout this book, we highlight ways to improve your after-tax returns. As we stress more than once, the profit you have left after the ATO takes its bite is all that really matters.

HOW LEVERAGE AFFECTS YOUR REAL ESTATE RETURNS

Real estate is different from most other investments in that you can borrow (finance) a large percentage of the cost of the asset. The loan can often amount to as much as 80 or 90 per cent of the actual purchase cost of the house, depending on your other assets and what your bank will agree to. Thus, you can use a relatively small deposit to buy, own and control a much larger investment. You can borrow money to invest in shares — although we don't recommend it. If you do borrow to invest in shares, you're unlikely to be able to borrow as high a percentage of the purchase cost and your mortgage rate is likely to be higher. (You're also likely to be subject to *margin calls* if the value of your security drops in relation to the loan amount, meaning you need to reduce your loan amount, contribute additional security or sell part of your investment.)

So, when your real estate increases in value (which is your aim), your returns are leveraged to take into account your total investment (your own deposit, plus the borrowed amount).

Take a look at this simple example. Suppose that you purchase a property for $600,000 and pay a $60,000 deposit. Over the next three years, imagine that the property appreciates 20 per cent to $720,000. Thus, you have a potential profit (on paper) of $120,000 ($720,000 minus $600,000) on an investment of just $60,000. In other words, you've made a 200 per cent return on your investment. (**Note:** This example ignores cash flow — whether your expenses from the property exceed the rental income that you collect or vice versa and any potential lenders mortgage insurance — and the tax benefits associated with rental real estate.)

But don't forget that leverage magnifies all of your returns and those returns aren't always positive! If your $600,000 property decreases in value to $540,000, even though it has only dropped 10 per cent in value, you actually lose (on paper) 100 per cent of your original $60,000 investment. See the 'Income- and wealth-producing potential' section later in this chapter for a more detailed example of investment property profit and return.

Risk

Real estate doesn't always rise in value. That said, market values for real estate don't usually suffer from as much volatility as share prices do. You're far less likely to experience roller-coaster ups and downs with real estate market values. The reason is land — even if the building is removed from a piece of land, the land itself generally retains its value. With an apartment block, the value of the land might be as little as 10 per cent of the full purchase price, which is far from ideal for investors. For some houses, the value of the land could be as much as 70 per cent.

Keep in mind, though (especially if you tend to be concerned about shorter term risks), that certain types of real estate in some areas, such as industrial locations, can suffer from price declines. If you make a deposit of, say, 20 per cent and need to sell your property after a 10 to 15 per cent price decline, after you factor in transaction costs, you may find that all (as in 100 per cent) of your invested dollars (deposit) are wiped out.

You can greatly minimise your risk in property investment through buying and holding property for many years — preferably a decade or two.

Liquidity

The ease and cost with which you can sell and exact your money out of an investment — known as *liquidity* — is one of directly held real estate's shortcomings. Real estate is relatively illiquid: You can't sell a piece of property with the same speed as you can whip out your ATM card to withdraw money from your bank account or sell some shares via an app. You generally also can't sell part of a house, although you can sell part of a shareholding.

We actually view property's lack of liquidity as a strength, certainly compared with stocks that people often trade in and out of because doing so is so easy and seemingly cheap. As a result, many stock market investors tend to lose sight of the long term and miss out on the bigger gains that accrue to patient buy-and-hold investors. Because you can't easily track the value of investment real estate daily online (although you can find out this information, it's not advisable to track it daily), and because real estate takes considerable time, energy and money to sell, you're far more likely to buy and hold properties for the longer term.

Income- and wealth-producing potential

Compared with most other investments, real estate can excel at producing income and capital growth for property owners. So, in addition to the longer term appreciation potential, you can also earn income year in, year out. Real estate can be both a true growth *and* income investment.

The growth in value of your investment properties compounds over years of holding them. The best part about capital growth is that you don't have to pay any tax on it until you sell the property and pay capital gains tax (CGT) — unlike any positive income from the property, on which you generally have to pay tax each year.

If you have property that you rent out, you have money coming in every month in the form of rent. When you own investment real estate, you should also expect to incur costs that include your mortgage repayment, property management agent, land tax (if your portfolio is above certain state-based thresholds), insurances as well as maintenance and repairs. The interaction of the revenues coming in and the expenses going out tells you whether you're positively geared or negatively geared (see Chapter 15 for a full explanation of gearing).

For income tax purposes, you also get to claim an expense that isn't really an out-of-pocket cost — depreciation. Depreciation enables you to reduce your income tax bill and hence increase your cash flow. (We explain this tax advantage and others in the 'Tax advantages' section, later in this chapter, and in further detail in Chapter 15.)

TIP

Unless you have a large deposit, a positively geared property can be difficult to achieve in the early years of ownership — although some investors can achieve this from day one. During soft periods in the local economy, rents may rise more slowly than your expenses (and rents may even fall). That's why you must ensure that you can weather financially tough times. In the worst cases, we've seen rental property owners lose both their investment property and their homes. Please see the section 'Fitting Real Estate into Your Financial Plans', later in this chapter.

Over time, your net rental income, which is subject to ordinary income tax, should rise as you improve the property and increase your rental prices faster than the rate of increase for your property's overall expenses. What follows is a simple example to show why even modest rental increases are magnified into larger positive incomes and healthy returns on investment over time.

Suppose that you're in the market to purchase a family home that you want to rent out and that such properties are selling for about $800,000 in the area you've deemed to be a good investment. (*Note:* Housing prices vary widely across different areas, but the following example should give you a relative sense of how a rental property's expenses and revenue change over time.) You expect to have a 20 per cent deposit and take out an interest-only mortgage (at an initial rate of 5.5 per cent) for the remainder of the purchase price — $640,000. Here are the details:

Monthly mortgage payment		$2,933
Other monthly expenses (maintenance, insurance and so on)		$700
Monthly rent		$3,000

In Table 1-1, we show you what happens with your investment over time. We assume that your expenses (except for your mortgage payment, which we assume averages out at your initial rate) increase 4 per cent annually and your rent increases 4 per cent per year. We also assume that your property appreciates at 6 per cent per year. (For simplification purposes, we've ignored depreciation in this example. If we had included the benefit of depreciation, it would further enhance the calculated returns.)

TABLE 1-1   **How a Rental Property's Income and Wealth Build over Time**

Year	Monthly Rent	Monthly Expenses	Property Value	Mortgage Balance
0	$3,000	$3,633	$800,000	$640,000
5	$3,650	$3,783	$1,070,580	$640,000
10	$4,400	$3,968	$1,432,677	$640,000
20	$5,353	$4,192	$1,917,245	$640,000
25	$6,512	$4,464	$2,565,706	$640,000

Now, notice what happens over time. When you first bought the property, the monthly rent was below the monthly expenses (of $700 plus $2,933 mortgage repayments). Keep in mind that only the $700 monthly expenses are rising by 4 per cent annually.

By about year 6, income equals expenses. By year 10, income now exceeds expenses by around $432 a month. Consider why this increase in income happens. Your largest monthly expense, the mortgage payment, will rise and fall roughly in line with official interest rates (but for the purposes of this example, we assume that it has averaged the same rate of 5.5 per cent over the period). Rent is likely to stay a relatively stable percentage of the value of the property. So, even though we assume that the increase in expenses is 4 per cent per year, the compounding of rental inflation begins to produce larger and larger positive cash flow to you, the property owner. By around year 6, the asset is paying its own way — that is, it has moved from being negatively geared to being positively geared.

The real story, however, is in the Property Value column of Table 1-1. While the net income from the investment has been growing more modestly, the property has continued to increase in value. At the end of 25 years, the property has appreciated by more than $1.7 million! Granted, $1.7 million in 25 years' time is not going to have the same purchasing power as $1.7 million now but, combined with a positive income from the property, here is an asset that has some real value. (And remember, if you factor in the tax deductions for depreciation, your cash flow and return would be even higher.)

In choosing an interest-only mortgage option, a debt of $640,000 is still attached to the property, which is the most tax-effective way to hold investment property if you still have other debts that are not tax-deductible (such as a home loan). But your equity in the house could be further improved if you change the loan from interest-only to principal and interest when the net income turns positive.

Capital requirements

Although you can easily get started with traditional investments such as shares and managed funds with a few hundred or thousand dollars, the vast majority of quality direct real estate investments require far greater investments of hundreds of thousands of dollars. (We devote an entire part of this book — Part 2, to be precise — to showing you how to raise capital and secure finance.)

Ability to add value

With shares in a company listed on the stock market, you're usually a small owner of a large company and your ability to make actual improvements to the company or its business is limited. With your own rental property, however, the biggest hurdle to improving your property is your budget and your imagination. You're in control of your property and, therefore, have the opportunity to improve the property to make it more valuable. You can fix up a property or even develop it to allow you to raise the rental income. Perhaps through legwork, persistence and good negotiating skills, you can also purchase a property below its market value, which is why we often say you make money when you buy property.

Tax advantages

Real estate investment offers numerous tax advantages. In this section, we contrast investment property tax issues with those of other investments.

Deductible expenses

Owning a property has much in common with owning your own small business. Every year, you account for your income and expenses on a tax return. (We cover all the taxing points about investment properties in Chapter 15.) We can't stress too strongly the need to be diligent about your accounting. If you're not prepared to learn how to file properly (or pay an expert to do it for you), property investment may not be for you.

Depreciation and capital works allowances

Two types of expense that you get to deduct for rental real estate on your tax return don't necessarily actually involve spending or outlaying money. The first is depreciation. This is an allowable tax deduction that's essentially an acceptance that parts of the investment property have a finite life span and will need replacement one day. These depreciable items are largely fixtures and fittings, depending on the legislation at the time. The second deduction is the capital works allowance, often referred to as the building or capital depreciation allowance, which is a special write-off for structural costs. This book uses the more common term of *building depreciation.*

TECHNICAL STUFF

Buildings, technically, can last for hundreds of years. However, the ATO allows buildings built after September 1985 to be 'depreciated' (at various rates), allowing investors to claim an annual cost until the building, for taxation purposes, is worth zero (in most cases, that will be 40 years after it was built). The other sort of depreciation is for fixtures, fittings and other items that largely will have to be replaced — for example, every 5, 10 or 15 year, depending on the legislation at the time.

Negative-gearing losses

Unlike some countries (including the United States), at the time of writing Australian tax law doesn't limit deductions for income losses made on investments being applied to regular income. This is partly why some property investors have earned their reputation for being fans of negative gearing; however, capital growth is what will make you wealthy, rather than the ability to negatively gear for a few years before your property becomes neutral or positive.

REMEMBER

Strategic investment is about purchasing the best property in the best location for the best price. No-one ever got wealthy owning negatively geared properties.

If, according to the accounting treatment of your investment, your property 'lost' $15,000 for one year, you can write that off against the income you earn from your day job. So, if you earned $120,000 from your full-time job, but your property was negatively geared to the tune of $15,000, you have to pay income tax on only $105,000 ($120,000 − $15,000).

Sure, you've lost $15,000 on your investment but, if your property has increased in value by, say, $40,000 or more, you're ahead, possibly on several fronts, because of the way properties are taxed differently for income versus capital gains.

Halving of capital gains tax

Capital gains tax (CGT) has been tinkered with many times since it was introduced in the 1980s. Assets owned prior to 19 September 1985 are exempt from CGT. Any investment purchased after that date is a CGT asset, and tax is likely to be required to be paid on profits.

The most significant changes to CGT occurred in 1999. In a nutshell (it's covered in more detail in Chapter 15), any asset that's held for longer than a year qualifies for a 50 per cent reduction in the gain itself, before it's added to other income to be taxed. This reduction is not particular to property investment but, because property is an asset that usually requires a longer holding period, property owners tend to benefit from this change more so than share owners.

Determining Whether Investing in Real Estate Is for You

We believe that most people can succeed at investing in real estate if they're willing to do their homework, which includes selecting top professionals to work with. In the sections that follow, we ask several important questions to help you decide whether you have what it takes to succeed and be happy with real estate investments that involve managing property.

Do you have sufficient time?

Purchasing and owning investment real estate and being a landlord can be time-consuming in the beginning. If you fail to do your homework before purchasing property, you can end up overpaying or buying real estate with a mass of problems. Finding competent real estate professionals takes time. (We guide you through the process in Chapter 4.) Investigating suburbs and zoning also soaks up plenty of hours (information on performing this research is located in Chapter 10), as does calculating market value and understanding contracts (see Chapter 11).

As for managing a property, we recommend engaging a real estate agent to manage the property for you, which includes interviewing tenants, solving problems such as leaking taps and broken appliances, and completing entry and exit condition reports, to name but a few of the agent's duties. Of course, their fees do cut into your investment income, and this option still requires some of your time (see Chapter 13 for information on property management).

Can you hire and fire?

Even extensive research of the people you engage to help you with your property investment journey can't create perfect relationships. Sometimes your advisers (such as buyers' agents, solicitors, property managers and accountants) will stuff it up. (By the way, you will, too.) Accepting the occasional problem or two is okay. But if problems persist and those errors continue to cost money, you have to be strong enough to end relationships — it's *your* investment, after all, and *you* are ultimately responsible as the owner of this investment.

Does real estate interest you?

In our experience, some of the best real estate investors have a curiosity, interest and passion for real estate. If you don't already possess it, such an interest and curiosity can be cultivated — and this book may just do the trick.

On the other hand, some people simply aren't comfortable investing in rental property. For example, if you've had experience and success with stock market investing, you may be uncomfortable venturing into real estate investments. Some people we know are on a mission to start their own business and may prefer to channel their time and money into that outlet.

But, even if you prefer other investments, we hope you consider the diversification value that real estate offers. When the stock market tanks from time to time, investors in real estate are always grateful their holdings are generally appreciating in value and offsetting the fact that their stock market investments have turned sharply south.

Fitting Real Estate into Your Financial Plans

For most non-wealthy people, purchasing investment real estate has a major impact on their overall personal financial situation. So, before you go out to buy property, you should thoroughly examine your money life and be sure your fiscal house is in order. The following sections explain how you can do just that.

Ensure your best personal financial health

If you're trying to improve your physical fitness by exercising, eating junk food and smoking are going to be barriers to your goal. Likewise, investing in real estate or other growth investments, such as stocks, while you're carrying high-cost consumer debt (such as credit cards or car loans) and spending more than you earn impedes your financial goals.

TIP

Before you set out to invest in real estate, you should try to pay off or pay down your non-home-loan consumer debt. Not only will you be financially healthier for doing so, but you'll also enhance your future mortgage applications.

Eliminate wasteful and unnecessary spending (analyse your monthly spending to identify areas for reduction). This exercise enables you to save more and better afford your investments, including real estate. Try to live below your means. As Charles Dickens once said, 'Annual income twenty pounds, annual expenditure nineteen nineteen and six, result happiness. Annual income twenty pounds, annual expenditure twenty pounds ought and six, result misery.'

Protect your property and yourself with insurance

Regardless of your real estate investment desires and decisions, only the foolish would enter into a property investment wealth-creation strategy without having comprehensive insurance for themselves and their major assets, including the following (in order of importance):

- **Home and contents insurance:** You want homeowner's insurance because it not only protects you against the financial cost caused by a fire or other home-damaging catastrophe, but also provides you with liability protection.

- **Landlord insurance:** This specialist insurance is non-negotiable for investors because it provides additional insurance coverage for tenant-related losses. Things covered include loss of rent due to tenants breaking their lease or being evicted, or damage caused to your contents by tenants, such as drink spills on carpets. This insurance provides additional peace of mind for investors.

- **Income-protection insurance:** For most working people, their biggest asset is their future income-earning ability. Income-protection insurance replaces a portion of your employment earnings if you're unable to work for an extended period due to an incapacitating illness or injury.

>> **Life insurance:** If loved ones are financially dependent on you, term life insurance, which provides a lump-sum death benefit, can help to replace your employment earnings if you pass away.

>> **Car insurance:** This coverage is similar to homeowner's insurance in that it insures a valuable asset and also provides liability insurance should you be involved in an accident.

>> **Health insurance:** Major medical coverage protects you from financial ruin if you have a big accident or illness that requires significant hospital and other medical care.

None of us enjoys spending our hard-earned money on insurance — insurance is universally known as a 'grudge purchase'. However, having proper protection gives you peace of mind and financial security, so don't put off reviewing and securing needed policies. See Chapter 14 for more detail on the different types of insurance policies that can aid or protect your strategy to create wealth from real estate investment.

Consider superannuation and property investment

Most working Australians have a superannuation account. And, due to how the money managers who run those super funds invest that money, most Australians have some of their super invested in property. A high percentage of Australians' super invested in managed funds sits in balanced funds (where about 60 per cent is invested in growth assets and 40 per cent in income assets — see the following section). About 5 to 15 per cent of any given super fund is invested in property. Those real estate holdings are generally commercial property — office, industrial and retail buildings.

Self-managed super funds (SMSFs) are also able to own property, but with some restrictions. One favourite way is for a self-managed super fund to hold the commercial property of a related business entity. Consider, for example, a sole trader — we've named him Michael — who owns a business called ABC. Michael also runs his own self-managed super fund, and the super fund owns the premises that ABC operates from. ABC pays the super fund rent.

Super funds can also own residential investment property and, since late 2007, SMSFs can actually borrow to invest in real estate. However, some strong restrictions exist on how the borrowings can be undertaken, and anyone considering a geared property investment inside a SMSF needs to talk with suitably qualified financial advisers, accountants and lawyers. (We cover using an SMSF to invest in property in Chapter 8.)

Think about asset allocation

With money that you invest for the longer term, you should have an overall game plan in mind. Financial advisers use phrases such as asset allocation or, more simply, diversification. This allocation indicates what portion of your money you have invested in different types of investments, such as shares and real estate (growth assets), or lending vehicles such as bonds, cash or term deposits (income assets).

TIP

Here's one simple way to calculate an asset allocation that takes into account your age (but doesn't take into account your ability to cope with risk): Take your age and subtract it from 100. The resulting number gives a rough indication of what percentage of your assets you should have invested in growth assets (property and shares). For example, a 40 year old would take 100 − 40 = 60 per cent in growth investments. If you wish to be more aggressive, you can take your age and subtract it from 110, so that a 40 year old would have 70 per cent in growth investments.

REMEMBER

The preceding calculation provides simple guidelines, not hard and fast rules. If you want to be more aggressive and are comfortable taking on greater risk, you can invest higher portions in growth assets. What the preceding example is trying to show is that younger people should have more of their investments in the higher risk assets of shares and properties, because they have more time on their side to weather the ups and downs of riskier investments.

Being Mindful of Performance Statistics

Since the beginning of investing, the supporters of property and the supporters of share-based investments have been at war. The 'property versus shares' debate will, no doubt, be one that never ends. Blinkered proponents of either asset class will swear that theirs is the top long-term performer. And they'll have the studies and statistics to prove their argument.

This book doesn't enter that debate. So many different numbers can 'prove' both sides of the argument. Property and shares are both growth assets. They both have long-term total returns that (depending on which study you're looking at or which stage of the cycle you're comparing) are in the range of 8 to 10 per cent. In the case of property, that return is made up of rents and capital growth. With shares, the return is in dividends and capital growth.

We believe in both asset classes and believe that diversification is important for all investment plans. Importantly, we always recommend that you seek expert advice to learn which is the best investment path for you personally.

IN THIS CHAPTER

» Looking at residential properties

» Broadening your investments away from home

» Getting to know commercial real estate

» Examining undeveloped land

» Comprehending rentvesting

Chapter **2**

Covering the Landscape of Common Real Estate Investments

I f you lack substantial experience investing in real estate, you should avoid more esoteric and complicated properties and strategies. In this chapter, we discuss the more accessible and easy-to-master property options, from residential to commercial properties and vacant land. In addition to discussing the pros and cons of each, we provide insights as to which may be the most appropriate and profitable for you.

Investing in Residential Properties

Residential property can be an attractive real estate investment for many people. Residential housing is easier to understand, purchase and manage than most other types of property, such as office, industrial and retail property. If you're a homeowner, you already have some level of experience locating, purchasing and maintaining residential property.

If you've been in the market for a home yourself, you know that, in addition to freestanding (detached) houses, you can choose from numerous types of attached or multi-dwelling properties, including units, apartments and townhouses. In the following sections, we provide an overview of why some of these may make an attractive investment for you.

Freestanding houses

As an investment, *freestanding* houses have usually performed better in the long run than attached housing, units or apartments. In a sound real estate market, most housing appreciates, but traditional detached homes tend to outperform other housing types for the following reasons:

» Freestanding houses tend to attract more potential buyers — most people, when they can afford it, prefer detached dwellings, particularly for the increased privacy (and space).

» Attached housing, or units and townhouses, is less expensive and easier to build — and to overbuild. Because of this potential for surplus properties on the market, such property tends to appreciate more moderately in price.

» Land value is the major driver of property prices. The higher the land content, the more likely the capital growth. And a freestanding house, in most cases, has a higher proportion of land content than attached housing.

Because freestanding houses are the first choice for most Australians, market prices for such dwellings can sometimes become inflated beyond what's justified by the rental income that they can produce. Detached houses are likely to produce lower rental yields (rent as a proportion of current value, for the purpose of market comparison) than most other options, partly because of the higher purchase prices of houses versus units.

With a house, you (in conjunction with your property manager) are responsible for maintenance and repairs. If you engage one (as we recommend), your property manager will find the tradespeople and coordinate and oversee the work, while the fees for such work will come out of your returns. Also recognise that, if you purchase a house with many fine features and amenities, tenants living in your property won't necessarily treat it with the same tender loving care that you might.

TIP

A primary rule of being a successful landlord is to let go of any emotional attachment to a property. But that sort of attachment on the tenant's part is favourable: The more tenants make your rental property their 'home', the more likely they are to return it to you in good condition — except for the expected normal wear and tear of day-to-day living. (We discuss the proper screening and selection of tenants in Chapter 13.)

Attached housing

As the cost of land around major cities has skyrocketed, packing more multi-dwelling units into a given plot of land keeps housing somewhat more affordable. Here, we discuss the investment merits of units, apartments and townhouses.

Apartments and units

When you purchase a flat or apartment, you're actually purchasing the airspace and interior surfaces of a specific apartment as well as a proportionate interest in the common areas — the pool, tennis court, grounds, hallways, roof-top gardens and so on. Although you (or your tenants) have full use and enjoyment of the common areas, remember that the body corporate or owners corporation (the collective owners of all apartments in the block) actually owns and maintains the common areas, as well as the building structures themselves, which typically include the foundations, outside walls and doors, roof, and the plumbing, electrical and other building systems. Before purchasing an apartment, you should review the body corporate governing documents to check what's considered common areas, and take into account annual body corporate fees (see Chapter 9 for more on ongoing fees).

A unit, on the other hand, can be an attached or detached dwelling on a block of land, with shared common ground (such as driveways and gardens). For example, two, three or more dwellings that have been built on a single block of land.

One advantage that apartments and units have over other investment property options is that apartments tend to produce higher yields because of the lower purchase price points. Most bodies corporate deal with issues such as roofing and gardening for the entire building and receive bulk-buying benefits. *Note:* You're still responsible for maintenance that's needed inside your unit, such as servicing appliances and interior painting (for more on ongoing maintenance, see Chapter 9).

Although apartments may be somewhat easier to maintain, they tend to appreciate slower than houses and even units, unless they're located in a desirable urban area. This is in part because most apartment blocks lack the scarcity value of houses.

Townhouses

Essentially attached homes, townhouses are a hybrid between 'air space only' apartments and houses. Like apartments and units, townhouses are usually attached, typically sharing walls and a continuous roof. But townhouses are often two- or even three-storey buildings that can come with a courtyard or balcony and offer more privacy than an apartment. That generally means you don't have someone living above or below you.

REMEMBER

As with apartments, it's extremely important that you review the body corporate governing documents before you purchase a townhouse to see exactly what you legally own. Townhouses are usually organised so that no limitations are stipulated on the transferability of ownership of the individual lot that encompasses each dwelling and often a small area of immediately adjacent land or air space for a patio or balcony. Courtyards are often exclusive-use common property, because, although the owner has sole use of the area, the body corporate still owns it. The common areas are all part of a larger single lot, and each owner is a shareholder, in equal proportion, of the common area.

Apartment blocks

Apartment blocks tend to produce positive cash flow (rental income less expenses) in earlier stages of ownership. But, as with a house, the buck stops with you for maintenance of an entire apartment building. You can hire a property manager to assist you, but you'll still have oversight responsibilities (and additional expenses) in that event.

TIP

One way to add value, if zoning allows, is to convert an apartment block into strata-titled individual apartments. Keep in mind, however, that this metamorphosis requires significant research on the zoning front, some legal work to separate the titles, and possible remodelling and construction costs.

Deciding among the options

From an investment perspective, our top recommendations for first-time investors are houses or well-located units that offer scarcity value (such as Art Deco design elements) or those with desirable attributes (such as water views).

Apartments make more sense for investors who don't want to deal with building maintenance and security issues. Avoid shared-wall dwellings (particularly apartments) in inner-city areas where the availability of prime development sites (property allotments ripe for development) makes building many more apartment towers more likely. Apartment prices tend to perform best where nearby land has already been fully (or nearly fully) developed.

TIP

For higher returns, look for property where relatively simple cosmetic changes can allow you to raise rents, and so increase the market value of the property. Examples of such improvements may include, but aren't limited to:

>> Adding fresh paint and floor coverings

>> Improving the landscaping

>> Upgrading the kitchen with new appliances and new cabinet and drawer hardware

All the preceding changes can totally change the look and feel of the property.

TIP

Look for property with a great location and good physical condition but with some maintenance that the current owner has put off. Then you can develop a hit list of items to achieve maximum results for minimum dollars — for example, a property with a large yard but dead grass, a two- or three-car garage but peeling paint or a broken garage door. You could also add a remote garage door opener to jazz up the property for minimum cost. You might be surprised how much value you can add to a property owned by a burnt-out, absentee or totally uninterested owner who's tired of maintaining the property. (See Chapter 11 for more on this.)

REMEMBER

Unless you can afford a large deposit (20 to 30 per cent or more), the early years of rental property ownership may financially challenge you, depending on the type of property:

>> **Houses:** The early years of owning an investment property are usually the most difficult in which to achieve positive monthly cash flow, particularly with houses. The reason: Land value. Houses sell at a premium relative to the rent they command because the land itself has a lower rental value than the dwelling.

>> **Apartments or apartment buildings:** Apartments and apartment buildings, particularly those with many dwellings, occasionally produce a small positive cash flow, even in the early years of rental ownership.

With all properties, as time goes on, generating a positive cash flow gets easier because your mortgage expense stays loosely fixed (apart from interest rate fluctuations) while your rents tend to increase faster than your expenses. Regardless of what you choose to buy, make sure that you run the numbers on your rental income and expenses (see Chapter 11 for details on calculating the yield of a property) to see if you can afford the negative cash flow that often occurs in the early years of ownership.

Using Your Home as a Base for Investing

The first foray into property purchasing for most people is a home in which to live. In the following sections, we not only cover the advantages inherent in buying a home for your own use, but also explain why a home and an investment property are essentially mutually exclusive purchases (except in the case of holiday homes).

We also cover the implications of converting your home to a rental property, as well as fixing it up and selling it.

REMEMBER

An important concept to understand is that a 'home' is not an 'investment property' from the perspective of investing. The two types of assets have too many differences, particularly when it comes to tax treatment, for them to be talked about as the same thing. However, it is important to always consider every home you buy as an investment because of the significant financial outlay that is required. In this book, when you see the word 'home', we're talking about the dwelling in which you live (also known in tax terms as the principal place of residence). However, 'investment property' can pretty much cover any other property on which an income, usually rent, is earned.

REMEMBER

Although a home is not an investment property, for most people their home is the basis from which most investment property is bought. The equity that has built up, for people who have owned their own home for a few years and have seen the value of their home grow and their loan reduce, becomes the cornerstone from which real wealth is built. The equity can be used as security for other investments in property. Outside of a large cash deposit, banks see home equity as the best source of security for their customers to use to reinvest (we cover this in more detail in Chapter 5).

Why tax makes 'home' and 'investment' different

What separates the taxation treatment of homes from that of rented properties is the federal government's intention that the principal place of residence (home) should not be taxed, whereas investment properties should be taxed on the profits or income made in the same way that all other economic investments are taxed.

The first major difference is capital gains tax (CGT) — a 'home' is generally exempt from CGT when sold. How much money you've made on your home doesn't matter. If the property has truly always simply been your home, you do not pay CGT on any profit you make. If you initially paid $500,000 for your home and you sell it for $2 million, you won't have to pay CGT — not a cent. Making the same profit on an investment property is a different story. You do have to pay CGT (for more information on CGT and how it's charged, see Chapter 15).

The second major tax difference between your home and an investment property is in the treatment of expenses incurred in relation to a property. By expenses, we mean the ongoing costs of holding or maintaining a property, such as mortgage interest, construction or capital-improvement costs, maintenance costs and government imposts. Usually, these expenses aren't tax-deductible for home-owners, but are deductible for an investment property (further information on the ongoing costs of property are included in Chapter 9; tax-deductibility issues are also discussed in Chapter 15). Tax deductibility makes a big difference to the real cost of an item. Homeowners who pay $200 to change the locks on their front door get no deduction. But an investor who pays $200 for the same work can have a proportion of the cost returned through tax (depending on the investor's marginal tax rate), which effectively reduces the cost of the same work.

Buying a place of your own

During your adult life, you're going to need a roof over your head for many decades. You have two options: Either buy a place to live in yourself or pay some-one else rent to live in a property they own. Real estate is the only purchase or investment that you can either live in or rent out to produce income. Shares, bonds or managed funds can't provide a roof over your head — or anyone else's either!

REMEMBER

Unless you expect to move within the next few years, buying a property to call home probably makes good long-term financial sense. (Even if you relocate, you may decide to continue owning the property and rent it out.) Owning usually costs less than renting over the long haul (your loan gets locked in at the start and becomes progressively smaller in real terms as the years roll on, while rents continue to rise) and allows you to build *equity* in an asset (the difference between market value and loans against the property).

You can briefly consider your home as part of your investment portfolio when you use that home as the cornerstone of your wealth-creation plans. It's usually the biggest single investment that you make. It's also usually responsible for creating equity that you can later use to make further investments (such as buying invest-ment properties). Many people move to a less costly home when they retire (known as *downsizing*). Downsizing in retirement frees up the equity you've built up over years of home ownership. You can use this money to supplement your retirement income and superannuation, and for any other purpose your heart desires.

How your home is similar to an investment is that your home usually appreciates in value over the years, and you can use that money to further your financial or personal goals. You can also turn your home into an investment property if you decide to buy and move into another property. But at this point — particularly for tax purposes — the former home stops being a 'home' and becomes an 'invest-ment property', and your new home gets the tax advantages and disadvantages of becoming your home.

Converting your home to a rental

Turning your current home into a rental property when you move or upgrade is one way to buy and own more properties. Holding on to your current home when you're buying a new one can be advisable if you're moving into a larger home or moving interstate. This approach presents a number of positives:

>> You save the time and cost of finding a separate rental property, not to mention the associated transaction costs.

>> You know the property and have probably taken good care of it and perhaps made some improvements.

>> You know the target market because the house appealed to you at an earlier stage of life.

WARNING

Many people hold on to their current home for the wrong reasons when they buy another. This often happens in a depressed market — even though they're buying a new home at a lower price, at the same time they're facing the prospect of selling their former home for a reduced price. If you plan to move and want to keep your current home as a long-term investment property, you can. But turning your home into a *short-term* rental is usually a bad move because:

>> You may not want the responsibilities of being a landlord, yet you force yourself into the landlord business if you convert your home into a rental.

>> You may have to pay some capital gains tax (CGT) — proportionate to the time you owned the property as an investment versus a home — on any profit when you do sell it.

TIP

If you own a property as a home but don't live in it — because you've moved interstate, for example, and are renting while you live there — you may be able to hang on to it for as long as six years before you incur CGT, even if you put a tenant into the property. This law applies only if you don't claim another 'home' as a principal place of residence in the meantime.

TIP

If you do convert your home into an investment property, you may be able to claim tax deductions for portions of the capital improvements that you made to the property while it was your home, depending on the relevant legislation at the time (for information about tax deductions, see Chapter 15).

Diversifying away from home

One of the most important rules of investing is diversification. That's the mantra of 'don't put all your eggs in one basket'. Why? If you drop the basket, all your eggs break. However, if you spread your eggs among many baskets, you reduce the chance of breaking them all at once.

WARNING

The same rule holds true for property investment. Not only can it be dangerous for someone to have all their investment money in property only (many investors have some money invested in other asset classes), but investing exclusively in one geographical area is also dangerous. Most importantly, for first-time investors, that means buying in an area away from where you live.

If you own your own home, a good portion of your individual net wealth is affected by property prices in your neighbourhood. If your suburb sees a strong rise in values, that's great. It's obviously not so great if your home falls in value. So, what would happen if the only other major asset you owned was an investment property that you bought close to home? You'd be doubling up on your luck. If the area continued to grow, fantastic. If it fell in value, you'd be in double trouble.

The economic health of many large towns, regional cities and even suburbs in metropolitan cities can sometimes rest on the prosperity of one large employer. For example, say you live in a mining or tourism location. Many of your friends and family may be employed by those industries. What would happen if, for some reason, that industry experienced a significant downturn, and thousands of people lost their jobs? Such a collapse would be an economic disaster for those people and for all the local businesses where those people spent their incomes. A further effect would be to put a severe dampener on property prices, often for as long as a decade, as people moved on in search of work. If you owned your own home and an investment property in the area, a large part of your wealth would probably disappear overnight and stay that way for many years.

TIP

Although probably time-consuming, doing the required research to invest in an area away from where you live doesn't have to be difficult — and you can take advantage of a plethora of experts to help you. You can begin by finding out the pros and cons of a few suburbs on the other side of town or in a larger town or city with an economy that relies on a different set of fundamentals or has a diverse economy that features a number of different industries. And, after you've had some practice and experience in owning rental properties, you may even wish to further diversify your property holdings interstate. Just make sure you to tap into expert assistance if considering this strategy.

Holiday homes

A common way for people with the means to expand their real estate holdings beyond their primary home is to purchase a holiday home. For Australians, this expansion is usually a place by the beach, in the bush, or by a river or lake — a home in an area where they enjoy taking holidays.

Why is this so? Many Australians grew up enjoying holidays at the family beach house, or with friends who had one. After the stereotypical 'Great Australian Dream' of owning your own home, another strong desire is to own a holiday home.

WARNING

Many people hope to own a holiday home and rent it out when they don't want to use it, for perhaps as much as 90 per cent of the year. They often believe that they can own this wonderful place of their own and, because they also lease it out, claim the whole thing as a tax deduction. Wrong! The ATO only allows you to claim tax deductions for the portion of the expenses that are related to the income-producing activity (that is, when it is truly available for rent). If you occupy it yourself for significant portions of the year, the ATO only allows you to claim the portion of the year that the property was 'available for rent'. For example, if you use the property for 15 weeks of the year, you're able to claim only the portion of expenses that represents 37 out of 52 weeks of deductions.

Holiday homes are a strange mix of 'home' and 'investment property'. They can be both, but you need to be well aware of the special tax rules that apply.

The downsides to holiday homes can be numerous, including the following:

>> **Expenses:** With a second home, you have nearly all of the costs of a primary home — including mortgage interest, property taxes, insurance, maintenance and utilities.

>> **Property management:** When you're not at your holiday home, things can go wrong. A pipe can burst, for example, and it may be days or weeks before the mess is found if the property is not being rented out regularly to holidaymakers.

>> **Lack of rental income:** Most people don't rent out their holiday homes, negating the investment property income stream that contributes to the returns real estate investors enjoy (refer to Chapter 1 for a comparison of real estate with other investments). If your second home is in a holiday area where you have access to plenty of short-term renters, you could rent out the property. However, this entails all of the headaches and hassles of having many short-term renters. These requirements can be managed by property managers but higher costs are usually associated with this than with long-term rental properties. That said, you do gain some of the tax advantages of depreciation and expenses as with other rental properties.

TIP

Before you buy a second home, objectively weigh all the pros and cons. If you have a spouse or partner with whom you're buying the property, have a candid discussion. For most people, buying a holiday home is more of a consumption decision than it is an investment decision. That's not to say that you can't make a profit from owning a second home, if the chosen location experiences strong market conditions. However, your total potential investment returns shouldn't be the main reason you buy a second home. Don't forget to weigh up the value of your personal use versus the likely gains from income or capital gains. (See Chapter 10 for more on buying property in holiday areas.)

Considering Commercial Real Estate

Commercial real estate is a generic term that includes properties used for office, retail and industrial purposes. You can also include self-storage and hospitality (hotel and motel) properties in this category. More than a few Australians have turned a pub into both a successful business and a real estate holding.

WARNING

Commercial real estate isn't our first recommendation, especially for inexperienced investors. Residential real estate is easier to understand and also usually carries lower investment and tenancy risks.

With commercial real estate, when tenants move out, new tenants nearly always require extensive and costly improvements to customise the space to meet their planned usage of the property. And you may have to pay for some of the associated costs in order to compete with other building owners. Fortunes can quickly change — small companies can go under, get too big for a space and so on. Change is the order of the day in the business world, and especially in the small business world.

So, how do you evaluate the state of your local commercial real estate market? You must check out, for a number of years, the supply and demand statistics, such as how much total space (and new space) is available for rent, and how that has changed in recent years. What is the vacancy rate, and how has that changed over time? Also examine the rental rates, usually quoted as a price per square metre. (We provide some information on commercial leases in Chapter 10.)

Commercial real estate is a more advanced investment strategy and, as such, requires plenty of research as well as expert advice and assistance before proceeding with this option.

Uncovering Undeveloped Land

For prospective real estate investors who feel tenants and building maintenance are ongoing headaches, buying undeveloped land may appear attractive. If you buy land in an area that's expected to experience expanding demand in the years ahead, you may be able to make a tidy return on your investment. This is sometimes referred to as buying in the path of progress, but the trick is to buy before it's obvious to all that new development is moving in your direction. (Check out Chapter 10 for a full discussion on the path of progress.)

You may hit a winner if you identify land that others don't currently see as having value in holding for the future. However, identifying many years in advance which communities will experience rapid population and job growth isn't easy for the average person. Land in those areas that people believe will be the next hot spot already sells at a premium price, so getting ahead of the pack to find bargains takes a lot of research and usually a bit of luck. *Note:* You won't have much opportunity to get ahead of the curve and, if you guess wrong, you may need to hold on to some costly land for a long time!

WARNING

Investing in land certainly has drawbacks and risks:

>> **Care and feeding:** Land requires ongoing cash to pay the property taxes and ongoing expenses, while it most likely produces little or no income. Although land doesn't require much upkeep compared with tenant-occupied property, it almost always does require some financial feeding.

>> **Opportunity costs:** Investing in land is a cash drain and, of course, purchasing land costs money. If you buy the land with cash, you have the opportunity cost of tying up your valuable capital (which could be invested elsewhere), but most likely you put down 30 to 40 per cent in cash and finance the balance of the purchase price.

>> **Costly mortgages:** Mortgage lenders usually require higher deposits and interest rates on loans to purchase land because they see it as a more speculative investment.

>> **Lack of depreciation:** You don't get the tax benefits of depreciation because land isn't depreciable.

On the income side, some properties may be able to be used for parking, storage or 'pop-up' businesses — just make sure you're aware of the tax implications of this.

Although large-scale land investment isn't for the entry-level real estate investor, savvy property investors have made fortunes taking raw land and getting the proper building approvals and then selling (or better yet, subdividing and then selling) the parcels to developers of commercial and residential properties. If you decide to invest in land, be sure that you

>> **Do your homework.** Ideally, you want to buy land in an area that's attracting rapidly expanding companies and that has a shortage of housing and developable land. Take your time to really know the area or work with experts in this area.

>> **Know all the costs.** Tally up your annual carrying costs (ongoing ownership expenses such as property taxes) so that you can see what your annual cash drain may be. What are the financial consequences of this cash outflow — for example, will you be able to fully fund it from your ordinary income?

>> **Determine what improvements the land may need.** Aspects such as running utility, water and sewer lines, building roads and adding landscaping all cost money. If you plan to develop and build on the land that you purchase, research these costs. Make sure you don't make these estimates with your rose-tinted sunglasses on — improvements almost always cost more than you expect them to. (Check with the local council planning or building department for its list of requirements.)

Also make sure that you have road access to the land. Some people foolishly invest in landlocked properties. When they discover that fact later, they think they can easily get an easement for access, which may not be the case.

>> **Understand the zoning and environmental issues.** The value of land is heavily dependent upon what you can develop on it. Never purchase land without thoroughly understanding its zoning status and what you can and can't build on it. This advice also applies to environmental limitations that may be in place or that could come into effect without warning, diminishing the potential of your property (with no compensation).

Some areas, particularly older suburbs with strong design characteristics, have strong networks of local residents who can organise themselves quickly to fight developments and influence council officials. A change in zoning can be a disaster for the value of a piece of land if its rating is lowered. Each state and local council has different laws relating to zoning to stipulate what the land can be used for — the council usually has ratings to cover residential, commercial or industrial uses, for example. If a zoning suddenly changes for the worse, the alteration could significantly reduce what you can develop on a property and, therefore, the property's value.

Considering Rentvesting

An increasingly popular investment strategy over the past decade is what's known as *rentvesting*. In essence, this strategy involves investors, usually first-time ones but not always, buying a property elsewhere while continuing to rent in their location of choice. High property prices in cities such as Sydney and Melbourne are no doubt one of the reasons this investment strategy has become so popular, because it enables people to invest their funds without sacrificing their current lifestyle. For example, they may only be able to afford to buy property in an outer-fringe city suburb or even a regional area. They can make this investment, and get started in the property market, while continuing to rent in their current location.

Rentvesting is becoming such a common investment strategy that, according to the 2022 Property Investment Professionals of Australia (PIPA) Annual Investor Sentiment Survey, 29 per cent of first-time investors are using it, with 45 per cent of all investors indicating they would consider rentvesting personally as well.

Generally speaking, young people can afford to rent in locations that they would not be able to afford to purchase a property, so rentvesting gives them the best of both worlds so to speak — they are investing when they are younger while still enjoying all of the attributes of living in their suburb of choice.

Chapter **3**

Opportunities in Real Estate

Most property investors begin by buying a home for their own use, building equity in the property, and then using that equity to purchase investment properties. Some people, however, find the best way to quickly become a real estate investor is to purchase income-producing properties in other ways.

In this chapter, we take a brief look at some of the most common methods of acquiring investment properties or participating in the real estate market, and we tell you what we think about whether you should pursue these options. We start off with a discussion on how to purchase via private sales and auctions, as well as looking at some more unusual purchase options. We then look at how to buy and flip real estate and discuss the basic risks of property development.

Buying Property Strategies

Opportunities to purchase real estate are near boundless. Every city, town or suburb has people trying to sell for one reason or another. The task for the property investor is to sort the wheat from the chaff — finding the best properties from the pool of those available on the market. This is where real estate sales agents come in — they're a central place for buyers and sellers to channel their separate interests.

When you find a property, however, how does it change hands between owners? Obviously, through a sale. Properties are sold in three main ways — private treaty sale, public auction and tender. What are known as *off-market sales* are also available.

Private treaty sales

Across Australia, the most common way for properties to change hands is through private treaty sale, or simply private sale. When the owner of a property decides she wants to sell by private sale, she places the asking price she wants on the property listing and then waits for offers to come in, usually via the real estate sales agent she has appointed.

In most stages of the property cycle, both vendor and potential purchaser then negotiate. The seller wants $800,000. A buyer comes in with an offer of $785,000. The seller lowers her price to $795,000. The buyer raises her offer to $790,000. And the haggling and changing of position keep going until the property is sold. Or not sold. Properties put up for private sale can be sold very quickly — often before they've even really been advertised. But they can also take months (even a year or more) to sell in a particularly slow market or when the seller has unrealistic expectations of what the property is worth.

The private sale market is all about negotiation. Potential buyers usually have plenty of properties on the market to choose from. And there's usually no rush (when compared with auction, with the process of purchasing literally over within 30 minutes). Negotiations can last for days, sometimes weeks.

TIP

A non-negotiable sale is rare when it comes to private selling. For a start, most property sellers start with a price a little above what they really see as their lower limit. If they're really determined to get a minimum of $800,000 for the property, for example, they may start their sales campaign with a price of $825,000 in the hope they'll be able to negotiate a price somewhere between $799,000,000 and $810,000.

Prices are almost always negotiable. And it's sometimes up to the buyer to be persuasive about what they believe the market value of the property is. You can try to get a seller to reduce her expectations through a number of means (although you'll usually be dealing with the seller's agent, who'll be wise to most of these tricks). Often, it's as simple as getting a builder, building inspector or valuer to point out the property's flaws, showing how much it's going to cost to fix those problems. (See Chapter 4 for information on how to get a builder to do a pre-purchase inspection.)

Buyers' agents (also covered in Chapter 4) can be a very useful part of your team too, particularly during negotiations. Putting your professional buyers' agent up against a real estate sales agent can be like throwing suited lawyers into a locked room together. But buyers' agents know a sales agents' tricks and vice versa. Experienced buyers' agents take the emotion out — you're likely to be emotional, but they're not. And removing emotion is always important in property negotiations where you're talking about large sums of money.

Experienced real estate sales agents can be a curse to deal with, or they can be your best helper. A sales agent's primary and fiduciary responsibility is to their vendors (their clients) and they'll obviously be more loyal to their clients than to prospective buyers. But agents also often believe that their clients' expectations are unrealistic and will use all offers, sometimes even a very low one, as a way of conditioning the client that the price they expect for their property is too high.

TIP

In most states and territories of Australia, purchases made through private sale treaties come with a cooling-off period, where the buyer can change their mind and get out of the sale contract. The period starts at midnight on the day the contract is signed and lasts for up to five business days. A decision to exercise your right to a cooling-off period may incur penalties (usually quite small). Sellers don't have the right to a cooling-off period.

Public auctions

A good auction can be a thrilling spectacle, with the drama played out on suburban streets and footpaths — sometimes bidding is so intense, and the price achieved so out-of-the-box, that it causes uninvolved spectators to audibly gasp and even break into applause when a 'winner' is finally determined.

Auctions are commonplace in Melbourne, Sydney and Brisbane, and they're used by real estate agents in many other parts of the country. The aim of auctions is to create an intense atmosphere for the sales process. Within a period of 10 or 15 minutes (after the particulars of the property have been read out), a property can be sold — unless, of course, it's passed in because it hasn't reached the reserve price the vendor has set (see the sidebar 'Passed in: Post-auction negotiation'). Unless you're the one making the final bid, you're not buying the property, and you have to continue your search.

The auction process is always under scrutiny. Occasionally there are mooted moves to impose restrictions on auctions following media noise citing concerns from buyers who've missed out on properties or believe that agents have misled them over the likely sales price of a property. These concerns appear to be cyclical and seem to get the most airplay when property prices are rising, and people are feeling locked out of the market.

PASSED IN: POST-AUCTION NEGOTIATION

Auctions often fail to get sufficient interest or momentum from bidders to move bids to a point that's acceptable for the vendor to sell. Auctions can get off to a slow start and not get any faster. After a few lacklustre bids, the auctioneer declares the final bid to be insufficient and that 'the property will now be passed in'. What happens then?

If no genuine bidders turned up, or only one bidder, and no real auction took place, the house effectively reverts to a private treaty sale. If the agent can't get an acceptable bid, she'll place the property back on the market with a 'For Sale' sticker that afternoon.

If several bidders showed up, the house will be passed in. The highest bidder will probably be ushered inside (but not always) by an agent and told what the vendor's reserve is (say, $800,000). Other agents (sometimes two or three other agents, including the auctioneer, attend every auction) will try to keep the next highest underbidder (or underbidders) around to let them know they still have a chance. The highest bidder will usually have the first crack at the vendor's reserve. If she isn't prepared to pay the reserve price, then agents will likely offer the property to the other bidders.

Here lies the strangeness of this situation and an interesting insight into the pressure tactics used by agents. They already have the person who's offered the most money for this property inside — in a competitive auction, other interested parties have already fallen by the wayside, believing the price was too high. But agents want to keep the auction going by having one agent negotiating with the highest bidder and another agent working on getting another bid or two out of parties who've already thrown in the towel.

This tactic, somewhat surprisingly, works. And, Bruce admits, it has worked on him (to some extent). He was interested in a property that he'd valued at $280,000 many years ago. When the bidding stopped, he was the top bidder with $255,000. The underbidder was at $252,500. Bruce was taken inside, where he was told the reserve was $270,000. He could hear a second negotiation going on outside with the underbidder. After some discussion, Bruce made a further offer of $257,500, then $260,000 (believing he was still getting a bargain anyway). He heard the underbidder outside say he may have gone to $260,000, but not above. Bruce's $260,000 offer was now $7,500 higher than his rival's public offer, but still under his own valuation and no interested parties were left.

The negotiations continued for half an hour, but the vendor wouldn't budge. Bruce left his offer on the table overnight. When the agent called back the following day, claiming the vendor was prepared to sell if Bruce would lift his offer by $1,500 (so the vendor could get out of a three-year home-security contract he'd recently signed), Bruce offered him $800 — a total of $260,800 — and the deal was done.

Auctions are all about competition and pressure. If you've seen off your competitors, you're in the box seat. The market has spoken, and you value the property more highly than anyone else. If you value it a little higher (which you inevitably do because auctions rarely get the top bid out of the final bidder), there's no harm in raising your bid a little. But, for an investment property, don't go too high. This is a business decision — don't allow emotions to get the better of you. The fact that you were prepared to pay more (in Bruce's case, up to $280,000) is irrelevant, and the risk that vendors take when they decide to auction.

TIP

If, as an investor, you're considering bidding at an auction, set yourself firm limits before you attend. If you've spotted the property at the start of its marketing period, you usually have about three or four weeks before the auction to do your due diligence — you can't do that after an auction. No cooling-off period (refer to the preceding section) is offered in public auction sales. Several days before the auction, nail down what you believe is fair value for the property. Then try to bid only up to that price. If your research suggests that a fair price for a unit is $800,000, set your limit at that price with the aim of only picking up the property if it goes for $800,000 or below. As an investor, this purchase is about making money — it's much harder to achieve your goal if you overpay for the asset in the first place. Stay focused — and don't get emotional.

WARNING

Agents' auction practices tend to come under scrutiny when buyers watch prices soar 20 to 30 per cent (or more) above the estimate or comparative recent sales offered during the property's marketing period. The concern over what's known as *underquoting*, whether valid or not, has undermined confidence in the auction process in the past. If a property being auctioned has a reserve price from the vendors of, say, $800,000, agents often advertise the property in a variety of ways to attract potential buyers — including putting their estimated price range below this reserve.

The rule is an unwritten one, but agents tend to estimate their price range within about 10 per cent below the vendor's potential reserve. The vendor can then change their mind at the last moment to raise or lower their reserve. That's out of an agent's power.

A problem during booming market conditions is when bidders push the price well in excess of the estimated range — underbidders feel like they've wasted their time because the budget they have means they were never really in the running to buy the house.

TIP

Investors shouldn't get too worried about the debate over underquoting (or its opposite, *overquoting*, which is what agents often do to vendors to get their business in the first place). If you do your homework and look thoroughly at prices in the area, you'll have a reasonable idea of whether the property is within your price range. And, in any case, as soon as bidding tops what you believe is fair value, your interest should immediately stop. Even if it happens mid-auction, you should walk away from the property (in your mind, if not in body) and start thinking about the next property you're interested in.

Tenders

Many names exist and slightly different processes are used for what's essentially a *sale by tender* — you submit a bid via a number of methods by a set deadline. These bids are also known as *sale by set date*, *set sales* and *expressions of interest*. They all have varying degrees of similarity to tenders, although some might be part-auction, with negotiations opening up with the highest bidder.

The tender process is very rarely used for the sale of residential investment properties, but it's not unknown. Most properties offered through a tender-style process are commercial properties, particularly higher value properties.

Tenders require you to put your own value on the property. Prior to getting to this stage, you make your price estimation of the property by either comparing the prices of other similar properties in that suburb, or by getting a qualified valuer to do the job (see Chapter 10 for more on this). Normally you only get one shot, so the price you submit should be at, or very near to, the top price you're prepared to pay.

This scenario is the same with multiple offer situations in private treaty sales, with potential buyers generally only having one opportunity to submit their 'highest and best offer' on a property if a number of potential purchasers are competing against each other.

Off-market

The 'Holy Grail' of property buying opportunities are *off-market sales*. These properties are offered to a select group of potential buyers, including buyers' agents, before they are marketed publicly.

While these properties are generally still being sold by private treaty, they have not been publicly advertised. A vendor or a sales agent might want to use this sales method for a number of reasons. The vendor might not want the property sale to be in the public forum, usually due to privacy reasons or perhaps a divorce. It could be a marketing ploy in slower market conditions, because those buyers will think they are being offered a special opportunity to buy the property 'off-market' without as much competition.

AUCTIONS VERSUS PRIVATE SALES

The argument over whether auctions or private treaty sales produce the best returns is unlikely to be settled — it's a perpetual debate. But there seems to be little doubt that, under the right conditions, auctions have the potential to deliver results that seem to defy logic.

How does an auction achieve these results? Simply, two (or more) people attend the same auction with huge budgets at their disposal. They both love this house and have decided that its value to them is substantially higher than the figure put on it by the vendor, the agent or the majority of the rest of the people in the market.

It's not unheard of during a particularly strong property market for a property being advertised for $800,000 to $1 million to go for $1.2 million or $1.4 million. Five bidders may be prepared to pay $1 million, but when it hits that price, all but two bidders fall away and the last two slug it out, a few thousand dollars at a time, until the second-last person withdraws.

This situation is what a vendor dreams about — two bidders desperate to buy the property for one reason or another. Indeed, 'It only takes two' is a common saying in the real estate sector. The bidders may have no idea of the value of property in the area. They may have a vision for the property that others don't share. They may have been the underbidders on so many occasions that they're prepared to pay a premium just so they don't have to continue the search. In most cases, 'silly' prices achieved at auction aren't going to come from investors — unless they're developers who can see an enormous potential for the land. Prices that defy logic usually come from emotional home buyers.

And what happens to properties that get passed in during an auction? Little reliable data on those properties exists, except that they tend to be sold later through a private treaty sale. A good deal of those properties sell fairly quickly, but at what discount on the price the vendor was hoping for?

Private sales, on the other hand, don't put the same intense pressure on the buyer or the seller. People have time to think about the offer they're going to make, and sellers have time to think about whether or not they will accept it.

Off-market properties are much more prevalent in slower market conditions, but they can be available in a boom market, too. Regardless of the market conditions, it is vital that you not only understand the opportunity in front of you, but also ensure you know the market price for the property because you could easily over-pay for the 'privilege'.

Flipping Out over Buying and Flipping

Over the long term, property prices have shown a history of increasing at 'real' rates about 2 to 5 per cent above inflation — that is, rises of between 5 and 7 per cent. (This doesn't include rent, which is a part of a property's return, and can often average a further 3 to 4 per cent for inner-city properties.) This increase is a solid and sustainable rate of appreciation that rewards investors who have long-term investment horizons and take the buy-and-hold approach with their property assets. This buy-and-hold strategy works and should always be the foundation of your property wealth building.

But, in some areas, particularly in Australia's capital cities and larger regional centres, the demand for housing is so great that the limited supply of new and existing properties available in the market is insufficient. It's in these markets of high demand and rapidly escalating prices that renovators with a buy-and-flip strategy appear.

Flipping new and existing homes

A buy-and-flip strategy (where an investor buys a property, generally makes minor or cosmetic improvements, and then quickly sells it, hopefully for a profit) can work with existing homes located within in-demand property markets.

Some people attempt to flip new properties for a profit, but this practice is speculation rather than strategy. This is how they attempt to do it. These buyers seemingly know about the shortage of housing or build-up of demand for property, and they look to make a quick profit by putting down a deposit on a new home that a builder hasn't yet started. The buyers make a deposit on the property, betting that when the house is complete (or sooner), the market value will have risen to a point where they can make a quick profit by selling their stake before they close on the deal.

TIP

Investing in the first phase of a new residential home development can be quite profitable, but only in the right conditions. Successive phases tend to be priced at higher levels, so the investor who secures a place in the first phase has the potential to pick up when the development is finished and supply of property in this development has stopped. Many investors try to buy in on the ground floor of a new suburb being developed or a new multi-apartment development nearing the start of construction. But be warned: Buying a place that you have no intention of ever actually physically owning is more about having a punt than making an investment. You're gambling that in the next 6 to 18 months, while construction is under way, underlying demand for the development will increase *faster than supply comes online.*

WARNING

Considerable risks are inherent in a buy-and-flip strategy using a new development, particularly when it relates to multi-storey, or high-rise, developments. For a start, where one high-rise development is planned, almost inevitably another developer is going to be able to put one up nearby, even alongside. If you bought into a 100-unit block, then another 100-unit block goes up nearby (and many multiples of that over a period of years), you're going to be competing for tenants and other buyers with those newer properties. We're not fans of medium- or high-density properties for this exact reason — the supply of other properties is virtually unlimited, and properties largely gain in value through scarcity. While it may be possible to buy a planned property with a relatively small deposit, if the market moves against you (that is, down), your losses are magnified.

While it can be tempting to try to buy-and-flip new properties, the opportunities have largely disappeared due to banks changing their lending processes.

The buy-and-flip strategy can also work with existing homes that the investor can purchase from a motivated seller below market value. Some minor cosmetic work or simple improvements may be needed before reselling but, typically, buy-and-flip investors really make their money when they buy at a discount and then locate a buyer at full market value after affordable cosmetic improvements have been completed. This situation is risky, because the cost of buying and selling in Australia is usually around 10 per cent (stamp duties to buy, and agent and advertising fees to sell), even before a capital gain might be taxed. However, it can also be rewarding.

Heeding the risks

The buy-and-flip strategy may be perfectly acceptable, but we prefer the more conventional and lower risk strategy of buy, fix and flip. With the buy-fix-and-flip strategy, you invest in properties that you can add value to through repairs, upgrades and improvements, taking a distressed property and turning it into a solid and well-maintained property.

We strongly prefer this method because it has proven throughout the years to be a lower risk than betting on future supply issues, and gives you a higher probability of making money in real estate. Think of it as the tortoise in the old story of the hare and the tortoise, with the hare as the fast-money, high-risk, high-return strategy.

You may find a property market experiencing rapid housing price increases but be careful. If the demand for new housing in the area is too much, real estate speculators (rather than long-term investors or homeowners) can make up the majority of the purchasers. This imbalance can be dangerous when the majority of buyers in the market are looking for the quick profit rather than a long-term stable property investment. When enough of these speculators head for the exits and don't return, prices can quickly turn nasty. The remaining speculators are then forced to mitigate their losses by renting out their properties (sometimes for years) until the real estate market rebounds and they're able to sell the property to break even.

But we're pragmatists — we know that you may run into a property that turns out to be a buy-and-flip candidate, so we cover possible tax drawbacks in Chapter 15.

Property Development

Like buy-and-flip strategies (or buy-fix-and-flip strategies — refer to preceding section), another favourite, but also high-risk, way of making money from property is to become a property developer. Doing so is even more hardcore than a fix-and-flip strategy, with cosmetic renovations possibly costing thousands, and larger renovations potentially costing hundreds of thousands, of dollars. Property development usually requires substantially more money — nowadays development project budgets can cost hundreds of thousands or millions of dollars, depending on the size of the project.

In the following sections, we outline how the process works and highlight the risks involved. We then cover common development options.

Understanding the process and the risks

Property development essentially involves buying real estate where the current value of the buildings is non-existent, negligible or little without a major facelift. Developers look to buy land that hasn't been put to its highest and best use. A large block of land with a ramshackle or run-down small home could often become three, four or more townhouses or, if the property is big enough, a high-rise block of apartments.

WARNING

Several TV shows have shown the thrills and riches that can be made from developing or redeveloping tired properties. The business is high risk, costs more than buying a property itself and requires the skills of a talented builder or a highly organised project manager. Far too many Australians have 'had a go' at property development, believing it's easy money, only to find they can't cover their building costs, let alone their holding costs, such as interest, council rates and insurances.

In this book, we don't have the space to cover all aspects of property development. You'll need to find additional sources of information — and you must do plenty of research on it — before you become a property developer.

Property developers face a number of serious risks. These include, but aren't limited to, the following:

» **Long lead times:** The time between finding the right investment property, buying it, developing it and selling it to investors can take years, in which time the property cycle is likely to be at a different stage to whenever you bought it.

» **Land can't be subdivided or rezoned:** You bought the property believing the property could be subdivided or given a zoning that allows better use of the land for development, but laws or council policy don't change to allow it.

» **Angry residents:** When you're getting your development through the planning stage, you'll often be taking on residents who are either anti-development (sometimes known as *NIMBYs*, or Not In My Back Yard locals, or Save Our Suburbs campaigners) or just against your development because they think what you're doing is too big or doesn't fit with the local character.

» **Council objections:** Local planning laws are often defended and interpreted fiercely by local councils, and councillors may decide to side with residents in order to win votes.

» **Delays in the building process:** Development projects rarely run to their original timetable, and the schedule is inevitably out of your control and that of your builder.

» **Builders going broke:** This happens all too often. The best builders can be poor businesspeople and they're regularly going broke midway through jobs.

» **The economy and interest rates:** Over the course of the several years that it may take to develop your property, the economy can change direction and interest rates can move dramatically up and down.

» **Hard to sell:** At the end of your project, you may find that the area isn't taking off as you had predicted, leaving you with the decision to either hold the property and rent it out or sell at a less than optimal price.

Property development can be financially rewarding, but don't go in without having done plenty of research or having experience under your belt with cosmetic or structural renovations. Check for any hidden surprises about the property. Find out how much the land itself is worth (see Chapter 11 for information on the principles of valuation). Get an idea of how much the development is likely to cost you (get a builder or quantity surveyor to estimate).

WARNING

With all property development (as with anything to do with property), thorough research is the key. You need to know more about the local laws as they relate to property development, more about the type of current and future residents who are attracted to the area and how much money you need to spend to get the return you're seeking (overcapitalising on property developments is a common trap), and more about the likely future demand for property in the area. You also need to have deeper pockets and good access to cheaper sources of funding, because you and the property will be without income for the construction period.

TIP

As a property developer, you need to be an even better record keeper than a normal property investor. Before the start of a project, you need thorough estimates for the cost of everything to do with the development process (and don't forget the interest costs of holding the property without rent for an extended period) and know whether your plans are likely to develop the sort of reasonable profit you expect because of the risk you've taken.

WARNING

Spending $800,000 on vacant land, $600,000 in building costs for two units and $200,000 in holding costs over two years isn't worth doing if you sell the two properties for only a combined total of $1.8 million. A profit of $200,000 isn't significant enough for the risks you've taken — in this situation, such a result is considered a poor return, almost a loss. You need to be rewarded for the risk to your capital and for the time you spent organising and planning the development. Returns need to be a minimum of 20 per cent per year to make property development a worthwhile investment.

Vacant land

The most obvious type of property available for development is vacant land. Often the seller places the land on the market after receiving council's approval for a certain style or size of development, or an acceptable building *envelope*, which is the space on which building works can take place (councils may limit where dwellings can be built on vacant land, which can be an issue for larger land areas in particular). Know exactly what the land is approved for before you enter negotiations. What's been okayed may not be big enough to fit what you're planning to build.

But keep in mind that the seller won't always have building approvals in place before offering vacant land for sale. It's up to you to investigate or take a risk that you're going to be able to develop the land to your satisfaction. Find out exactly what can be done on the land. Otherwise, you're taking a risk that the land can't be developed at all and you're stuck with a property that will also be difficult to onsell to the next wishful thinker. At the very least, find out what has been approved in the area recently, so you have an idea of what the council and residents are prepared to accept.

The knock-down job

Some dwellings are virtually unfit for human habitation. Houses that aren't regularly maintained eventually fall into disrepair or obsolescence. When the situation gets to this stage, properties often come onto the market because the owner hasn't the money or the inclination to redevelop (or even because the owner has died).

In some cases, even though the land includes a building (of some description), the property is more valuable to someone with an eye for development. Knocking down a house, even one that's in danger of falling over, almost inevitably requires a permit. The same goes for trees on a property. You're wise not to knock anything over until the local council grants permission. And don't forget to factor in the time approval may take.

Redevelop or renovate?

An older building may have a sound building structure, but the inside may have gone to ruin, and most people wouldn't live in it. Whether what you're intending to do is a redevelopment or a renovation is really a matter of degree. A redevelopment is a larger, more expensive job that requires significant construction work, whereas a renovation suggests more cosmetic changes.

Sometimes $100,000 spent updating bathrooms, laundries and kitchens, plus $20,000 spent on carpets and repainting can turn a tired property into a sought-after property for rental or resale.

IN THIS CHAPTER

» **Putting a team together**

» **Starting with a solicitor**

» **Seeking lending professionals**

» **Hiring an accountant**

» **Choosing a building inspector**

» **Finding buying and selling agents**

» **Selecting property managers**

» **Maintaining a professional team**

Chapter **4**

Building Your Team

For some investments, you can simply turn your money over to professional money managers or financial advisers who then act on your behalf and make the day-to-day investment decisions, buying and selling investment assets within your portfolio. Managed funds are an example of this type of passive investment. You invest your money with your favourite fund and periodically evaluate how your fund managers are doing.

Decision-making responsibilities for investment in most real estate assets can't be left to others. And, for most property investors, real estate investing is complicated enough to require the services and knowledge of several professionals. Although you may be skilled in your chosen field, it's unlikely that you possess all the varied and detailed skills and knowledge necessary to find and manage your properties.

Evaluate proposed real estate investments carefully and methodically before you make the ultimate decision to purchase. The uniqueness of each potential opportunity means you need to patiently critique the investment. You should understand the economic climate, the potential for growth, the current physical condition of the property, the status of tenants and leases, and the property's value in the marketplace. Then you must ensure that the transfer of real estate is handled properly and that tax issues don't ruin the investment. Some of these steps require skills you may not have.

In this chapter, we discuss the different professionals involved in real estate who you can team up with as you search for real estate investment opportunities and proceed with the purchase of property. These experts range from solicitors to buyers' agents, accountants and valuers.

Establishing Your Team Early

Some real estate investors make the mistake of looking for a property to buy without spending any time up-front identifying the professionals whose help should be hired.

TIP

Having your team in place before you begin your serious property searching is necessary for two reasons:

» **You can move quickly.** The speed at which you can close a transaction is an advantage in any type of market. In a buyer's market, some sellers are desperate for cash and need to exit quickly. In a seller's market, sellers typically won't tolerate a long settlement if another buyer can get them their asking price sooner.

» **You can effectively research the property before making an offer.** Prudent investors conduct their research before they make an offer. You don't want to waste time on a property that can't meet your goals or your budget.

TIP

For individual residential properties, if you do find yourself in a position where you have to move quickly, consider making a *conditional offer* for a property — one that's subject to finance, for example, which should be standard for all purchases anyway, apart from those bought at auction. In many senses, doing extensive research on the property — getting building and pest inspections — is pointless if the seller's asking price isn't in your ballpark. Making a conditional offer can help determine whether the seller's asking price has any leeway. We recommend making offers only when you've done enough investigating to feel comfortable that your further thorough review of the property interiors (and rental track record in the case of larger residential and all commercial properties) probably won't reveal any surprises that will lead to cancelling the purchase.

WARNING

Never make unconditional offers to buy property without having first consulted your key professionals — your banker, mortgage broker or lender, and your solicitor. Avoid making an offer if you don't have the cash or finance ready; also avoid making offers if you haven't had a solicitor (or conveyancer) cast their eyes over the legal documents. You may invest dozens of hours and several thousand dollars to perform the necessary due diligence (meaning your research), but this amount is small compared with the potential loss from the purchase of a property with problems. (We cover this pre-purchase research in Chapters 10 and 11.)

Getting Good Legal Advice

Don't think for a second that you can get away with buying property without getting proper legal advice. This is simply dangerous. Given that vendors sell their property by *caveat emptor* (Latin for 'let the buyer beware'), buyers have an underlying responsibility to know what they're buying. That's understandable. Why would sellers point out reasons for you not to buy their property?

The legal transfer of property from one owner to another is called *conveyancing*. It's not as simple as signing a few documents. It's also about making sure the right taxes and duties are paid, that the correct titles are changing hands and the required legal checks are undertaken.

Choosing your solicitor

You may think that adding a lawyer to your real estate investment team is a luxury you can't afford. Well, property conveyancing isn't all that expensive (usually between $1,000 and $2,000) and, unless you're fluent in property law, that's a cheap price to pay to have someone look after it for you.

TIP

We strongly suggest you consult with an experienced real estate solicitor from day one of your life as a property investor. If you've already engaged a solicitor, as soon as you find a property that you're considering making a bid for, you can send your solicitor the sale documents to look over for any interesting or unusual conditions, caveats and easements.

With more complicated transactions, have the solicitor review all documents. A good property solicitor can help ensure you avoid some pitfalls before even making an offer.

REMEMBER

If you're going beyond single-home dwellings, seek a solicitor who has experience in purchasing and lease transactions. Ideally, you'll find one solicitor or law firm that can assist with you not only your transactions, but also the drafting and review of other documents. In particular, look for solicitors who have specialised knowledge of tenancy laws and the complicated issues surrounding commercial leases.

Find a solicitor with the communication skills to explain legal terms simply to you. As with any professional, the old adage that 'you get what you pay for' holds true more often than not. So, remember that paying a lower hourly rate for a solicitor isn't necessarily your best option.

Solicitors versus conveyancers

Property buyers can use either solicitors or conveyancers, but which is best? The difference in cost between the two is minimal — you can expect to pay somewhere between $1,000 and $2,000 for either, which may not include inescapable fees for some government searches and additional searches.

Solicitors claim that, as a profession, they offer buyers better legal protection if something goes wrong. Conveyancers argue that, if any extra legal protection is involved, it's actually to protect the lawyers themselves from their clients.

REMEMBER

Choosing between a solicitor and a conveyancer is up to you, and often depends on what your legal needs are. For example, simple real estate transactions generally only require the services of conveyancers, but more complex deals, such as purchasing a unit block or a property with development potential, may need the expertise of a solicitor.

Lining Up a Lender or Mortgage Broker

Before looking at specific property opportunities, you need a budget. And, because your budget for real estate purchases is directly a function of how much you can borrow, you need to determine the limits on your borrowing power. If you can't afford a property, how great the deal is doesn't matter at all.

Reviewing roles

Postpone that appointment to look at investment properties until after you've examined the loans available. You have two resources to consult:

>> *Lender* is a generic term for any firm, or officer of that firm, that lends you the cash to purchase your property. Most often, your list of possible lenders includes banks, credit unions, building societies, non-bank lenders, and private lenders, including property sellers (see Chapter 5 for more details on sources of capital).

>> A *mortgage broker* is a service provider who presents your request for a loan to a variety of different lenders in order to find the best financing for your particular needs. Just like insurance brokers, a good mortgage broker can be a real asset to your team. (We cover mortgages in detail in Chapter 6, and the advantages and disadvantages of working with mortgage brokers versus direct lenders in Chapter 7.)

Lenders and mortgage brokers are in the business of making loans. That's how they make money. A lender's product is cash, and they make money by renting it to people and businesses that pay them the money back plus interest, which is the cost of renting the money. Money is a commodity just like anything else and its availability and pricing are subject to an assortment of variables.

WARNING

Lenders and mortgage brokers want to find you money for your next real estate purchase, but they're not necessarily objective advisers to provide counsel for how much you should borrow. They're trained to calculate the maximum that you may borrow. Don't confuse this figure with the amount that you can truly afford or that will fit best with your overall financial and personal situation.

REMEMBER

If lenders and mortgage brokers want to find you money, then why is getting a loan so difficult sometimes? Because lenders want to make loans to those investors who are a good credit risk, with a high probability of meeting the repayments. Lenders have costs of doing business and need to make a profit. Because the money they lend often belongs to their depositors, lenders need to be careful and selective about the loans they make. (See Chapter 7 for more information on the necessity of a good credit rating when investing in real estate.)

The lender requires collateral for protection against the borrower not being able to make the debt service payments as required. Collateral is the real or personal property that's pledged to secure a loan or mortgage. If the debt isn't paid as agreed, the lender has the right to force the sale of the collateral to recover the outstanding principal and interest on the loan. Typically, the property being purchased is the pledged collateral for real estate loans or mortgages.

Building relationships

A good lender or mortgage broker can help you understand how your financial situation is likely to affect how much you're able to borrow, before you begin your search for an investment property.

TIP

Get together with your lender or mortgage broker and provide him with your latest financials, which includes your income and expenses, as well as your assets and liabilities. Always be truthful. One way to sabotage a relationship with a lender or mortgage broker is to exaggerate or stretch the truth about your financial situation or the potential of your proposed property acquisition.

The lender will require supporting documents for your income and assets and will obtain a credit report. Banks weren't born yesterday — they still issue their share of loans that turn sour, but they don't issue a lot of them because they have thorough systems in place. Expect the lender to check and recheck every line item. When you don't oversell yourself or your proposed property, lenders are often more willing to work with you and even offer better terms.

Lenders can also serve a valuable role in preventing you from making serious mistakes. Particularly in overheated markets, where prices are rising irrationally with no fundamental economic support, lenders, through their lending process, can keep you from getting caught up in a buy-at-any-price frenzy, similar to what occurred in some locations before the global financial crisis (GFC) and during the COVID-19 pandemic boom.

In these rapidly rising markets, lenders tend to be more conservative and will limit loan amounts and require larger deposits, as they did in Australia in 2008 and 2022 when global credit issues emerged. These factors provide the lender with additional protection should market prices fall, but they're also a signal that the lender feels the requested loan exceeds the intrinsic value of the property that they'll be stuck with if you default. Small loan offers with high deposits are a clue that you may be paying more than a property is worth or buying at the market's peak.

Adding an Accountant

An accountant may not be the first person you think to consult when making a real estate transaction. However, our experience is that a good accountant who is a specialist in property investment can provide terrific feedback on the benefits and pitfalls of different strategies. Accountants aren't legally allowed to provide investment advice in Australia (without having additional qualifications). But their knowledge of tax issues can be useful. Of course, make sure your tax professional has experience with property investment, preferably with specialist qualifications, and understands your needs and goals. (We cover the basics of accounting and tax in Chapter 15.)

TIP

Although you may pick up a lot of information about real estate and discover some of the advantages of property investing by speaking with some tax people, don't rely on generic information ('Investing in real estate offers a terrific tax dodge', for example). You need specific feedback and ideas from a specialist accountant regarding your unique financial situation and which types of real estate investments will work best for you.

Based on your age, income and other important factors, the benefits you seek from real estate may be entirely different from what other investors are after. Many investors look for immediate cash flow from their properties. But others have sufficient other income currently and prefer to look at real estate as a wealth builder via capital growth to improve their retirement. These investors may be prepared to consider negative gearing as a way of accelerating the potential growth. While some real estate investors are looking for **tax benefits, the ability to** negatively gear property should never be the sole reason for investing in property.

The role of your accountant is to evaluate the potential tax ramifications of your investment and how they will affect your financial position. Remember the old adage, 'It's not what you make that matters, but what you keep'.

A good accountant with property experience can advise you on the proper structures to consider from a tax perspective and what your best real estate investment might be — the direct ownership of residential investment properties, perhaps, or units in a commercial property trust with lower returns but fewer management headaches, for example. Accountants are tax experts and the ownership structure you choose for your real estate investments can be an important determinant of your success as a property investor.

Meet with your accountant and get to know the benefits and pitfalls of your proposed real estate investments before you start making offers, even if only so your accountant can suggest which ownership option is best for you. (See Chapter 11 for a discussion of the different types of title.)

Inspecting with a Building Expert

Whether or not the building you're buying is brand new, you should never buy a property before you've had a well-qualified builder conduct a thorough inspection of the property. New properties can have serious problems if the builder was shonky or cut corners. And older properties inevitably have maintenance issues.

The two reports you should purchase prior to buying a property are a building report and a pest-inspection report — each of which cost about $400 to $600, depending on a few factors, including size and location of the dwelling. Only commission these reports when some of the other pegs on the property have fallen into place. Building and pest inspections are like getting a full medical for the building — they give you a great insight into current problems and what problems are lurking that are likely to require action within a few years. (See Chapter 12 for more on due diligence.)

TIP

The timing of building and pest inspections is important. If you're buying privately, you should make your purchase offer conditional on satisfactory building and pest-inspection reports, which can give you an out for your offer if the reports show major flaws or costly problems. However, you can't do this if you're buying at an auction, where bidding is final. These reports can take a few days to put together, so book in your inspections about a week prior to auction.

The building industry professionals who do your building and pest inspections are able to report on the quality or condition of a range of items, including the structural integrity of the building, plumbing and drainage, insulation, evidence of asbestos, rising damp or termite infestation, roofing quality, sub-floor ventilation, condition of walls and paintwork, and whether additions have had proper council approval.

In the worst-case scenario, they may find serious problems that will cost big money to fix. The cost of fixing these problems may be prohibitive and your interest in the property may end. In most cases, the amount of serious work that needs to be done is quite small.

TIP

The builder's report can sometimes be used to renegotiate the price with a vendor. If costly problems that require fixing arise, pointing them out could see the vendor, particularly one who's had the property on the market for longer than average, reduce his price expectations.

Inspection reports are important because they're one way of being able to control the risks associated with your property purchase. They allow you to plan ahead for those expenses.

One of the largest national groups that does inspections is the architect's association Archicentre (www.archicentre.com.au). Another way to find a company that does building inspections in your area is to search online and check out the reviews posted for each company. You can also ask your expert team members for their recommendations.

Working with Real Estate Professionals to Buy and Sell Property

The real estate industry is a considerable sector in Australia, and real estate agents are responsible for the buying and selling of property, and for managing rentals (we discuss managing rentals in 'Dealing with Property Managers', later in this chapter). Although the primary job of agents is to market and sell property, a second, smaller industry group, known as *buyers' agents*, can source and secure property for you.

We cover working with these professionals in the following sections, as well as looking at what to be aware of when buying property through spruikers and developers.

Understanding what agents do

Buying property in Australia almost always involves dealing with a licensed real estate agent (although some people do sell their own properties — or attempt to, as it usually turns out). Agents are hired by vendors to sell their property with the aim of getting the highest price possible. In a nutshell, the agent's responsibility is to look after advertising and marketing the property, showing potential buyers through the property, answering queries and then, if it gets to the negotiation stage, acting as the intermediary between buyer and seller.

In most instances, agents charge a commission based on the price a property sells for. This fee is paid by the seller and generally ranges between 1 and 4 per cent, depending on location, value of the property, reputation of the agent and competition in the area (see the section 'Commission? You bet', later in this chapter).

Obviously, in order to get a sale, the buyer and seller must agree on a price. If a buyer is offering to pay only $760,000 for a property and the seller wants $790,000, no sale occurs. The agent's responsibility in this common situation is to get the buyer and the seller to come together. This usually involves the agent trying to convince the buyer to raise his price and also convincing the vendor to lower his price expectations — known as *conditioning* a vendor.

TIP

No matter what you think of real estate sales agents, it doesn't pay to put them offside if you're looking around an area and you're likely to bump into them frequently at house inspections. Be friendly to them and make polite conversation. But, as a potential buyer, don't get sucked in by questions designed to find out how big your budget is. Nothing is better for an agent than knowing how much a potential buyer is looking to spend or could spend if the right property surfaced.

If you say that you're looking to spend up to $900,000, the agent now knows that's how much money you can spend. This could hurt you in several ways. An agent has no incentive to show a $700,000 property to a buyer who has $900,000 to spend, even if the investment may be better. And, if you're bidding at auction, the agent and auctioneer know your limit.

On the lookout: Buyers' agents and QPIAs

Licensed buyers' agents and qualified property investment advisers (QPIAs) are industry professionals who work independently and exclusively for buyers to help them find and secure a home or investment property.

WARNING

The number of buyers' agents and QPIAs has been rising in Australia over the past decade — as has a less qualified cohort. Some people present themselves as being a buyers' advocate, for example, but don't have the skills, experience or qualifications to back up their claims. When considering buyers' agents or QPIAs, make sure you check their qualifications and their bona fides, such as their membership of relevant industry associations, the Property Investment Professionals of Australia (PIPA) and the Real Estate Buyers Agents Association of Australia (REBAA), before agreeing to work with them.

The most professional, educated and experienced buyers' agents and QPIAs will provide you with a tailored investment plan that is bespoke to you personally and will charge you a fee for their professional service, as is their right. They will also happily disclose any commissions that they are paid, and by whom, because they are committed to transparency.

Understanding the advantages of buyers' agents

Buyers' agents are becoming a bigger part of the investment property landscape, especially for time-poor investors. They can add significant value and potentially save you thousands — if not tens of thousands — of dollars by being able to deal impartially with the seller's agent. They can also use their deeper local connections in the area or industry to source the best properties for you specifically.

Many property investors do their own homework and research and are prepared to save themselves the buyers' agent fee to find their own properties, especially if they're looking to invest in single-home dwellings. But experienced buyers' agents can remove many risks for you, which can far outweigh their direct cost, especially for investors seeking properties interstate to take advantage of different market conditions.

Firstly, they're often able to spot under market value properties and can potentially negotiate the price of properties down, which may potentially save you far more than the fee you've paid for their professional services. Secondly, they usually have a clear investment strategy you can take advantage of.

TIP

Make sure the buyers' agent you're considering has a solid track record and that you understand what his investment strategy is and how that might be different from your own. Some buyers' agents recommend property that minimises tax (such as property that is negatively geared or new). Others have a different focus — for example, they only purchase properties that are new, are neutrally geared, are a certain distance from a central business district, have certain types of characteristics, or are located in growth hotspots around the nation.

REMEMBER

Each property investment strategy has its benefits and drawbacks, and understanding how these might apply to your situation is crucially important. For example, if you don't have a lot of spare income, a negatively geared property may have too big an impact on your personal cash flow. A less aggressive option may suit your circumstances better. Similarly, if cash flow isn't your issue, a neutrally geared property may not be as beneficial to your long-term wealth-creation plans.

A third possible advantage is that you have a professional dealing with a professional — a buyers' agent dealing with a sales agent. When that's happening, the emotion is completely removed from the discussions between these two professionals, especially in the negotiation phase of the real estate transaction.

Fourthly, your buyer's agent can give you back your time. Choosing property can be a horrendously time-consuming process, from searching through the properties online, to attending inspections, to objectively assessing them (or trying to), to getting the inspections done, to making offers or bidding at auction, to settling the purchase. It can take dozens and dozens (even hundreds) of hours to find property that suits your needs. Depending on how you value your time — and you should put a dollar value on your time — the cost of a buying professional could be justified simply on the time they save you (outside of the other benefits already covered in this section).

Considering the costs of buyers' agents

Professional buyers' agents and QPIAs provide a service for a fee. You need to understand what that service is as well as their specific investment strategy (because they generally have one) to ensure it fits in with your own personal real estate goals.

REMEMBER

You should expect to be charged a fee for the services provided by buyers' agents and QPIAs because they are professionals and deserve to be paid for their time and their advice. Some buyers' agents charge a percentage commission on the purchase price of the property they help you purchase, while others charge a flat fee for their services.

The most experienced operators provide a variety of services, including the following:

>> Finding and negotiating on a property in an area primed for future growth

>> Sourcing your new home based on your specific instructions

>> Preparing a property investment plan for you

>> Taking over the negotiation on a property that you have already located

All of the options provided by buyers' agents are generally fee-for-service. If someone purporting to be a buyers' agent or advocate offers to undertake these services for free, you should be very wary, because they are being paid by someone, somewhere, and are likely not working for you independently at all.

The top property investment professionals always disclose any commissions they might be paid — for example, for referrals to other people in the industry such as mortgage brokers. If they don't, or won't, you should question why.

Commission? You bet

Real estate sales agents are generally motivated to see a transaction go through, usually because they're compensated only when a sale is made. Compensation for sales agents is typically a *commission* — a percentage of the price paid for a property. As a result, property agents do have an interest in the property going for a higher price. But their primary interest is getting a sale, and it doesn't matter what percentage the commission is — the commission on a property that sells for $750,000 is always going to beat the commission on an $800,000 property that doesn't sell.

Commissions vary based on the property and the size of the transaction. In Australia, commissions are typically between 1 and 4 per cent. That range covers most properties — houses, apartments, commercial properties and vacant land. Commissions are sometimes higher in towns with a smaller population and less competition, or for small commercial properties. They can be lower for very large properties, such as a significant block of flats.

The commission charged on a property is related to the service given, and (if using a buyers' agent who charges commission — refer to the preceding section) you should always ask exactly what you're going to get for your fees. Get everything in writing — what's included, in the way of services and research, and what isn't.

TIP

Don't forget the first rule of being a consumer — you inevitably get what you pay for. If you beat an agent down to a price, or percentage, that won't make much money for him out of the deal, don't expect to get as much in the way of service. If agents would normally make $25,000 out of a sale of this type and you get them to halve their commission to $15,000, for example, don't expect $25,000 worth of service.

Making the most of real estate professionals

If you do decide that you want to employ a professional to help you with your property purchase, make sure you do sufficient research to find the right one. Look for professional buyers' agents with the following qualifications:

>> **Expertise in the geographic market:** Find someone who knows the area you want to buy in, and the specific property type you're seeking. This is especially important if you don't live nearby.

>> **Professional licence status:** Check with the state's real estate institute to make sure the professional holds the proper accreditation. Also, check that they belong to the key industry associations, such as the Real Estate Buyers Agents Association of Australia (REBAA).

>> **Bona fide references:** Get the names and numbers of three to five clients that the agent has worked with in the past year. Then make sure you call them. Ask the clients which parts of the provided service were most valuable. Did the buyers' agent assertively represent the client?

>> **Willingness to communicate:** The number-one complaint about real estate professionals is that they don't keep their clients informed. Look for someone you're comfortable with and can talk to.

>> **Negotiation skills:** Especially with buyers' agents, you want a representative with strong negotiating skills who will exhaust all avenues to get you the best deal possible.

>> **Reputation for honesty, integrity and patience:** The reputation of your representative can be critical when it comes to dealing with other agents or gaining the cooperation of an adversarial seller.

Getting friendly with sales agents in your area of interest can also be worthwhile. Agents don't care where their buyers come from and a once-a-week phone call, email or text to keep a potential buyer up to speed with what's happening in the suburb can be a winner for them.

TIP

Our advice is to make friends with experienced sales agents in the area who specialise in the types of properties you're looking for and know the local market. These agents know buyers and sellers, and also have contacts for other services and products you're likely to need as your property portfolio expands.

To get the best deals, timing is critical. You want to be the first one contacted about the best properties coming onto the market, or even about properties before they hit the market. This can be another advantage to working with a professional buyers' agent, but being on good terms with the local sales agents also helps. You want an agent to think of you first. If you're not interested in or not able to purchase a property at the time, explain your situation and thank the agent for thinking of you.

REMEMBER

In many metropolitan areas, looking at the properties online isn't enough. The best deals are often the ones that aren't advertised. This is where insider information from agents can make you the bride and not the bridesmaid.

Many property owners don't want the disruption caused by openly listing a house and avoid the problem by quietly talking to one or two top agents in an area, with the understanding that the potential transaction is kept confidential. This leads to some great opportunities for agents and their clients.

And, although having agents on your team can be an excellent strategy that may give you a competitive edge, don't completely ignore current listings. Such sources often include properties that other investors overlook because they didn't have the vision to see a potential opportunity.

Spruiker alert!

Property spruikers have been around for decades, but their numbers seem to have spread like mushrooms in recent years. You can see them advertising in all media (print, radio, television and online), telling you they can make you property millionaires in just a few years. Sigh.

The old adage 'if it sounds too good to be true, it probably is' is more true of those promising big short-term profits in property than such promises made in almost any other part of the investment universe. Property takes years to grow wealth and the transaction costs are considerable. It's most certainly not a get-rich-quick scheme, which some property promoters seem to suggest it is.

WARNING

Instant riches aren't possible in any game (outside of lotto-style gambling), but this doesn't stop property spruikers from promoting their seminars to help you get onto the property wagon and — automatically, they seem to suggest — get you on a path to your first, second and third million in real estate.

While you can almost always learn something from a seminar, be wary of people or companies that use free seminars to lure you into expensive specialist courses that they run (some of which cost up to $30,000), or that take you straight from a seminar to buying your first investment property (usually from an entity related to those running the seminar, or one where the seminar runners receive a substantial but undisclosed kickback).

Obviously, not all companies selling real estate through seminars are shysters. You can find some very reputable property companies that are making an honest buck from explaining property investment legitimately and fairly to potential customers. But plenty have fallen foul of the investments watchdog, the Australian Securities and Investments Commission (ASIC), for misleading advertising or making false claims. Others, it would seem, ASIC would love to shut down, but they're operating just enough inside the law to be considered legal.

TIP

If you do feel compelled to answer an advertisement to go to a property seminar, here's one suggestion. Don't sign anything that day. If you get something positive out of the experience, sleep on it. If the following day, or a few days later, you're still tempted to take things further, you can give the person or company a call. Signing up a few days later gives you the space to let ideas settle in. And, in any case, any seminar that has to be signed up for at the time on a 'one-time special offer' is more likely to be a high-pressure sales pitch than a genuine offer to help you increase your wealth.

At the end of the day, always check the qualifications, experience and industry association memberships of anyone purporting to be an independent property investment adviser. Ideally, they should be licensed for every state they operate in as well as being members of PIPA, REBAA, and their local real estate institutes. If they're not, ask them why.

Dealing with developers

Most property developers are out to deal with potential purchasers honestly and fairly. Their main role is to find underutilised land to develop in a way that provides housing to those who seek it, and creates a profit for themselves.

However, buying directly from developers brings its own risks — primarily, that you can overpay for a property. It seems that whenever a housing downturn occurs, the first properties to start struggling are the higher density developments, which are inevitably the realm of developers.

TIP

We have a personal rule never to purchase brand new properties as an investment, unless you have worked with a qualified buying expert in this space. (However, we consider purchasing a home to be in a different category, because it's different from an investment property.) This is because we believe that brand new properties come with costs that don't exist with established properties. Firstly, GST applies to new housing, but not off-the-plan units. Secondly, the developers need to make their margins. And, thirdly, developers often have to hire good salespeople to sell their building, which is a cost that's then passed on to the purchaser. We have seen time and again that the same properties sold directly by the developer come back onto the market one to three years later at a similar or lower price than paid by the original purchaser. With property that's still relatively new, the depreciation benefits are still usually considerable (see Chapter 15 for more on depreciation), so it can often make good sense to purchase into a development that's a few years old — especially when you're dealing with a motivated seller who doesn't have the same profit imperative as the developer did.

Dealing with Property Managers

Attempting to manage your investment property as a first-time investor is not a good idea. You have to know far too many laws, and ignorance of the law is no excuse if you treat a tenant unfairly. The cost of a property manager is usually only about 5.5 to 8.8 per cent of the collected rent, including GST, meaning having a real estate agent handle the property management is a price worth paying. (Rental management is covered in more detail in Chapter 13.)

Most suburbs and towns have a number of real estate agencies that look after rental properties. Property management–only agencies are also available these days. In most instances, appointing an agency in the area where your property is located is desirable. They not only know the area but are also able to attend to the property to give tradespeople access when required.

If you have a choice of agents in an area, here are some questions to put to them to determine their suitability:

>> **How many properties do you manage?** One real estate agency may be managing significantly more properties than its competitors for a very good reason. This reason could be either service or price. The places that have the most properties available for rent are going to have the most potential tenants coming through their offices.

>> **What is your vacancy rate?** Find out how many vacancies the agency has and work it out as a percentage of its total portfolio. A higher vacancy rate than other agencies in the area may indicate problems with its management style.

- **What is your fee structure?** You want to see in writing the agency's main charges for collecting rent (usually 5.5 to 8.8 per cent), what that fee includes (meeting contractors for repairs, for example) and all its other fees and charges (for services such as postage or attending the tenancy tribunal on your behalf).

- **How many staff are looking after the rental properties?** Unlike agents who sell property, property managers can sometimes be overworked and underpaid. If they don't have enough time to answer a property owner's calls, how are they going to treat a tenant?

- **How experienced are the staff?** Property managers are often new to the industry and are doing their time in the rental department before trying their hand with the more glamorous sales side of the industry. Having someone with a track record on the selling side of the business is a plus.

- **How do they screen tenants?** You want to know exactly how the managers are going to make sure you end up with decent tenants. What reference checks do they do?

- **How do tenants report issues?** Some agents now have online portals for tenants to quickly report maintenance issues, and for owners to track how these issues are responded to by the agent. This system often means smaller issues are reported before they become bigger problems.

- **How is rent collected and disbursed?** Best practice is for rent to be collected from tenants and directly disbursed into your bank account at an agreed timeframe — say, weekly, fortnightly or monthly. You will also receive a statement of income and expenses at the same time, either via email, text or your property manager's specialised online portal.

Keeping Relationships Professional

As your property investments grow or develop into a portfolio, you'll need the services of industry professionals more and more. Make sure you treat those service providers professionally. To start with, be courteous and businesslike in all your dealings, just as you'd expect professionals to be. You also want the people you're dealing with to be honest, and you should be honest in return.

But you also need to be assertive when something goes wrong. If one of your team messes up, then you need to be clear with that person about how he needs to fix up the error and get things back on track.

WARNING

Mixing business and family works for some people and not for others. If you have a relative (sister, father-in-law, cousin) who you're thinking of taking on as part of your team, make sure you can be firm with that person if it's required. It's no good getting family discounts if the service is substandard or going to cost you money in other ways. Sacking or no longer using family members who you once employed can also cause family tension — and make family get-togethers rather unpleasant.

2

Financing: Raising Capital and Sourcing Loans

Work out the amount of money you need to get started, and the best places to source those funds in the likely event that you'll need to borrow money for your real estate plans.

Understand the key issues you need to consider in deciding the terms of your financing — because getting these steps right can help reduce the risk associated with the large debts that property investors inevitably have.

Find out about traditional lending sources and the types of banking products that may aid your investment program, and how to make the most of your bank as your portfolio grows (along with your debt and your reliance on good credit terms).

Consider the pros and cons of geared property investment within a self-managed super fund.

Uncover the ongoing costs of property investment that you need to figure into your funding strategy.

IN THIS CHAPTER

» Knowing how much you need to get started

» Getting the required cash together

» Finding lenders

» Drawing on home equity

» Going straight to an investment property

» Tapping into advanced funding strategies

Chapter **5**

Sources of Finance

For many people, the trouble with real estate investing is that they lack the access to cash for the deposit as well as the expertise to select the most strategic holding. The old adage that 'it takes money to make money' is usually true in our experience. So how do you get started in real estate if you don't want to own distressed properties in the worst suburbs or regions and you don't have a six-figure deposit to pay top dollar in the best suburbs? Successful real estate investing requires patience and a long-term vision. Our method of building real estate wealth over time is to create an investment portfolio that's sustainable and provides generous returns on your investments.

You don't necessarily have to be wealthy to begin making attractive real estate investments. In this chapter, we present a wide range of funding options that offers something for virtually everyone's budget and personal situation.

Calculating the Costs of Entry

At some point in your life, you've surely had the experience of wanting to do something and then realising that you didn't have sufficient money to accomplish your goal. Perhaps it was as simple as lacking the change to buy a chocolate bar as a child. Or maybe it happened on a holiday when you ran low on funds and tried to do business with a shop owner who took only cash when you carried only a credit card. No matter — the world of real estate investing is no different. You can't play if you can't pay.

Determining what you need to get started

Most of the time, real estate investors make a deposit and borrow most of the money needed to complete a purchase. That's the 'conventional way' to purchase investment properties and is likely to be the most successful method for you in the long run (as it has been for us).

For most residential investment properties, including free-standing houses, semi-detached housing such as some townhouses and apartments, and even small multi-unit developments, you can gain access to good financing terms by making at least a 10 per cent deposit or offering significant equity (see the section 'What is equity?', later in this chapter), depending on your personal financial situation and the lending environment at the time.

WARNING

Most banks in Australia charge *lenders' mortgage insurance* (LMI) when the size of the deposit (or equity guarantee) is less than 20 per cent. LMI is an exponential charge that increases as the deposit offered by the property buyer decreases. For more about LMI, see 'Overcoming deposit limitations', later in this chapter. (We also cover getting finance in Chapter 6, and delve into lenders' mortgage insurance more deeply in Chapter 7.)

REMEMBER

A minimum deposit of at least 10 per cent is recommended for first-time property buyers. You can escape being charged LMI if you have a deposit (or equity) of at least 20 per cent.

You won't find such wonderful financing options for commercial real estate and vacant land. Compared with residential properties, these types of investments usually require larger deposits and/or higher interest rates and loan fees.

Determining how much cash you need to close on a purchase is largely a function of the estimated purchase price. Here's an example: If you're looking at buying a modest house priced at $800,000, a 20 per cent deposit equals $160,000. You then add another 4 to 6 per cent for settlement costs (including stamp duty, title-transfer fees, bank fees and legal fees) to reach the estimated deposit of $200,000 that you would need to get the best financing options.

Most first home buyers will struggle to save a deposit of this magnitude, with many first-timers usually presenting a 5 to 10 per cent deposit as well as making the most of various state government grants and stamp duty concessions.

Don't forget stamp duty

After the actual cost of the property itself, the next biggest cost in buying properties in Australia is *land transfer duty* or *stamp duty* — a generally nasty, big, regressive tax levied by state and territory governments. Each government charges stamp duty in a different way, and it's usually tiered so that lower valued real estate is charged less stamp duty as a proportion of the value of the property. Investors often pay higher rates of stamp duty as well. For what reason, we're not sure.

Stamp duty usually ranges from about 3 to 5.5 per cent of the value of a property (although above certain amounts, it can be very close to 6 per cent). For example, buying a $650,000 established or new property in Victoria incurs a stamp duty of $34,070 if it's your home or principal place of residence — and if it's an investment property. If you're a first home buyer, you may qualify for a concession, which would result in a reduced stamp duty fee of $11,356.

However, in Queensland (which applies the cheapest stamp duty), buying a $650,000 property incurs a stamp duty of $15,100 for existing and new homeowners — however, this increases to $22,275 for investors.

TIP

For details of exactly how stamp duty is charged in your state or territory, contact your local state revenue office or department of treasury. The following list of website addresses can help you get started:

>> **Australian Capital Territory:** www.revenue.act.gov.au/duties

>> **New South Wales:** www.service.nsw.gov.au/

>> **Northern Territory:** www.nt.gov.au/employ/money-and-taxes

>> **Queensland:** www.treasury.qld.gov.au/budget-and-financial-management/revenue-and-taxation/

>> **South Australia:** www.revenuesa.sa.gov.au

>> **Tasmania:** www.sro.tas.gov.au/property-transfer-duties

>> **Victoria:** www.sro.vic.gov.au/land-transfer-duty

>> **Western Australia:** www.wa.gov.au/service/financial-management/taxation-and-duty

Overcoming deposit limitations

Many people, especially when they make their first real estate purchase, are strapped for cash. In order to qualify for the most attractive financing, lenders typically require that your deposit be at least 20 per cent of the property's purchase price. In addition, you need to reserve money to pay for other settlement costs such as stamp duty, title-transfer fees, and loan fees. (Banks usually require commercial property buyers to put up 30 per cent, plus costs, as a deposit.)

TIP

If you don't have 20-plus per cent of the purchase price, don't panic and don't get depressed — you can still own real estate. We've got some solutions:

>> **Lenders' mortgage insurance:** Most lenders can still offer you a mortgage even though you may be able to put down only 5 to 20 per cent of the purchase price. These lenders are likely to require you to pay lenders' mortgage insurance (LMI) for your loan. This insurance usually costs several thousands of dollars and is designed to protect the lender, not you, if you default on your loan. When you do have at least 20 per cent or higher equity in the property, you can usually eliminate the LMI. (For more information about this insurance, see Chapter 7.)

>> **Delayed gratification:** If you don't want the cost and strain of extra fees and bad finance terms, postpone your purchase. Boost your savings. Examine your current spending habits and plan to build up a nest egg to use to invest in your first rental property. For more tips on saving, see the section 'Make saving a habit', later in this chapter.

>> **Thinking smaller:** Consider lower priced properties. Smaller properties and those that need some work can help keep down the purchase price. For example, a duplex where you live in one unit and rent out the other is also a cost-effective way to get started. (We also discuss ways to get started in the section 'No Home? No Worries!', later in this chapter.)

Rounding Up the Required Cash

Most successful real estate investors we know, including ourselves, started building their real estate investment portfolios the old-fashioned way — through saving money and then gradually buying properties over the years. Many people have difficulty saving money because they don't know how, or are simply unwilling, to limit their spending. Easy access to consumer debt (via credit cards, car loans and 'buy now, pay later' schemes, for example) creates huge obstacles to saving more and spending less — many Australians holding credit cards don't pay off their debt in full each month. Investing in real estate requires self-control, sacrifice and discipline. As with most good things in life, you must be patient and plan ahead to be able to invest in real estate.

Make saving a habit

As young adults, some people are naturally good savers. Those who save regularly have usually acquired good financial habits from their parents. Other good savers have a high level of motivation to accomplish goals — retiring young, starting a business, buying a home, prioritising time with their kids and so on. Achieving such goals is much harder (if not impossible) when you're living payday to payday and worried about next month's bills.

If you're not satisfied with how much of your monthly earnings you're able to save, you have two options (and you can take advantage of both):

» **Boost your income:** To increase your take-home pay, working more may be a possibility, or you may be able to take a more lucrative career path. But keep your priorities in order. Your personal health and relationships shouldn't be put on the backburner for a workaholic schedule. We also believe in investing in your education. A solid education is the path to greater financial rewards and can lead to all of the great goals we discuss here. Education isn't only a key to your chosen profession, but also to real estate investing.

» **Reduce your spending:** For most people, this is the path to increased savings. Start by analysing how much you spend on different areas (for example, food, clothing and entertainment) each month. Then decide where and how you can cut back. Would you rather eat out less or have takeaway food delivered less often? How about driving a less expensive car versus taking lower cost holidays? Although the possibilities to reduce your spending are many, you and only you can decide which options you're willing and able to implement. If you need more help with this vital financial topic, a number of books and budgeting tools are available these days that can help guide you.

Tap into other cash sources

Saving money from your monthly earnings will probably be the foundation for your entry into your real estate investing program. However, you may have access to other financial resources for deposits. Before we jump into these, we offer a friendly little reminder: Monitor how much of your overall investment portfolio you place into real estate and how diversified and appropriate your holdings are, given your overall goals (refer to Chapter 1 for more guidance).

As you gain more comfort and confidence as a real estate investor, you may wish to redirect some of your dollars from other investments — such as shares, bonds and managed funds — into property. If you do, be mindful of the following:

>> **Diversification:** Real estate is one of the prime investments (the others being shares and small business) for long-term appreciation potential. Be sure that you understand your portfolio's overall asset allocation and risk when making changes. Check out Chapter 1 for more details.

>> **Tax issues:** If you've held other investments for more than one year, you can take advantage of lower capital gains tax rates if you now wish to sell. The effective maximum federal government tax rate for long-term capital gains (investments sold for more than they were purchased for after more than 12 months) includes a 50 per cent reduction in the gain itself, for assets held longer than a year.

Primary Sources of Finance: Lenders Big and Small

When the Hawke–Keating federal government deregulated the banking system in the mid-1980s, the number of lenders in Australia exploded, as did the competition between them. At first, foreign banks rushed in, many of which later retreated or scaled back their activities after failing to understand the subtleties of the local market. But banks aren't the only institutions that now lend money for investment property in Australia. Alternative mainstream lenders include building societies, credit unions and non-bank lenders.

In the following sections, we describe the different types of mainstream lenders that you can approach to finance property investment, and briefly cover how they operate.

Banks

Traditionally, banks are deposit-taking institutions. They accept deposits from some customers and then lend this money to other customers. Because they're the backbone of the Australian financial system, banks are heavily regulated by federal government entities, including the Australian Prudential Regulatory Authority, the Australian Securities and Investments Commission and the Reserve Bank of Australia.

When Australians think of banks, most call to mind the 'big four': The Australian and New Zealand Banking Group (ANZ, at www.anz.com), the Commonwealth Bank of Australia (CBA, at www.commbank.com.au), the National Australia Bank (NAB, at www.nab.com.au) and Westpac Banking Corporation (Westpac, at www.westpac.com.au). These banks are protected by the federal government's four pillars policy, which bans mergers between the four club members. And, between them, these banks account for more than 80 per cent of all loans from mortgage borrowers in Australia.

The big four aren't the only banks in Australia. Most states have at least one or two other banks, many of which are also expanding beyond their traditional state boundaries. These include the Bank of Queensland (www.boq.com.au) and Suncorp Bank (www.suncorp.com.au) in Queensland, Bendigo Bank (www.bendigobank.com.au) in Victoria, Banks SA (www.banksa.com.au) in South Australia, and Bank-West (www.bankwest.com.au) in Western Australia (owned by the Commonwealth Bank of Australia).

The foreign banks with significant presences in Australia include HSBC (www.hsbc.com.au), Citibank (www.citibank.com.au) and ING (www.ing.com.au), to name just a few.

For information on the different types of interest rates and the types of mortgages you're likely to be offered if you approach a bank to finance your property investment, see Chapter 6.

Building societies and credit unions

Prior to the mid-1980s, building societies and credit unions were the places you went to for a loan when the banks knocked you back. These institutions charged higher interest rates than the banks to cover the bigger risks they were taking to provide mortgages. They were also usually less efficient. These building societies and credit unions were traditionally operated as not-for-profit organisations to provide loans to their members.

Today, most building societies and credit unions offer interest rates that rival their larger banking competitors' rates and tend to differentiate themselves by providing customised service.

Non-bank lenders

The deregulation of the banking system in the 1980s eventually paved the way for non-bank lenders to become mainstream. The first and most successful of these was Aussie Home Loans (www.aussie.com.au), which arrived in time to ride the first big wave of anti-bank sentiment in the 1990s (generated by branch closures and sacking of staff to make higher profits) and undercut the banks' interest rates.

WARNING

As well as Aussie Home Loans, now called Aussie, other small and nimble providers have also entered the market to offer an array of loans in recent years. Some have the reputation of being a little fly-by-night, often appearing attractive because of very low interest rates. As a property investor, price shouldn't be everything in your decision of which lender to use, and using a well-established lender should be a priority.

The main difference between banks, building societies and credit unions on the one hand and non-bank lenders on the other is how they source the money they lend out to property buyers. The traditional lenders source their money from depositors, whereas the non-bank lenders tend to raise their money from international money markets — international investors seeking fixed-interest returns from reasonably secure investments, such as Australian mortgages.

Non-conforming lenders

The emergence of non-conforming lenders is a relatively new innovation in mainstream lending. Pioneers in this area include Liberty Financial (www. liberty.com.au) and Bluestone (www.bluestone.com.au). These lenders emerged in the late 1990s, when competition created a vacuum in the middle market — they filled the gap between traditional lenders and solicitors' funds, which lend on property at lender-of-last-resort interest rates.

Non-conforming lenders use a method called *risk-based pricing* to set individual mortgage rates for their borrowers. That is, customers are charged an interest rate that reflects the risk they pose of defaulting on the mortgage. Non-conforming lenders' terms are aimed at borrowers who find it very difficult to get a loan from mainstream lenders because they may have failed to provide enough paperwork to satisfy traditional lending criteria — for example, customers who have an impaired credit record, are self-employed or have jobs with irregular income streams, such as consultants, freelancers, professional sportspeople and actors. A non-conforming loan usually starts with a premium on the interest rate, but as borrowers prove their ability to pay, the premium is reduced.

Here's an example: If the current interest rate charged by a bank is 5 per cent, the non-conforming lender may agree to lend the money based on an interest rate premium of, say, 4 percentage points. When the borrower gets her loan, she must pay an interest rate of 9 per cent for the first year. Assuming the borrower meets all the repayments during the first 12 months, the lender may then reduce the loan to, say, 8.5 per cent for the second year, then to 7.5 per cent in the third year and to 6.75 per cent for the fourth. By this stage, the borrower may be able to refinance to a different lender at normal interest rates.

REMEMBER

Non-conforming lenders, like non-bank lenders, source their funds through international money markets rather than deposits.

Borrowing Against Property Equity

Many real estate investors begin building their real estate portfolio after they have bought their own home, but we are seeing an ever-increasing number of people buying an investment property (and even two or three) *before* purchasing a home to live via the rentvesting strategy (refer to Chapter 2). However, tapping into your home's equity may be a good deposit source for your property investments.

The family home is often the primary source of capital for those who have developed equity. Lending against property is the primary business of banks. Banks are comfortable doing so, because they've developed systems that allow them to judge the risks associated with lending to an individual or to a sector in general (and, as we discuss further in Chapter 7, banks can take out lenders' mortgage insurance — or LMI — on you failing on your mortgage, and get you to pay the premiums for this insurance anyway). Because the bank maintains the mortgage over a property, it's usually happy to lend against the value of that property, knowing that if anything happens to the borrower, the bank can take possession of the house and onsell it to recover any losses incurred.

What is equity?

Equity is the difference between the value of an asset and the loan secured against that asset. For example, a home valued at $900,000 that has a loan attached for $650,000 has 'equity' of $250,000. Equity can be built in a property in two ways: By paying the loan down or when the value of the asset increases.

As a general rule, most people see their equity grow faster from asset price growth than from paying down the loan. For example, say a homeowner bought her house ten years ago. The house was bought for $500,000 with a $400,000 loan and is now valued at $800,000. But the owner owes only $300,000 on her mortgage, meaning equity of $500,000 has been built from initial equity of $100,000. Home equity provides the best and the cheapest form of financing for subsequent investments in real estate, because this is the asset that banks feel most comfortable lending on and what they charge the lowest interest rates for. Assuming all the other financial pegs are in order, most banks would allow the homeowner to 'access' that equity.

Now, say the homeowner found a $700,000 investment property she wanted to purchase. She would go to her bank and request approval for a loan (which, in this case, would probably be approved), if she hadn't already received pre-approval. Often, the bank would approve the client for a facility to access the extra equity for the deposit for a new investment loan — in this case, 10 per cent of the purchase price. When settlement occurs (usually in 30, 60 or 90 days — see Chapter 12 for more details), a new investment loan will be created for the new holding.

The homeowner-cum-investor now has two loans to service — the existing home loan of $370,000, which she has been paying for ten years and now includes the $70,000 accessed for the investment property deposit, and the new investment property loan of $630,000, which she'll have to fund with the aid of rent from the tenant, tax savings (if applicable) and other income. (The investor would also need to find the funds to cover additional purchase costs such as stamp duty, which generally needs to be paid for out of cash reserves.)

In some cases, particularly where more than 90 per cent of the investment property price has been borrowed and no other security except the investor's home is offered, the investment property loan may be tied to the home loan (known as *cross collateralisation*). It may appear as a separate loan, but if the investor were ever to default on the investment property loan, the bank would have the power to take control of (and sell) both properties in order to recoup its loans.

TIP

We recommend avoiding tying your investment loan to your home loan when possible. You have two ways to prevent this. The first is to put up a substantial cash or equity deposit of perhaps 20 per cent of the total purchase price. The other is to take out a non-recourse loan. (For an explanation of recourse financing, see Chapter 6.)

REMEMBER

If you fall outside the confines of what banks think are 'normal' credit risks, all is not lost. Australia's major banks have so much competition nowadays that you can generally find another lender who will offer you reasonably favourable terms (refer to 'Primary Sources of Finance: Lenders Big and Small', earlier in this chapter).

Some investors use a strategy of turning their original home into an investment property. However, you have a number of tax implications to take into account before considering this strategy (see Chapter 15).

WARNING

Before you go running out to borrow to the maximum against the current value of your home, be sure that you

>> **Can handle the larger payments.** If you're going to borrow the maximum against your home, make sure that you're going to be able to service the

higher mortgage payments that are likely to accompany that strategy. Excessive leveraging can be dangerous and could come back to haunt you! Refer to Chapter 1 for the big picture on personal financial considerations.

>> **Understand the tax ramifications of all your alternatives.** Interest charged on the portion of the mortgage against your own home is not tax-deductible, whereas the interest paid on investment borrowings generally is, even if secured and charged against your home mortgage.

>> **Fully comprehend the risks of losing your home to foreclosure.** The more you borrow for any reason, the greater the risk that you could lose the roof over your head to foreclosure should you not be able to make your mortgage repayments.

Watch those bank valuations

When using equity in your home loan to borrow more money for investment, it's important to keep an eye on the valuation that the bank puts on your home when it's assessing your lending eligibility.

When a borrower applies for a new property loan, one of the bank's duties is to value the borrower's current assets. Until recently, most banks paid a valuation company to conduct a *kerbside valuation*. This is almost as literal as it sounds. The valuer gets a rough description of the house, has a look at what properties have recently sold for in the area via various online means, and then drives by the property. From the kerb, the valuer makes a few judgements on the value of the property. These days, sales records are more extensively used, and more and more banks require valuers to physically attend and assess the property in question.

Although most banks will share valuation details with you if you ask, not all banks do. Sometimes, the bank will ask you for your own valuation of your property before it sends someone out there. You need to follow up with a request to find out the figure your property (or properties) is valued at. To find out how valuers generally make valuations, see Chapter 11.

TIP

If you don't believe the valuation, query it. If you have proof that your property is worth more — perhaps the bank and valuer are relying on data that's a little out of date — show the bank proof of recent sales. Sometimes it might also be worthwhile to ask for another valuation, this time including an inspection of the inside of the house and the backyard! This can be especially important if the front of your house hasn't received as much love and attention as the inside and back. We have both regularly had valuations raised following internal inspections by a valuer.

Be aware, also, that valuers and valuation companies tend to be conservative by nature. They have to provide figures that hold up to their employer's scrutiny. They generally need to provide a figure to the bank that they believe the property can or would sell for, if a sale were required with a reasonable degree of urgency. Not a fire-sale figure, but a price they believe the property would achieve it was sold on that very day.

No Home? No Worries!

Property investors don't need to own their own home before launching into buying their first investment property. Far from it — buying an investment property is often a cheaper way to get into the property market than buying your own home. After all, you have a tenant who can help repay the mortgage. (An increasingly popular strategy, this is now commonly known as *rentvesting* — refer to Chapter 2.)

After getting fired up about property investment from reading a personal finance book, Bruce decided that he wanted to buy a home to live in. After a discussion with his wife, Genevieve, he was persuaded not to buy a home until the two of them could afford to buy one together. He decided to buy an investment property instead.

Bruce bought the property, a detached unit in a block of three, in Heidelberg West in Melbourne, near the old village for the 1956 Melbourne Olympic Games. The unit cost $141,000 back in the day. By the time Bruce and Genevieve had saved enough money between them to buy a home, about 15 months later, the Heidelberg West property had appreciated and was worth $170,000. This is a strategy increasingly being used by younger people still living at home with their parents. They're often paying a peppercorn rent to their parents and have managed to save enough money for a house deposit. Or they may be share housing and still paying a relatively low rent. People may want to invest in property while continuing to live in their current home for many reasons, including not yet wanting the responsibilities that come with living in a home, wanting a foothold in the market or wanting to buy a place that they can move into later.

Rentvesting enables more people to purchase an investment property, perhaps in a more affordable suburb in their home city or even interstate, while they stay renting in their location of choice. As a property investor, you are also able to take advantage of the rental income from tenants as well as tax deductions where appropriate.

Advanced Funding Strategies

Sophisticated investors who develop an extensive real estate investment portfolio can employ a range of strategies to source capital. In the following sections, we outline those strategies, along with our advice for how to make them work.

Leveraging existing real estate investments

Over time, if the initial properties that you buy do what they're supposed to do, they'll appreciate in value. Thus, you may be able to use the equity from your successful investments as security to make more purchases or duplicate your real estate investments. As we discuss in the section 'Borrowing Against Home Equity', earlier in this chapter, many investors begin by using equity in their owner-occupied home to fund other real estate purchases. By the same token, as you acquire more properties and they then appreciate, you can tap their equity for other purchases (see also Chapter 16 for information on how to build your investment portfolio).

WARNING

As you build a real estate portfolio, you should be mindful of exactly how much debt you take on. Property can go through downturns and, in some situations, you could find yourself with vacant properties and falling rents. Excessively leveraged real estate investors can end up in serious financial problems.

Partners and investors

To accomplish larger deals, you may need or want to invest with a partner or other investors for the sake of diversification and risk reduction. Bringing in a partner can also provide additional financial resources for deposits and capital improvements, as well as greater borrowing capability.

TIP

Partners can be the best thing or the worst thing that ever happened to you. Although the additional financial resources may be essential when you're starting out in real estate, attempt to find partners with complementary skills to really take advantage of the potential of investment partnerships.

With the assistance of a good lawyer, prepare a legal contract to specify (among other issues) what happens if a partner wants out. A buy/sell agreement makes a lot of sense, because it outlines the terms and conditions in advance for how partnership assets can be redistributed. With life events (such as death, divorces and new marriages) constantly changing partnerships, having a buy/sell agreement in place at the time the partnership is established helps to prevent bickering down the road. Partnership disputes often enrich lawyers and accountants, rather than the partners or their intended beneficiaries.

Family members sometimes make good partners, but some families aren't suited to partnering to buy and operate real estate. Disputes over management style, cash distributions versus reinvesting in the property, and how and when to sell are difficult in any partnership but particularly in families, where members may have different goals based on their age, risk profiles or personal desires. To minimise the potential problems, we strongly suggest documenting any real estate investment or lending relationship in writing just as diligently as you would with a non-family member. Check out Chapter 11 for more on partnerships.

Seller financing

You may be able to find some properties that your research suggests offer potentially attractive investment returns and that the seller may be willing to extend finance for. This can be a beneficial way to buy real estate when your cash position is limited but is far from a common scenario.

REMEMBER

Don't get sucked in by great financing alone; only consider purchasing a property with seller financing that you would be willing to buy conventionally. The seller financing should just be an extra benefit, not the only benefit! See Chapter 6 for more details.

Getting in the door with good credit

Lenders, property sellers and potential partners all prefer to deal with someone who has an established reputation for paying bills. This means a good to great credit rating is essential. As keen investors, we all began building our credit rating through the responsible use of credit cards and, to this day, our high credit scores have allowed us to borrow at favourable rates and terms, and potentially save thousands of dollars a year in financing costs.

Don't underestimate the importance of establishing good credit, because the best returns on real estate rely upon the leverage of using OPM — other people's money. Why pay more for money when you can show the ability to handle it properly and be rewarded with a lower price? We cover the importance of good credit and ways to remove unsightly blemishes on your credit history that may keep you from getting solid interest rates in Chapter 7.

IN THIS CHAPTER

» **Understanding lender financing options**

» **Selecting the best mortgage for your situation**

» **Checking additional lending fees**

» **Knowing which mortgages to avoid**

» **Seeking vendor's terms**

Chapter **6**

Financing Your Property Purchases

You can't play if you can't pay. We know property investors who spent hundreds of hours finding the best locations and properties only to have their deals unravel when they were unable to gain approval for needed financing.

You probably also have questions about how to select the mortgage that's most appropriate for the property you're buying and your overall personal and financial situation. This chapter covers the financing options you should consider (and highlights those you should avoid). In Chapter 7, we cover the actual process of applying for and locking up the specific loan you want.

Taking a Look at Mortgages

Although you can find thousands of different types of mortgages (thanks to all the various bells and whistles available), you need to understand the four basic mortgage types, covered in two groups. The first group focuses on the type of interest rates you can choose — *variable* interest rates or *fixed* interest rates. The second group involves a decision on whether your repayments will be *interest-only* or also repay part of the borrowed capital, called a *principal and interest* (P&I) loan. All mortgages combine at least one element from the first group — variable or fixed interest — with one from the second group — interest-only or P&I repayments. But mortgages can combine both elements of each group — the interest rates can remain fixed for a number of years and then have a variable interest rate after that, and the repayments can start off as interest-only and then later switch to principal and interest. In the following sections, we discuss these major loan types, what features they typically have and how you can intelligently compare them with each other and select the one that best fits with your investment property purchases.

Going with the flow: Variable-rate mortgages

The vast majority of all mortgages taken out in Australia — whether for investment purposes or to buy your own home — are taken out as variable-rate mortgages, usually for terms of 25 or 30 years (although some lenders are now offering 40-year terms). Variable-rate mortgages carry an interest rate that changes over time, usually tracking the changes made by the Reserve Bank of Australia (RBA) to the 'official cash rate'. In fact, for more than the 15 years before the GFC, whatever change the RBA made to the cash rate was matched equally by the major lenders. However, lenders' 'costs of financing' changed dramatically following the GFC and banks no longer move in lock step with the RBA. The RBA can commonly make, say, a cut of 0.5 percentage points, but the banks then only pass on 0.3 or 0.4 percentage points. And when the RBA has increased rates by, say, 0.25 percentage points, the banks have sometimes increased their rates by 0.3 or 0.4 percentage points.

A variable-rate mortgage starts with a set interest rate, but can move up or down each and every month during the course of a 25- or 30-year mortgage. In practice, variable rates tend to move probably only a few times each year. Because a variable interest rate changes over time, so, too, does the size of the loan's monthly repayment. Variable rates are attractive for a number of reasons:

>> At most points of the interest rates cycle, variable rates are lower than fixed rates. So, given the economics of a typical investment property purchase, variable rates are more likely to enable you to achieve positive cash flow in the early years of property ownership.

>> Should interest rates decline, you can realise most, if not all, of the benefits of lower rates without the cost and hassle of refinancing. With a fixed-rate mortgage (which we discuss next), the only way to benefit from an overall decline in the market level of interest rates is to refinance, which can result in expensive exit fees from your current loan.

Depending on the individual lender's policies, variable-rate loans usually come with many more features and options than do fixed-rate mortgages. But variable rates also come in two broad types — standard and discount variable rates.

Standard variable rates

The standard variable rate (SVR) is generally a lender's full-service loan product. Although it has a different name at almost every banking institution, SVR is the figure most often quoted by the media when they talk about mortgage interest rates, or rising or falling interest rates. The SVR is usually the highest rate charged to general mortgage customers, but often comes with other products thrown in, which can be useful to some customers, such as offset accounts, redraw accounts and fee-free general banking (see Chapter 7 for more information on these products).

But, despite the fact that the SVR is the most often quoted interest rate, few customers actually pay it. Customers — particularly property investors, who tend to have higher average total loan balances — find that most banks discount the offered interest rate from the SVR.

Discount variable rates and 'no frills' loans

Discount variable rates are in essence SVR loans with a discount applied to them.

REMEMBER

Generally speaking, you should be able to receive a discounted rate to the SVR — unless you have recently rolled off a fixed rate and didn't request a discount or, potentially, you forgot to pay your package fee and lost the package benefits, which include discounts off the SVR.

The advertised discount on the SVR is usually between 0.70 and 1.30 per cent across the lenders. However, these amounts are the *minimum* that will be offered with packaged products — and certainly not the maximum. In fact, they can be negotiated on request and the discounts that can be achieved are on average twice as high as the advertised discount.

Also available are 'no frills' loan that may be attractive to some borrowers at the start of their investment journeys. Generally, these loans won't offer access to products such as offset accounts, redraw accounts and fee-free banking.

These lower rate products may suit you when you're starting out with your first, relatively low value, investment property. However, even if you're buying a more expensive first investment property, a bank, if asked, will offer all the extras available with a standard variable rate, but at an interest rate normally associated with a discounted loan (see Chapter 7 for more information on banking products).

The basic or 'no frills' loans may offer lower rates than the standard SVR; however, don't just use this as your comparison rate. You should be able to negotiate having access to the SVR products while still receiving a discounted rate. The basic loans are usually offered with a rate that's approximately an additional 0.20 to 0.60 per cent lower than the SVR rates with the advertised discounts. But you're often able to negotiate the SVR discount further, ending up with a discount SVR rate that's the same or lower than the basic product rate (depending on total loan size and other factors).

Honeymoon rates

Lenders often offer an introductory rate for a mortgage, known as *honeymoon* or *introductory* rates. These rates usually offer a discount of about 0.60 to 1.20 per cent. Don't be fooled, though: You won't pay this tantalisingly low rate for very long. These rates are inevitably offered for periods of as short as six months, or as long as two years. This rate is referred to as a honeymoon rate because the lower initial interest rate gives the borrower a gentle easing-in to the longer term costs of a mortgage. The introductory rate is often set artificially low to entice you into the product. In other words, even if the market level of interest rates doesn't change, your variable-rate mortgage is destined to increase at the end of the defined honeymoon period.

Crucially, you need to know what your interest rate will 'revert' to when, as they say, the honeymoon is over. What's the point in having a low introductory rate if you're just going to have to repay those 'savings' and more when you change to the higher rate? Saving $500 now only to have to repay $1,000 or $2,000 six or 12 months later is rarely (probably never) going to make sense. And the 'extras' might come not just in the form of higher interest, but higher fees and charges. In most cases, the honeymoon rate will revert to a standard variable rate (refer to 'Standard variable rates', earlier in this chapter).

Concerns over borrowers being duped by low honeymoon rates has reduced dramatically since the introduction in recent years of average annual percentage rates (AAPR), under the general principle of 'truth in advertising', by lenders.

Average annual percentage rates

Much more important than an artificially low introductory interest rate is the average cost of the loan over a given period — that is, if the rate is cheaper at the start and more expensive later, what's the average cost over, say, seven years?

This concern over borrowers being seduced or duped by low introductory rates led some industry figures and state governments to introduce the concept of average annual percentage rates (AAPRs) to interest-rate advertising by Australian lenders. The AAPR, also sometimes referred to as a comparison rate or a true rate, is designed to force lenders to bundle all of the associated costs of a loan — such as interest rates, fees and charges — and average them over a seven-year period for the purpose of advertising the 'true' cost of the mortgage. This bundling creates an average interest rate that makes it easier for customers to compare rates offered by various lenders — and to realise that a honeymoon rate, for example, might not be such a great deal.

What does this mean for potential borrowers? It means you'll often see an interest rate advertised for a product with a different comparison rate alongside it. Almost inevitably, the lower rate is the loan's advertised interest rate. The higher figure is likely to be the AAPR rate, or the one that takes in the cost of the lower introductory rate, the higher ongoing rate, plus the other bank fees and charges due over the course of a seven-year period.

For example, a one-year honeymoon rate (refer to the preceding section) may have an advertised rate of 3.6 per cent, and an AAPR of 3.96 per cent. As another example, a two-year honeymoon rate may be 3.74 per cent, versus an AAPR of 4.46 per cent.

But finding a loan with the lowest AAPR isn't necessarily the most important factor in determining which loan is best for you. Loans may have low AAPRs because they don't have some other loan functions that you may want or need (see Chapter 7 for other loan features that you may wish to consider as part of your mortgage funding requirements). The AAPR is just one way to compare a part of one loan with another.

The security of fixed-rate mortgages

Less common than variable-rate mortgages in Australia, fixed-rate mortgages tend to be offered for periods of between one and ten years, depending on the individual lender. The interest rate remains constant over the life of the agreed loan term. Because the interest rate stays the same, your monthly mortgage payment stays the same.

For the purpose of making future estimates of your property's cash flow, fixed-rate mortgages can offer you certainty and some peace of mind for fixed periods, because you know precisely the size of your mortgage payment next month, next year and up to ten years from now. (Of course, the other costs of owning investment property — such as property taxes, insurance and maintenance — will still escalate over the years.)

Peace of mind has a price, though. The following points examine some of the conditions of fixed-rate mortgages:

TIP

>> Fixed-rate loans are usually inflexible. Many lenders won't let you make extra repayments or, if they do, only under restricted conditions. Should you find that you need to sell your property — and, therefore, don't need the loan anymore — you might find that you face hefty exit fees.

>> Depending on the stage of the credit cycle, with fixed rates you normally pay a premium in the form of a higher interest rate, compared with loans that have a variable interest rate over time. In other words, you're paying a premium for your 'peace of mind'.

>> If, like most investment property buyers, you're facing a tough time generating a healthy positive cash flow in the early years of owning a particular investment property, a fixed-rate mortgage may make it even more financially challenging. A variable-rate mortgage, by contrast, can lower your property's carrying costs in those early years. (Refer to the section 'Going with the flow: Variable-rate mortgages', earlier in this chapter.)

>> Fixed-rate loans carry the risk that, if interest rates fall significantly after you obtain your mortgage and you're unable to refinance, you're stuck with a relatively higher cost mortgage until the loan term completes its fixed period. Also remember that, even if you're able to refinance, you'll probably spend a significant sum in exit fees and new loan fees by doing so. Many borrowers who had fixed rate mortgages before the COVID19 pandemic missed out on once-in-a-lifetime low interest rates, for example.

REMEMBER

While fixed rates can increase your property's carrying costs, they can be invaluable if the interest rates are locked in at a low point of the interest rate cycle. If, for example, you've locked in a rate of 3 per cent and then interest rates rise, say, two to three percentage points (as they did in 2022 as Australia emerged from the COVID-19 pandemic), you have a very cheap source of financing until your locked-in period finishes.

Tax-effective interest-only loans

Many Australians have been brought up with a fear of debt. From the time many of us start to learn about money, it's rammed into our heads that when you get a loan (for any purpose), your primary goal is to get that loan repaid as quickly as possible. In the extreme, some people believe you should put your enjoyment of life itself on hold until the loan is repaid. But buying property — be it a home or an investment — almost inevitably requires borrowed money. And, although it may shock some to hear this, in many cases, it makes financial sense to never actually pay the bank its money back! Just pay interest — that is, rent the bank's money — forever.

Australia's tax laws at the time of writing state that interest paid on money borrowed to fund investments is tax-deductible, whereas repayment of investment capital and personal, non-investment debt is not deductible. So, if you have an interest-only loan on an investment property, in most cases, all of your interest costs qualify as a tax deduction. However, if you repay some of the original money you borrowed, that portion of repaid capital does not qualify as a deduction. All repayment of money for personal loans (including your home, cars, holidays and credit cards) is also not deductible against your other income.

Whether the loan interest is tax-deductible or not is the basis of what is often referred to as the *good debt/bad debt* principle. If you have a number of loans, some of which are investment (good debt) and some of which are personal (bad debt), then you should always aim to pay off the bad debt before attacking repayment of any of the good debt. The only exception may be if the interest rate on the good debt was significantly higher than the rate on your bad debt (which is rarely, if ever, the case with investment property).

TECHNICAL STUFF

Here's an example of the good debt/bad debt principle: Assume an investment property loan of $600,000, with an interest rate of 4.5 per cent. If the loan is interest-only, the repayments required each year will be $27,000. Under most circumstances (assuming that the property is rented or available for rent) and with most investment properties, that entire $27,000 will be a tax deduction. However, if the same loan is a 25-year principal and interest (P&I) loan, the annual repayment in the first year will be about $40,000. Of that sum, $27,000 will be interest and $13,000 will be repayment of principal and won't be deductible. Only the $27,000 will be a tax deduction. Although no difference exists between the two sums that qualify as a deduction, the investor still has to find more than $13,000 extra each year for repayment of principal that he won't have to find on an interest-only loan.

'But at least the loan is being repaid!' is the reaction of many to suggestions that people not aim to repay principal quickly. If this is the only loan that an investor has, an interest-only loan might not be an option, as many lenders may insist on principal being repaid. And nothing is wrong with repaying loan principal because it will need to be repaid in some way at some point in time. However, it's not always the most tax-effective solution for an investor. In particular, if investors who have other non-deductible debt accelerate payments on their personal debt, they're usually better off in two ways. Most investors have some money owing on their own home. By focusing repayment of principal onto the home loan, the investor is both minimising the non-deductible interest on the home loan and maximising tax-deductible interest payments on the investment loan.

To take the previous example one step further, if the investor uses that $13,000 to pay down his own home loan, he'll save interest on the home loan (which would compound the following year).

REMEMBER

Some lenders only insist on principal being repaid from one of their loans. If you have a home loan and an investment property loan (or many investment property loans) with the same lender, the lender may want you to repay principal on the home loan, but allow long-term, interest-only repayments on the remainder — until such time as the home loan is paid off, when the lender will generally want to convert one of the other interest-only investment loans to principal and interest (P&I).

The downside of interest-only loans is that the amount of money owed against the property doesn't fall. If you buy a property with a $600,000 loan, after three years of interest-only repayments, you'll still owe the bank $600,000.

Making a dent with principal and interest loans

For a principal and interest (P&I) loan, the borrower agrees to pay the lender not only the interest on the loan, but also some of the initial capital each week, fortnight or month. Over the term of the loan, which usually starts at 25 or 30 years for mortgages in Australia, the initial sum borrowed is repaid in full and the mortgage comes to an end.

Apart from the effect of changes to official interest rates, P&I loan repayment amounts are constant throughout the term of the loan. What changes during that period is the amount of money within that repayment that's assigned as interest and the amount that's designated as repayment of capital. The reduction in the principal component of the loan is worked out by a mathematical formula known as *amortisation*. Initially, the majority of the repayment is designated as interest repayments and a small amount is to repay the initial capital, or principal. And as the principal gets paid down, the amount of interest reduces, and the amount used to pay off principal increases.

TECHNICAL STUFF

Here's an example: A 25-year, $600,000 principal and interest loan with a 4.5 per cent interest rate will require repayments of about $3,334 a month. In the first month of repayment, $2,250 will go towards interest and about $1,084 will be repayment of principal. At the end of the first year, the amount being directed to interest versus principal repayment won't have changed very much — $2,204 will be interest and $1,130 will go towards principal. However, at the end of the 12th year, the $3,334 will be split as $1,481 for interest and $1,853 for principal.

The final repayment, when the loan is finally paid out, will be $12.46 in interest and $3,322 as the last principal repayment.

An owner has two ways to increase the amount of equity in a property (refer to Chapter 5 for a discussion of home equity). The first is that the value of the property itself increases; the second is that the value of the loan decreases. P&I loans are one option where investors can exercise control in increasing their equity ownership in a property.

Making Some Decisions

You can't (or at least shouldn't) spend months deciding which mortgage may be right for your situation. You can also work with professional mortgage brokers to undertake most of this research for you. (See Chapter 7 for more on mortgage brokers.) However, in the following sections, we help you zero in on which type of mortgage may be best for you.

Deciding between variable and fixed

Choosing between a variable-rate and a fixed-rate loan is an important decision in the real estate investment process. Consider the advantages and disadvantages of each mortgage type and decide what's best for your situation prior to refinancing or purchasing real estate.

How much risk can you handle in regard to the size of your property's monthly mortgage payment? If you can take the financial risks that come with a variable rate — the main risk being that your mortgage could rise considerably if the Reserve Bank, or your bank, raises interest rates — you have a better chance of saving money and maximising your property's cash flow with a variable-rate rather than a fixed-rate loan. Variable interest rates tend to start lower and stay lower, if the overall level of interest rates stays unchanged. Even if rates go up, they'll likely come back down over the life of your loan. If you stick with a variable loan for better and for worse, you should come out ahead in the long run.

Variable rates make more sense if you borrow less than you're qualified for. If your income (and applicable investment property cash flow) significantly exceeds your spending, you may feel less anxiety about a fluctuating interest rate. If you do choose a variable loan, you may feel more secure if you have a sizeable financial cushion of a few months' expenses reserved, which you can access if rates go up.

Some people take variable rates without thoroughly understanding whether they can really afford them. When rates rise, property owners who can't afford higher payments can face a financial crisis. If you don't have emergency savings you can tap into to make the higher payments, how can you afford the monthly payments and the other expenses of your property? Bank loan approval processes generally build in a buffer when trying to determine whether a borrower can afford to meet higher repayments, in case interest rates rise. If interest rates at the time of an application were 5 per cent, for example, the bank would generally want to be satisfied that the customer could meet repayments if interest rates were to rise to 7 or 8 per cent. The banks' system is obviously not foolproof, and smaller or less scrupulous lenders may not be as diligent in assessing a customer's repayment power before approving a loan.

Over the longer term, variable-rate mortgages tend to be cheaper (because the investors making their money available for banks to lend on fixed terms expect a higher rate to lock their money away). But don't ignore fixed-rate mortgages. If you see a fixed rate that you believe is affordable and may allow you to sleep more soundly at night, consider locking in that rate for a term.

Some property people recommend locking in for a long time if you find a suitable rate, whereas others believe it's best to fix rates for only short periods when you believe the market has temporarily mispriced the likely future interest rate movements.

Fixed interest rates tend to reflect the level that lenders believe rates are heading towards over the fixed rate term. If investors believe that interest rates are likely to fall over the next couple of years, one-and two-year fixed rates may be lower than some variable interest rates. If they believe that interest rates are heading up, fixed rates may be higher than variable rates. You also can have short- and long-term fixed rates on different sides of current variable rates. If investors believe that the Reserve Bank is likely to cut interest rates over the short term (possibly to add extra stimulus to the economy) but raise them in the medium to long term, one-, two- and three-year fixed rates may be below current variable rates, while five-, seven- and ten-year rates may be above. This scenario can also work in the reverse.

You may also consider a split loan, which combines features of variable- and fixed-rate mortgages. Most major lenders allow borrowers to choose to fix a percentage of their home loan and have the rest of the loan as variable. This apportionment is designed to give the borrower partial protection against future interest rate rises. If rates do rise, only half your mortgage will require higher repayments. The opposite applies if rates fall, where you may be stuck paying a higher interest rate on the fixed portion of your loan.

Deciding between interest-only and principal and interest

The decision on whether to take an interest-only or principal and interest (P&I) loan should be a simple one. If you have other non-deductible debt (such as a home loan, car loan or personal loan), it usually makes more financial sense to take out an interest-only loan for your investment property. Any savings should be redirected to repaying the principal on loans that can't be claimed as a tax deduction, particularly your principal place of residence (refer to 'Tax-effective interest-only loans', earlier in this chapter).

However, many investors won't feel comfortable with an interest-only loan, and that's okay. Repaying principal on an investment loan is a good thing. It's just not as tax-effective because the repaid principal can't be claimed as a tax deduction.

Some other investors — young people buying an investment property before buying their first home and older people who've paid off their home — won't have any non-deductible debt and may want to repay the principal on their investment loan as a way of building equity faster, but this may mean they are unable to add to their portfolio as quickly as they may have done otherwise.

Deciding on a loan term

Most mortgage lenders offer you the option of 25-year or 30-year mortgages. Borrowers can also ask for shorter loan terms if they want, but rarely do so. So, how do you decide whether a shorter or longer term mortgage is best for your investment property purchase?

The difference in repayments between 25- and 30-year loan terms isn't significant. On a $600,000 loan at 4.5 per cent, a 25-year term would have P&I monthly repayments of approximately $3,334, whereas a 30-year term would have $3,040. This decision is often a function of whether you choose to pay interest-only or P&I. If you choose P&I because you'd rather repay your debt faster, you may also want a shorter term.

TIP

If you decide on a 30-year mortgage over a 25-year mortgage, or a 25-year mortgage over a 20-year mortgage, you may still maintain the flexibility to pay the mortgage off faster if you choose to. You can make larger payments than necessary and create your own 25- or 20-year mortgage. You can also fall back to making only the payments required on the original schedule when the need arises. Some loans, usually fixed-rate loans, have restrictions on prepayments and may charge a fee for early repayment of capital. We dislike mortgages with *prepayment penalties* (penalties for paying off your loan before you're supposed to).

Normally, pre-payment penalties don't apply if you pay off a loan because you sell the property, but when you refinance a loan that has pre-payment penalties, you have to pay the penalty. And while the Australian Government moved to ban exit fees on home loans many years ago, exceptions to the rules always occur — so make sure you find out what exit fees your lender charges ahead of finally making the decision to pay out the loan.

Reviewing Other Common Lending Fees

Whether the loan is variable or fixed, mortgage lenders typically levy other up-front fees and charges. These ancillary fees can really amount to quite a bundle with some lenders. Here's our take on the typical extra charges you're likely to encounter — what's reasonable and what's not:

>> **Application fee:** Most lenders charge a few hundred dollars to process your paperwork and see it through their loan-evaluation process. If your loan's rejected, or if it's approved and you decide not to take it, the lender usually won't charge this fee.

>> **Valuation fee:** The property you're borrowing money to buy needs to be valued. If you default on your mortgage, a lender doesn't want to be stuck with a property that's worth less than you owe. The cost for valuation ranges from $0 to $800 for typical purchases.

>> **Settlement fee:** Many lenders charge a fee to attend to the actual process of settlement — the final signatures that transfer the ownership of the property and finalise mortgage documents for the new owner.

You need to know the total of all lender fees so you can accurately compare different lenders' loans and determine how much settling on your loan is going to cost you.

TIP

Most banks or mortgage brokers will run your application through a pre-approval process for free, which usually gives you a fairly clear indication of whether the bank is going to lend you the money and how much they'll lend you. If this process indicates that you'll be approved for a loan, you can ask for the pre-approval in writing, which will allow you to bid or negotiate confidently for a property (depending on you staying within the bank's guidelines).

Alternatively, to reduce the possibility of wasting your time and money applying for a mortgage you may not qualify for, disclose up-front any credit issues you have and ask the lender if your situation suggests any reasons that you may not be approved. By raising your credit issues and explaining them, you may find that the lender is willing to look around the issue or that their processes are too inflexible to do so. Either way, it may be better than going through the entire process, only to be knocked back.

Mortgages That Should Make You Think Twice

As well as the more standard loans (refer to the section 'Taking a Look at Mortgages', earlier in this chapter), you may come across other loans such as interest-capitalising loans and recourse loans (where a lender can come after your own home if you fail to meet repayments on your investment property). Here, we present our thoughts on the risks associated with these loans.

Interest-capitalising loans

A relatively recent mortgage to hit the market is the interest-capitalising loan — that is, the investor doesn't pay the interest and the interest itself is added to, or is capitalised on, the loan. Although this loan, in theory, is even more tax-effective than an interest-only loan, we consider that taking this loan is taking one risk too many.

When you add interest to a loan, you add a compounding impact, just like interest paid on a savings account. In the first year of capitalising your interest on a $600,000 loan (at 4.5 per cent), your loan grows to more than $627,000. In the second year, the loan balance grows to more than $655,000. By the end of the 10th year, the loan will be more than $931,700. This means that, if you sold the house after ten years, its value would need to have increased by 4.5 per cent a year, compound, just to repay the loan.

WARNING

The Tax Office is constantly monitoring these sorts of loans and has occasionally challenged them in the courts and won. Borrowers entering into these sorts of loans should be wary of the potential that an adverse ATO ruling could have on their personal finances. They are best steered clear of.

Recourse financing

Among the many factors to explore before agreeing to any loan, you also want to consider whether the loan is non-recourse or recourse, or even limited recourse (for self-managed super funds):

>> **Non-recourse loans:** In the event that you fail to fulfil the terms of your loan, this type of loan limits the lender to foreclosing only on the property financed

by the loan. Foreclosure is the full and complete satisfaction of the loan, and the lender can't seek a deficiency judgement or go after your other assets, such as your home. These types of loans are very rare in Australia for personal property loans.

>> **Recourse loans:** These loans lower the lender's risk because they offer additional protection. If the terms of your loan aren't fulfilled, the lender has the legal right to go after your other assets to cover any shortfall, should the value of the property financed by the loan not fully cover the outstanding debt balance. Remember that, after a loan is in default, the interest penalties and legal fees can add up quickly. If you're already in default on the loan for your rental property, you may not want a lender taking your home or other viable rental properties to satisfy the shortfall. Full recourse loans are the most common type of loan offered for personal property loans.

>> **Limited-recourse loans:** These loans are a legal requirement of loans to self-managed super funds (SMSFs), which we take you through in Chapter 8.

Lenders prefer recourse financing. If you're prepared to put up other properties (including your home) as security, a lender feels more secure and can possibly offer you funds at a lower rate. If you don't want to put up other homes as surety (non-recourse), you may have to pay a higher interest rate or put up more of a deposit for the property.

As long as you're not too aggressive and don't over-leverage your rental properties, real estate investing can be relatively safe, and the chances are you won't be faced with losing other properties by defaulting on your loan. But you are limited in your ability to control all the diverse factors that can affect your property. For example, your cash flow is likely to suffer if the major employer in your area suddenly leaves, which can be a devastating problem in rural or regional areas where one employer is responsible for a large portion of a town's employment.

Non-recourse financing (if available at all for a property investment loan) has more stringent qualification standards, such as higher debt-coverage ratios, and generally results in a lower loan amount. These loans may also attract a much higher interest rate than recourse loans. Just as with borrowers who use longer term mortgages or, in some cases, interest-only loans, simply so they can borrow as much money as possible, the closer you live to the edge, the more likely you'll regret it.

In Australia, the loans you'll consider for your investment property are highly likely to be full recourse. We recommend that you properly consider the risks you're taking when you use recourse financing. The possibility that you could lose your home to your investment property strategy could stop you from sleeping at night — giving up your health for an investment strategy isn't worth it.

WARNING

You may occasionally find that you're offered a partial recourse loan. A partial recourse loan allows the lender to seek payment through other assets up to a certain limit if you default. Although such a loan may make sense for some great real estate investment options, be careful before agreeing to such terms, and include in your overall analysis the consequences to your overall financial status in a worst-case scenario.

Vendor's Terms

A common way of selling property a century or so ago, when banks were only for the rich, was to effectively borrow the money from the vendor, to be repaid over an agreed term. Vendor's terms is a transaction in which the seller (the vendor) accepts terms other than all cash at closing, such as borrowing the remaining funds from the vendor and repaying them as you might a regular mortgage, or offering partial settlement through swapping another asset (property, business interest or a vehicle).

Not every seller needs or even wants to receive all cash up-front as payment for a property, so you may be able to finance part or even all of an investment property purchase under vendor's terms with the property seller's financing. This is a rare way to buy a property in Australia, but it is possible.

Some vendors are financially well off enough that they don't need all of the sales proceeds immediately for their next purchase, or they're buying another property for less money — or maybe not buying a replacement property at all — and prefer to receive payments over time. They may be looking for the payments to replace their income in retirement or they may prefer to receive the funds over time for tax reasons.

TIP

The best candidates for vendor's terms are vendors with significant equity or, best of all, those who own the property outright.

Occasionally sellers will offer this option but, in other cases, you need to pop the question. We can think of two good reasons to ask for the seller to help finance an investment property purchase:

>> **Better terms:** Mortgage lenders, typically banks or large monolithic financial institutions, aren't particularly flexible businesses. You may well be able to obtain a lower interest rate, lower or waived fees and more flexible repayment conditions from a property seller. Conventional loans also carry many expenses that a property seller may not require, including loan-application fees, account-keeping fees and a valuation. Some sellers may not even want a

loan application or credit report, but they'd be wise to retain these requirements.

>> **Loan approval:** Perhaps you've had prior financial problems that have caused mortgage lenders to routinely deny your mortgage applications. Some property sellers may be more flexible, especially in a slow real estate market or with a property that's challenging to sell. A seller can also make a decision in a few days, whereas a conventional lender will often take weeks.

Be careful when considering a property if a seller is offering financing as part of the deal. This factor may be a sign of a hard-to-sell property. Investigate how long the property has been on the market and what specific flaws and problems it may have.

REMEMBER

Some of the reasons sellers may offer their own financing are

>> **They're attracted to the potential returns of being a mortgage lender.** This reason shouldn't concern the buyer as long as the terms of the seller financing are reasonable.

>> **They have significant equity.** Another win–win opportunity for both the buyer and seller to use seller financing.

>> **Their current financing has pre-payment issues.** This can be a problem for the buyer if the underlying financing has a due-on-sale clause and the lender becomes aware of the sale of the property and demands the full payment of the outstanding loan balance on short notice.

>> **They're seeking a price that exceeds the normal conventional loan parameters, or the property doesn't qualify for a conventional loan for some reason.** Examples of qualification issues include a cracked slab and environmental issues. This is a risky scenario for buyers and may be an indication that they're over-reaching or pursuing a property that's not a good investment.

TIP

When financing on vendor's terms, make sure that the agreement is non-recourse (refer to 'Recourse financing', earlier in this chapter) and watch out for a due-on-sale clause. A due-on-sale clause is a requirement that stipulates that, if you sell the house while you still owe the original vendor money, your first obligation is to pay the original vendor out the remaining owed funds (meaning you can't effectively take the loan and transfer it to your next property). This clause is fine in an agreement, but you need to be aware of it, because it may affect your future financing options.

IN THIS CHAPTER

» **Understanding the best ways to look for mortgages**

» **Weighing up economies of scale**

» **Evaluating banking products for property investors**

» **Going professional for your banking needs**

» **Getting around hidden fees**

» **Accounting for rental income, from the lender's perspective**

» **Overcoming common loan problems**

Chapter **7**

Shopping for and Securing the Best Mortgage Terms

I n Chapter 6, we consider the differences between the many loan options available so you can select the one that best suits your personal and financial situation. If you've started delving into the different types of real estate investment financing, you may have already begun the process of speaking with different lenders and surfing home loan comparison sites online.

In this chapter, we provide our top tips and advice for shopping for and ultimately securing the best financing that you can for your real estate investment purchases and refinances. We also cover how to attribute rental income and deal with common loan problems that may derail your plans.

Shopping for Mortgages

Mortgage costs of your real estate investment purchases are generally the single biggest ongoing expense by far, so it pays to shop around and know how to unearth the best deals. You're likely to find that many lenders would love to have your business, especially if you have a strong credit rating. Although having numerous lenders competing for your business can save you money, it can also make mortgage shopping and selection difficult. The following sections should help you to simplify matters.

Putting your existing relationship to the test

In Australian society today, with so much money moving around through cyberspace via digital transactions, virtually everybody needs a bank account. The most basic of all accounts is a savings account, but most people considering a property investment have probably tested a number of other products, including credit cards, a personal loan, a car loan and even a home loan. Having any sort of account means you have a relationship with a lender. And, if you believe you have a reasonable relationship with that lender, why not ask if you can extend the friendship?

As a first port of call, ask to speak to a loans manager at your local institution, whether that's a big or small bank, building society or credit union. A general rule of business — but particularly in banking — is that it's far cheaper to keep a customer than to find a new one. Businesses hate losing good customers. And, if you have a good credit record, you may find that your bank wants to keep you.

But this is just a first step. If you're buying property for the first time, and particularly if it's your first time getting a loan, don't accept the first offer made to you by your own bank. Treat your first application as a practice interview, if you like, while you find the best source of financing for you.

The rise of mortgage brokers

Mortgage brokers came to the fore in the early 1990s, when banks went through a cost-cutting period, which involved culling staff and shutting branches. The former branch and lending managers were among those to be sacked. But banks still needed to write loans, so mortgage brokers — usually they were ex-branch managers, but the sector is now a career in its own right — began writing loans for lenders.

Mortgage brokers can be very useful for property investors. For a start, they have access to a wide range of lenders on their books, potentially saving you a lot of time in trying to compare products. They should also be able to answer all of your questions about the various products that you may, or may not, want to consider as part of your funding package (although we cover much of what you need to know about the important products later in this chapter).

Look for mortgage brokers who have at least a dozen lenders on their books, but preferably 30 or 40. Brokers are paid by the banks via an up-front fee and a trailing commission.

TECHNICAL STUFF

As with all sales industries, the finance industry continues to debate whether commissions affect the quality of advice given. The argument goes that fee-for-service brokers are likely to recommend the best product for the customer because they get paid the same amount of money no matter what product they recommend. One concern is whether commission-based brokers are likely to recommend a product that doesn't pay them a commission. Or, perhaps, whether they are less likely to recommend a product from a bank that pays them significantly less commission than another bank's product. Usually, a commission-based broker is a cheaper up-front option for the customer. In effect, the customer pays nothing, because the bank pays the fees to the broker. The bank also pays a trailing fee, which continues for the life of the loan, to the broker. A *trailing fee* is essentially paid in recognition that the broker will continue to provide service to the customer.

TECHNICAL STUFF

In 2019, the Royal Commission into Misconduct in the Banking, Superannuation and Financial Services Industry handed down its findings, including 76 recommendations to fix the finance industry — and, in particular, the banking and superannuation sectors — in Australia. One of the recommendations that has been implemented is the *Best Interests Duty* for mortgage brokers, which is a statutory obligation for brokers to act in the best interests of consumers (*best interests duty*) and to prioritise consumers' interest when providing credit assistance (*conflict priority rule*). These two obligations combine to form the Best Interests Duty. Based on the Royal Commission's recommendations, it aims to align 'consumers' expectation and interest with that of the interest of the mortgage broker'.

Keeping up with commissions

A mortgage broker is typically paid a percentage, usually between 0.5 and 0.65 per cent, of the loan amount drawn down, which means commissions are not paid on funds not used, or held in an offset or redraw account by the borrower. In most circumstances, a trailing commission is also paid to the adviser, in the vicinity of 0.15 per cent.

Even if you plan to shop on your own, talking to a mortgage broker is also a good idea. At the very least, you can compare what you find with what brokers say they can get for you.

Counting a broker's contribution

A good mortgage broker can make the following contributions to your real estate investing team:

>> **Advice:** If you're like most people, you may have a difficult time deciding which type of mortgage is best for your situation. A good mortgage broker can take the time to listen to your financial and personal situation and goals, and offer suggestions for specific loans that match your situation.

>> **Reviewing:** Even after you figure out the specific type of mortgage you want, dozens of lenders may offer that type of loan. (You'll find fewer lender options for commercial properties.)

A good mortgage broker can save you time and money by reviewing the options for you. Brokers can be especially helpful if you have a less-than-pristine credit report, or you want to buy property with a low deposit — 10 per cent or less of the value of a property. (Purchasing commercial, industrial or retail property with less than a 20 to 30 per cent deposit or equity is quite difficult.)

>> **Paperwork and presentation:** An organised and detail-oriented mortgage broker can assist you with completing the morass of forms most lenders demand. Mortgage brokers can assist you with preparing your loan package so that you put your best foot forward.

The larger the loan, the more involved and complicated the paperwork. Have your personal financial statement prepared in advance so it can be easily updated, because each time you seek a loan for an investment property, you're required to provide current financial statements to the broker (and all potential loan sources).

>> **Closing the deal:** After you sign a contract, you still have much to do before settlement (see Chapter 12 for information on due diligence and settlement). A competent mortgage broker can make sure you meet the important settlement deadlines.

Relying on referrals

Some sources of real estate advice simply tell you to get referrals in your quest to find the best mortgage lenders. Sounds simple and straightforward — but it's not. For example, loans for commercial investment properties have different lender-underwriting requirements and terms compared with residential loans.

Good referrals can be a useful tool for locating the best lenders. Here are a few sources we recommend:

>> Start with a bank or credit union you currently have a relationship with and then seek referrals from them if they're not interested in making the specific loan you have in mind.

>> Collect referrals from people who you know and trust and who've demonstrated some ability to select good service providers. Start with the best professional service providers (buyers' agents, QPIAs, tax advisers, lawyers, financial planners, real estate agents and so on) you know and respect and ask them for their recommendations.

Don't take anyone's referrals as gospel. Always be wary of businesspeople who refer you to business contacts or colleagues who have referred business to them over the years. Whenever you get a recommendation, ask the people doing the referring why they're making the referral and what they like and don't like about the service provider. And ask if any money changes hands between the two businesses — that can be an indication of the motivation of the referrer.

Working with Economies of Scale

Most consumers understand the concept of economies of scale, even if they don't understand the actual meaning of the term as used by economists. In economic terms, economies of scale are where the cost of a unit decreases because large quantities of the item are being produced or bought. A simpler version for consumers is: When you walk into a supermarket, a single can of soft drink may cost you $2. But if you buy a box of 30 cans of soft drink, the box may cost you $30, or $1 per can. Buying banking products is no different.

Buying banking in bulk

Lenders are prepared to offer you discounts if you purchase enough banking products through them. How much extra work is needed to look after you if you have both a home loan and an investment mortgage with a bank? Twice as much? Probably not. What happens if you have a home loan, two investment property mortgages, a credit card, and a car loan and various insurance products? The bank is making a margin on a bunch of products. In this situation, a competitor might cut its margins slightly in order to win your business. So, to keep your custom, a smart lender will keep you satisfied with special discounts. The concept is no different from any other aspect of business — bigger customers get better rates.

In fact, most banks offer volume discounts even if you have a single loan product. Home mortgage loans of more than $250,000 often incur a discount to the standard home loan rate. Still-larger discounts may be offered to those with more than $500,000 or $700,000 worth of home loans (see 'Considering a Professional Package', later in this chapter).

Property investors obviously tend to have larger-than-average loan volumes. They often have a home mortgage and also need a mortgage on their investment property. If you buy a second or a third investment property, you can quickly find yourself with more than $2 million of debt. And, for a lender, that's an attractive amount of money to be charging interest on.

Taking on bigger and bigger debt

To begin property investing, you need to have a solid understanding of debt. And you need to be comfortable with large debt. Moving from having a mortgage on your home to having a mortgage on your home and an investment property often means a doubling of debt (but not a doubling of your net interest costs, thanks to the deductibility of interest on investment loans). Large investment property debt is covered in more detail in Chapter 16.

When you've been investing in property for a while, you may even accumulate multimillion-dollar debts on your property portfolio. Big debt scares a lot of people off property investment. But getting comfortable with larger debt is the best (and most tax-effective) way to build a portfolio of property assets.

Sizing Up Banking Products

Literally thousands of mortgage products and options are on offer, and hundreds of lenders, some of which offer dozens of combinations of loans each. How on earth are you supposed to find the perfect one for you? Relax. You probably won't find the perfect one. The best thing to do is make sure the loan you settle on suits you and your situation and offers a level of service you find acceptable.

The starting point for finding a suitable loan is to find out about the basic products and whether or not you need or want them.

Interest rates: Is cheaper always better?

The biggest ongoing cost of property investment is usually the interest being paid on the loan. That is almost certainly the case in the early stages of an investment if you use a loan to fund most of your purchase. So, putting in the groundwork to find a good relationship and a cheap source of funding makes sense.

The sharp increase in the number of lenders since the mid-1980s has meant a considerable increase in competition. Competition has been good for borrowers on two main fronts. The first is that competition puts a major squeeze on interest rate margins — making loans considerably cheaper — and the second is that the variety of lending products has expanded dramatically.

REMEMBER

The global financial crisis (GFC) put an end to the interest rate squeeze suffered by banks, which had been so wonderful for consumers. Interest rate margins — the difference between the interest rate banks pay to get the money and the rate at which they lend it out — have been increasing since early 2008. The foundation of the GFC was actually a global credit crisis and those lending the credit to banks to on-lend to borrowers started demanding two things. First, they wanted higher rates paid for their credit. Second, they wanted less risk. Both of those demands then increased the cost of funding to the banks, which was passed on in the form of higher interest rates to consumers.

The cheapest source of funding isn't necessarily always the best source of funding. Usually, the cheaper the interest rate on a loan, the fewer bells and whistles attached. Nothing is wrong with hunting down the cheapest investment loan rate when you're sourcing an investment property, but you may find that a product with a slightly higher interest rate may save you money in the long run.

Most lenders can quote a range of interest rates, which often only serves to confuse potential customers, but generally speaking the SVR with a discount applied is the most common — refer to Chapter 6 for more.

Merging your home and investment finances

Most people approaching their first investment property have already bought their own home and probably still have a home loan. Taking on extra investment debt can have advantages — you might find that banks are keener to keep you, or lure you, with lower interest rates or extra products that may be useful in your personal life, such as free credit cards, redraw and offset accounts or rewards programs.

DON'T BE TAKEN FOR GRANTED

A while ago, an investor couple Bruce knows managed to buy three investment properties within a few years, running up debt of more than $800,000. Each time the couple wanted a new property, they went back to the same lender and requested another loan. The couple owned their own home outright, had sufficient income to repay the loans and were good customers.

For their first property, the bank started them off on the normal rate for a loan of that level, about $250,000. When they came back and borrowed another $260,000, the bank lent them the money at the same rate. And the same with the third property, another $300,000 of debt.

They finally asked Bruce about their situation. He said that, with that much debt, most banks would, at that time, offer to beat their existing bank's interest rate by 0.6 per cent, purely because they had more than $800,000 worth of debt. Unfortunately, the original lender had steep exit fees. However, the couple bit the bullet, paid the exit fees and transferred to another lender. The interest savings effectively paid off the exit fees within 18 months and the couple were ahead by nearly $5,000 a year after that on their existing loans — and had further savings as their property portfolio expanded. Since then, the couple received further discounts and were achieving a 0.9 per cent discount to the standard variable rate charged by the bank.

Few banks offer particularly rewarding discounts if you have loans of less than $250,000. So, the addition of an investment property mortgage — which will usually be more than $600,000 these days— may give you loans of more than $850,000. If you have two investment properties and your own home, for example, then it's reasonable to assume that your total aggregate lending is $1 million or more, which would attract the largest discounts. A mortgage broker can be vital in securing the best discounts for you in this scenario (refer to the section 'The rise of mortgage brokers', earlier in this chapter).

Having $1 million or more in aggregate lending will make you considerably more appealing to a lender. Previously you may have been paying full price on a standard variable loan and the associated frills, or have been on a discount variable rate, without the benefits. With most banks, if you're about to sign up for an additional investment property mortgage, you only have to ask in order to get all the benefits of a standard variable loan for the price of a discount variable loan — or get your mortgage broker to do the heavy lifting for you.

TECHNICAL STUFF

Here's an example of how increasing your debt can give your bank an incentive to lower your interest rate: You may have been paying a standard variable interest rate of 4 per cent for a $600,000 loan. But the addition of a $600,000 investment property loan gives you $1.2 million of total business with the bank. You could rightly expect to see your interest rate cut by up to 0.15 to 0.40 percentage points, depending on the lending environment at the time. Although this is obviously good news for the investment property loan, the interest on your home loan has just fallen as well.

Linking an offset account

One of the potentially more valuable extras that isn't available with all loans is an offset account. An *offset account* works by allowing the borrower to have spare cash sitting in an account linked to the mortgage, with any savings in the offset account offsetting interest charged against the mortgage.

That means that if a borrower with a loan of $650,000 had a monthly average of $40,000 in a linked offset account, the lender would charge interest on only $610,000 ($650,000 – $40,000).

TIP

Banks usually only allow customers one offset account with a loan package. And, if you still have a home loan, that's the mortgage to which you should attach the offset account. Here's why: Even if rates are the same on both the home and the investment property, the interest on the home loan is not tax-deductible.

Paying ahead into a redraw account

Redraw accounts work similarly to offset accounts, with a few important differences. A redraw account contains money repaid early from a loan. If a borrower had repayments of $2,000 a month for her mortgage, but paid $3,000 a month for a year, she would have repaid an extra $12,000. Many lenders will now have that money sitting in a redraw account — an account that allows the borrower to redraw it when she wants to have the money. The act of redrawing may, or may not, have an associated bank fee.

WARNING

As a property investor, you need to be wary about redraw accounts attached to your investment property loans. The Tax Office has declared that any principal repaid on an investment loan is deemed to have been permanently repaid. One investor couple known to Bruce put the $80,000 they'd cleared from the sale of their own home into the redraw account of one of their investment properties while they were waiting for their new home to be built. This meant that their $156,000 loan had been reduced to $76,000 for six months. But their accountant informed them that, although they could take the money back out of the loan account, increasing its balance back to $156,000, they would now be able to claim interest only against $76,000, not $156,000.

TIP

If you have both a home loan and an investment property loan, you may want to consider having the redraw account attached to the home loan. Many borrowers use a redraw account as a way of hiding money away for a rainy day.

Other useful products

A lender may offer you a few other optional extras as part of a loan package if your total loan balance is attractive enough. Usually, the bank offers these credit products in the hope you'll misuse them, often incurring interest. But they may give you the advantage of using the bank's money for free each month.

REMEMBER

The most useful products the banks may offer you these days are credit cards. In the wrong hands, credit cards can be a danger to financial health but, used correctly, they can save you money on your mortgage each month. Most credit cards come with an interest-free period, usually 55 days. If your monthly debt is paid off in full each month — and, therefore, no interest is paid — you've used the bank's money for free during that period.

For example, if you run up an average monthly bill of $3,000 on a credit card, and repay it during the interest-free period, $3,000 of your own cash is constantly sitting in your offset account or earning interest for you in a savings account. And, if this money is held in an offset account that's linked to your home loan (for the options, refer to 'Linking an offset account', earlier in this chapter), you could be saving approximately $240 a year on your mortgage — 8 per cent of $3,000. But don't use a credit card this way unless you're positive that you're going to be able to pay off the full credit balance each month.

Considering a Professional Package

Professional packages, often abbreviated to *pro-packs*, were originally designed as specially marketed packages for high-income earners, such as those in the medical, legal and accounting professions. Nowadays, however, pro-packs are often available to anyone who does enough business with the bank — which usually simply means having a big enough loan or loans. Competition means that banks have continued to expand these offers and most borrowers find that for about $395 a year they can have access to all the additional products offered (refer to the preceding section), along with no account or transaction fees.

Two more features of most professional packages can be stand-out advantages to property investors. The first is that you get access to all these potentially useful products while also getting a discounted variable interest rate. A second advantage is that you often get free (or steeply discounted) loan-application fees in subsequent years. Loan-application fees can be $600 to $1,000 with some lenders. If you're intending to build a property portfolio, not having to pay a loan-application fee every time you purchase a property can compensate for the annual fee.

Avoiding Some Big Hidden Nasties

Outside of the normal lending fees discussed earlier in this chapter, two major costs (potentially thousands of dollars each) you want to avoid, if possible, are lenders' mortgage insurance and exit fees. And you can avoid them under some circumstances within your control.

Lenders' mortgage insurance

An unusual and slightly nasty charge, lenders' mortgage insurance (LMI) is the bank getting you to pay the bank's insurance premium in case you default on the loan. The bank takes the risk, but you pay the premium for its insurance. The percentage rate charged for LMI rises exponentially in direct relation to the percentage of the property's cost you're seeking to borrow.

If you want to borrow less than 80 per cent of the purchase price of a property, you usually won't have to pay LMI. If you want to borrow slightly more than 80 per cent, you may find you have to pay only a few hundred dollars (or a fraction of a per cent of the entire loan's value). If you're borrowing 90 per cent or more of the value of the property, LMI could be several thousand dollars (or perhaps 1 to 2 per cent of the loan's value). If you're borrowing more than 95 per cent of the value of the property, you could pay many thousands of dollars (or 3 to 4 per cent of the loan's value).

However, banks take into account other equity you have in assets and loans you hold with them, if you're prepared to cross-collateralise your other loans or take out recourse loans (refer to Chapter 5). If you're buying your first investment property, but already have substantial equity in your own home, you may have a good chance of escaping LMI.

Exit fees

Exit fees were effectively banned by the federal government in mid-2011 to allow borrowers to be able to switch lenders charging interest rates that were unfair.

Borrowers had long been concerned that they would get locked into a loan and not be able to leave a lender that was either providing uncompetitive interest rates or consistently bad service. However, the law made big inroads on this, and you can now much more easily leave a bank with which you're unhappy.

The ban on exit fees is not retrospective. If you have a loan that pre-dates 1 July 2012, you might still have to pay exit fees. Make sure you ask precisely what fees will be charged before you try to exit your loan.

The ban on exit fees doesn't always mean you won't face any fees for leaving a bank, or that you won't still find moving banks difficult. The new bank, or the application process, may see you incur a new series of fees, including application fees and mortgage discharge fees (which are fees paid to the government for the registration and deregistration of mortgage documents).

Even though exit fees are banned on new loans, you should still ask your lender what fees you will incur if you need or wish to end the loan early. Ask the specific question: If I want to get out of this loan after one, three or five years, what extra costs will be incurred?

Attributing Rental Income

You'd think that rental income is rental income, right? If a tenant pays $2,300 a month to rent your investment property, you've received $2,300 in rent, correct?

No. Banks don't see it that way. Banks discount the rent that can be attributed to you as income, and the calculation differs from lender to lender. Depending on the lender's individual rules, they may allow you to attribute only between 70 and 90 per cent of that $2,300 to your income (for the purposes of deciding if you can afford the loan). That's somewhere between $1610 and $2070. Lenders' reasoning for making this calculation makes some sense. They realise that properties have ongoing expenses (see Chapter 9 for a rundown of ongoing property costs) and that the rent you receive won't all go towards your loan.

Note: The Tax Office doesn't see income and expenses the same way. They allow only attributions of actual income and actual expenses.

Ask your proposed lender how much of the rent you receive they will allow to be attributed to you as net rental income. If the figure is substantially below 80 per cent, that lender may not be a great long-term partner for your property-investment future.

Solving Loan Predicaments

In Chapter 6, we discussed the different types of mortgages and how to select the one that best fits your situation. But remember that, just because you want a particular mortgage, doesn't mean you'll be approved for it.

REMEMBER

The best defence against loan rejection is avoiding it in the first place. To head off potential rejection, disclose anything that may cause a problem before you apply for the loan. For example, if you already know your credit report indicates some late payments from when you were out of the country for an extended period or your family was in turmoil over a medical problem, write a letter to your lender that explains this situation. Or perhaps you're self-employed and your income from two years ago on your tax return was artificially much lower due to a special tax write-off. If that's the case, explain that in writing to the lender or mortgage broker.

Even if you're the ideal mortgage borrower in the eyes of every lender, you may encounter financing problems with some properties. And, of course, not all real estate buyers have a perfect credit history, lots of spare cash and no debt. If you're one of those borrowers who must jump through more hoops than others to get a loan, don't give up hope. Few borrowers are perfect from a lender's perspective, and many problems aren't that difficult to fix.

Polishing your credit report

Late payments, missed payments or debts you've never bothered to pay can tarnish your credit report and squelch a lender's desire to offer you a mortgage. If you've been turned down for a loan because of your less-than-stellar credit history, secure a copy of your credit report to assess what the issues may be.

TIP

We advise you to get a credit report before you even apply for a loan. In Australia, you can access your credit report from a number of places online, including the following:

>> Equifax, www.equifax.com.au/personal, phone 138 332

>> Experian, www.experian.com.au, phone 1300 783 684

>> illion, www.illion.com.au, phone 1300 734 806

According to the Office of the Australian Information Commissioner, a credit reporting body must give you access to your consumer credit report for free once every three months.

You can also request a free copy if:

>> You've been refused credit within the past 90 days

>> Your credit-related personal information has been corrected

At other times a credit reporting body may charge a fee, but it mustn't be excessive.

If problems are accurately documented on your credit report, try to explain them to your lender. Getting the bum's rush? Call other lenders and tell them your credit problems up-front and see whether you can find one willing to offer you a loan. Mortgage brokers may also be able to help you shop for lenders in these cases.

REMEMBER

Sometimes you may feel you're not in control when you apply for a loan. In reality, you can fix a number of credit problems yourself. And you can often explain those you can't fix. Some lenders are more lenient and flexible than others. Just because one mortgage lender rejects your loan application doesn't mean that all the others will.

As for erroneous information listed on your credit report, get on the phone to the credit bureaus. If specific creditors are the culprits, call them too. They're required to submit any new information or correct any errors at once. Keep notes from your conversations and make sure you put your case in writing and add your comments to your credit report. Getting mistakes cleaned up on your credit report can take the tenacity of a bulldog — be persistent.

Another common credit problem is having too much consumer (or bad) debt at the time you apply for a mortgage. The more credit card, car loan and other consumer debt you rack up, the smaller the mortgage you're likely to qualify for. If you're turned down for the mortgage for this reason, consider it a wake-up call to get rid of this high-cost debt. Hang on to the dream of buying real estate and plug away at paying off your debts before you make another foray into real estate. (Refer to Chapter 5 for more information on entering the real estate market.)

Conquering insufficient income

If you're self-employed or have changed jobs, your income may not resemble your past income or, more importantly, your income may not be what a mortgage lender likes to see in respect to the amount you want to borrow. A simple (although not always feasible) way around this problem is to make a larger deposit. For example, if you put down 20 per cent when you purchase a rental property, you will have a much wider range of possible lenders for getting a loan.

If you can't make a large deposit, another option is to get a guarantor for the loan — your relatives may be willing. As long as they aren't overextended themselves, they may be able to help you qualify for a larger loan than you can get on your own. As with partnerships, make sure you put your agreement in writing so that no misunderstandings occur. And understand that if you default, you're also putting the guarantor's finances at risk. Asking someone to be your guarantor isn't a request that should be asked lightly. And if the relative doesn't feel comfortable becoming a guarantor, that's your problem. You shouldn't make it hers.

Dealing with low property appraisals

Even if you have sufficient income, a clean credit report and an adequate deposit, the lender may turn down your loan if the appraisal of the property you want to buy comes in too low. This situation happens more in rapidly moving market cycles — that is, a property not being valued for what a buyer agrees to pay is usually because prices have risen or dropped quickly. This was the case in 2022 after the 'pandemic boom' came to a screeching halt due to rapidly increasing interest rates.

TIP

Assuming you still like the property, try to renegotiate a lower price with the seller using the low appraisal. If the appraisal is too low for a property you already own and are refinancing, you obviously need to follow a different path. If you have the cash available, you can simply put more money down to get the loan balance to a level for which you qualify. If you don't have the cash, you may need to forgo the refinance until you save more money or until the property value rises.

IN THIS CHAPTER

» Taking advantage of super's tax concessions

» Working out what makes SMSFs different from other super funds

» Buying your business premises through your SMSF

» Using new gearing rules to boost returns and increase diversification

» Getting a grip on the legal requirements for SMSF property investing

» Lending to SMSFs

» Incorporating rules on negative gearing and capital gains tax

» Taking note of the complexities

Chapter **8**

Property in Self-Managed Super Funds

The way the media talked about self-managed super funds (SMSFs) about a decade ago could have led you to think they were a brand-new phenomenon that was hot to trot! But they were not new at all. SMSFs have existed for decades. And while they used to be generically known as DIY (do-it-yourself) super funds, they've had the difficult-to-say acronym of SMSFs since the mid-1990s.

According to the Tax Office, as at 30 June 2021:

>> Almost 598,000 SMSFs were registered, an increase of 4 per cent on the previous year, and an increase of 6 per cent over the five years from 2016–17.

>> Almost 1.115 million people were members of SMSFs.

>> SMSFs collectively held $822 billion (25 per cent) of the $3.3 trillion in super assets under management.

These trends are not new. The number of SMSFs has been growing exponentially over the past two decades, as more and more Australians decide to take control of their retirement planning and become the trustee of their own SMSF. Using these funds, they become responsible for all aspects of their super, from the investments the fund makes, to its relative performance, to making use of some of the powerful tools available to SMSFs that simply aren't available to those who have 'regular' super funds — such as industry or retail funds.

A major change in SMSF regulations may have, in part, be behind their growing popularity. SMSFs have always been allowed to invest in property. However, from late 2007, they were also allowed to borrow to invest in property. Given that the GFC followed soon after this change (making many people more cautious about their super investments), it has only been since about 2011 that SMSF trustees have been realising the true value of this potential opportunity. However, the number of SMSFs with residential property investment is believed to only be around 5 per cent, with about 10 per cent investing in non-residential (or commercial) real estate.

In this chapter, we cover all you need to know about investing in property through an SMSF, to help you decide whether this option works in with your overall property investment strategy. We take you through the tax advantages, gearing regulations and legal requirements, while also offering a word of caution on taking your time to understand all the intricate details.

Superannuation's Great Tax Advantages

Superannuation (super) has been around in Australia for decades and our superannuation system is the envy of much of the world. Super was introduced to reduce the burden on governments in regards to the provision of government age pensions by getting employers and individuals to save for the individual's retirement through long-term investment and by offering tax incentives. Those tax incentives are considerable. They cost the federal government billions of dollars each year in lost tax revenue that it would otherwise receive as income tax and company tax. And they mean that employees are having money put away for their future that, ultimately, they could have received and spent now.

In order to encourage people to use superannuation as a form of retirement savings, the Australian Government uses a carrot and stick approach. Largely, it's carrots. That is, it taxes the income and earnings of superannuation at a lower general rate than it does individuals or companies. As for the stick? The stick is the regulations that force employers and employees to comply. The Superannuation Guarantee, introduced in 1992, forces employers to pay a percentage of employees' wages into a superannuation fund for the employees' retirement. As of mid-2022, that rate is 10.5 per cent of an employee's wages.

So why hold property in a super fund? Fair question. But the answer, in its simplest form, is the same reason you would potentially want to hold property in your own name, or that of a trust or other entity (see Chapter 11 for the different ways property can be held). Property, along with shares and owning your own small business, is a growth asset that has proven over longer periods to appreciate at greater than the rate of inflation and create real wealth for investors. The real added advantage of holding property in super is that the fund is also a low-tax savings or investment vehicle, designed to help fund your retirement, and provides a good form of asset protection from creditors.

Super: A low-tax environment

Part of superannuation's attraction is that it is, generally, taxed at lower rates for income and capital gains than other tax entities in Australia, including individuals and corporations.

Individuals in Australia are taxed at what's known as *marginal tax rates*. These are set thresholds, over which you pay a set percentage rate in tax. For example, from 1 July 2022, if you earn less than $18,200, you don't pay income tax (and if you did have some tax withheld during the year but ended up earning less than $18,200 for the entire year, you'll get your tax refunded). If you earn between $18,200 and $45,000, you pay 19 per cent of the income earned in excess of $18,200, but less than $45,000. And the marginal tax rates increase from there. (Table 8-1 shows all the marginal tax rates for 2022–23.)

The rates shown in Table 8-1 don't include the Medicare Levy, which in 2022 was set at 2 per cent. The Medicare levy is 2 per cent of your taxable income, in addition to the tax you pay on your taxable income, depending on your personal financial circumstances. Superannuation funds that are in the accumulation phase of their life (that is, before they start to pay pensions to a member) are charged two tax rates. Income is taxed at 15 per cent, while long-term capital gains are effectively taxed at 10 per cent.

TABLE 8-1

Australia's Marginal Tax Rates (FY 2022–23)

Earnings	Marginal Tax Rate
0–$18,200	0%
$18,201–$45,000	19%
$45,001–$120,000	$5,092 plus 32.5 cents for each $1 over $45,000
$120,001–$180,000	$29,467 plus 37 cents for each $1 over $120,000
$180,001+	$51,667 plus 45 cents for each $1 over $180,000

To clarify, where assets are held for greater than 12 months, the funds receive a one-third discount on the capital gains, which effectively brings the tax rate down to 10 per cent. The methodology is similar to if you held an asset in your name and for greater than 12 months — in that situation, you would receive a 50 per cent discount on the capital gains and that amount is added to your tax return.

TECHNICAL STUFF

Income to a super fund includes bank interest, dividends, coupons, distributions and, most importantly for the purposes of this book, rent. *Concessional contributions*, which include the 10.5 per cent that your employer pays into your account and *salary sacrifice* that you elect to contribute to super, are also treated as income.

TIP

Salary sacrifice allows Australians to contribute pre-tax money to their super fund and be taxed at only 15 per cent, rather than their marginal tax rate. Obviously, if you're earning $100,000 a year and your marginal tax rate is 32.5 per cent (plus another 2 per cent for the Medicare Levy), salary sacrifice can be quite appealing. If you were to salary sacrifice $10,000 into superannuation, this amount would be taxed at 15 per cent on the way into the super fund. However, if you were to take the amount as salary, you would lose up to 32.5 per cent of that money. Salary sacrificing the $10,000 gives you a tax saving of $1,750.

TECHNICAL STUFF

Two main types of contributions can be made into super (others are possible, but are beyond the scope of this book). The first is *concessional contributions* (employer contributions and salary sacrificed contributions made by the employee), which have a limit of $27,500 a year (for 2022–23). The other is *non-concessional contributions*, which have a limit of $110,000 a year (for 2022–23), or up to $330,000 under the *bring-forward provisions* under certain circumstances. The bring-forward provisions allow those under 75 to contribute up to three years of non-concessional contributions at once — that is, up to $330,000 under certain circumstances (check with your financial adviser or accountant for more information). However, using the pull-forward rule means that you won't be able to make further non-concessional contributions for up to three financial years. As an example, if you were to put in $330,000 in non-concessional contributions on 1 January 2022, this would represent your full non-concessional contributions for the 2022–23, 2023–24 and 2024–25 financial years. After turning 75, or if your total superannuation balance is more than $1.7 million, you can't use the bring-forward provisions. Concessional contributions can be considered as monies contributed into super wherein someone is claiming a deduction — for example, the employer or the member. Personal concessional contributions can be included.

From 1 July 2018, Australians have also been able to use the *five-year catch-up provisions* to put extra concessional contributions into their super fund. This is essentially to cover not using your $27,500 concessional contribution cap in the four previous years. You can only use the concessional contributions cap if your total superannuation balance is under $500,000 at the start of a financial year. You can generally find out your previous years' contributions by logging on to your mygov account (my.gov.au).

Non-concessional contributions come from personal savings, where tax has already been fully paid before it enters the fund. These contributions are not taxed at 15 per cent as they enter the fund (unlike concessional contributions). Non-concessional contributions also make up a tax-free element of your fund, which can have positive implications when a pension is paid from the fund, or when the super fund's assets pass to others upon your death. New changes effective from 1 July 2022 include the removal of the work test for personal non-concessional up to age 75 as well as the bring forward rule being applicable for individuals to age 75.

You're best to speak to a financial adviser for more detail on concessional and non-concessional payments, because getting contributions wrong can lead to considerable tax penalties.

Super: A no-tax environment

Obviously, swapping a tax rate as high as 45 per cent for a 10 or 15 per cent rate can be pretty appealing. The average Australian worker earns around $90,000 a year. When workers earning this much make concessional contributions to their super fund, they're swapping either 32.5 or 34.5 per cent (if we're including the Medicare levy) tax rate for the 15 per cent rate in super.

A super fund's primary reason for existence is to provide retirement benefits for members. Retirement benefits can come in the form of lump sum payments from the super fund, or the preferable option of a super pension. While a super fund is in *accumulation mode* — that is, a pension is not being drawn from the fund — it pays tax at the rates covered in the preceding section. However, when a pension starts being drawn from the super fund, the fund switches from being in the accumulation phase to being in a *pension phase*. At that point, assets in the pension fund are no longer taxed for balances transferred into the pension fund of up to $1.7 million (for the 2022–23 financial year).

REMEMBER

Under a *transition to retirement* arrangement — where you continue to work some hours while also accessing some of your super — up to age 65, pension payments from your super fund are subject to the 15 per cent income tax.

However, a pension fund (after 65) generally pays no tax on income or capital gains. Imagine if the fund was earning net rent of $50,000 each year from a couple of properties. Not a cent of tax to pay. And if a property bought for $600,000 is sold for $900,000, no tax is paid on the gain if the asset was in the pension fund. Hold that same asset in your personal name and you could be paying tens of thousands of dollars in capital gains tax (see the section 'How SMSFs pay low, or no, CGT on property' later in this chapter for more).

REMEMBER

You don't have to retire from work in order to take a pension from your super — you just need to hit your preservation age. Depending on when you were born, your preservation age at the time of writing is between 55 and 60 years old. If you were born before 1 July 1960, you have a preservation age of 55. If you were born on or after 1 July 1964, you have a preservation age of 60. On 1 July of each year between 1960 and 1964, the preservation age increases one year from 55 to 60. For example, someone born on 1 September 1962 has a preservation age of 58.

Comparing SMSFs with Other Super Funds

Roughly six different types of super funds exist in Australia: Industry funds, corporate funds, government funds, retail funds, defined benefit funds and self-managed super funds.

The first five come under the purview of the Australian Prudential Regulatory Authority (APRA), while SMSFs are regulated by the Australian Tax Office (ATO).

Most super laws apply to all super funds, but not all. And while super laws apply to everyone, super funds need to operate under a trust deed. The trust deed can't be more lenient than the law, but can operate up to the law's limits. As a general rule, APRA-regulated funds, which are larger funds for potentially tens, or hundreds, of thousands of super members, need to create a trust deed that caters to all of the members of the super fund and can be monitored and implemented efficiently. As a result, they tend to have simplified rules in place.

For example, nothing in the law stops APRA-regulated super funds allowing their members to purchase an investment property as part of their super account. However, because direct property ownership is complicated, for the sake of streamlined management of funds, APRA-regulated funds won't allow this.

APRA-regulated funds also have investment options limited to particular managed funds and shares, and may have only one potential insurer on the panel.

SMSF trust deeds can be highly flexible. They can allow investment in any asset class that a super fund is allowed to invest in (SMSFs can invest in most assets, but some restrictions do exist). These investments can include directly held property (residential and commercial), the wide-world of managed funds and shares, directly held bonds and property trusts, and a bank account or term deposit that's happy to accept their money. And, potentially, the likes of artwork and wine. SMSFs also have broader ranges of insurers they can use and have far more powerful estate planning provisions that could allow for the passage of your super assets more tax-effectively to others.

A SMSF is restricted to a maximum of six members. And while APRA-regulated funds can have thousands of members, they normally have only a handful or two of trustees. With SMSFs, 'all trustees must be members and all members must be trustees'.

Therefore, a SMSF's members (and trustees, of course) usually include just one person, or a mum and dad, or mum and dad and up to four kids, or even two business associates and their partners. Other combinations are possible, but restrictions do exist on who can be members. For example, employees who aren't relatives of other members can't become a member of a SMSF in which an employer is a member.

TIP

If you're considering setting up a SMSF with someone other than your spouse and children, you should seek expert advice from a suitably qualified financial adviser, because this is a potentially dangerous area that can lead to non-compliance (and horrendous tax consequences for the SMSF).

WARNING

SMSFs are a highly complex area of superannuation, trust and tax law, and the penalties for making mistakes can be considerable. Being the trustee of a SMSF is not the same as making a few decisions about how you're going to invest your existing super fund — for example, changing the investments from a 'balanced' fund to a 'growth' or 'conservative' fund. The strategies discussed in this chapter, particularly as they relate to geared property investment, require high-level technical compliance. And the penalties for making mistakes as a trustee of a SMSF can be severe — including having the Australian Tax Office (ATO) declare your fund non-complying, meaning it can tax up to 45 per cent of the fund's capital and earnings. If, after reading this chapter, you believe that you might be a candidate for buying a property in a SMSF, contact a knowledgeable financial adviser to help you with that process.

Owning Your Business Premises Inside Your SMSF

A long-term favourite of SMSFs trustees who also happen to be business owners is to have their SMSF own the premises from which their business operates. The SMSF owns the business real property and the member's business pays rent directly to the SMSF for leasing the commercial business space. You would think that this situation should lead to a harmonious relationship between tenant and landlord!

SMSFs have always been able to purchase commercial property. Since 2007, changes to the gearing rules within super have meant that many more super funds have been able to buy the commercial property out of which a related party business operates, with the aid of a loan, earlier than they would otherwise have been able to consider doing so.

TIP

Unlike residential property, it is further possible, where the property is already owned by the business owner/s, or the company itself, to transfer that property into a SMSF. The process is known as an *in-specie transfer*. This is a complicated process and suitably qualified professionals must be consulted. Under certain conditions — potentially if the current owner is an individual or individuals and the ownership matches the members of the SMSF — the property can be transferred, in-specie, without having to pay stamp duty again. The rules here, however, vary from state to state, so you need to check these details thoroughly.

WARNING

Even if you can escape stamp duty on an in-specie transfer of the ownership of your business property, you can't escape capital gains tax. At the point that the property is transferred into the SMSF, it will trigger a capital gains tax event and tax may need to be paid. (See Chapter 15 for more on CGT.) The potential upside of paying the CGT at the point of transfer is that, at worst, it will be entering a low-tax environment and, at best, a no-tax environment if the property eventually forms part of the pension fund. (Refer to the section 'Superannuation's Great Tax Advantages', earlier in the chapter for more.) Each situation is different and whether the transfer is worthwhile depends on the economic circumstances of the time. When looked at as a long-term option, the extra tax paid now can often be worthwhile, when compared with a low or no-tax environment inside super.

Transferring the commercial property into a SMSF means that the value of the property must be accounted for as a contribution — either a concessional or non-concessional contribution. Strict limits are in place on contributions to superannuation and heavy tax penalties applied for breaching them. (Refer to the section 'Super: A low-tax environment', earlier in this chapter, for more on contribution limits.)

Some of the advantages of the business premises of a SMSF member being owned inside the super fund should be reasonably obvious:

>> The business and the SMSF have parallel goals in the financial advancement of the member.

>> The rent is no longer dead money (not that rent is 'dead' money, per se, because it's generally a cheaper alternative to buying in the short to medium term).

>> The SMSF owns an asset that members know the tenant is going to look after satisfactorily.

>> Work completed on the property should benefit both the business and the SMSF.

>> The enrichment of the business should lead to an enrichment of the SMSF.

Again, this is an extremely complex area so you should speak with your accountant or financial planner about the potential to minimise tax on transfer.

WARNING

While using your SMSF to own your business premises should mean rent collection demand letters are a thing of the past, SMSF trustees do need to be aware that the business needs to pay a commercial rate of rent to the owner of the property, the SMSF. The business should not pay too much, or too little. The rent paid to the SMSF should be market-based — that is, what the business would pay if the landlord or owner was an unrelated party. The reason for this is directly related to the strict contributions limits that surround how much people can contribute to superannuation and to the sole purpose test. If a business paid too little rent to the SMSF, the owner of the business could be seen as deriving a benefit from his SMSF prior to reaching preservation age. If a business paid too much rent, the ATO (the government regulator for SMSFs) could determine that the excess rent is essentially a contribution to the fund, which would need to be counted against one of the two contribution limits (concessional or non-concessional), which has the potential to see the member go over his contribution limits and be subject to significant penalty taxes, which can be substantial. If you're considering this as a potential strategy, seek the advice of a suitably qualified SMSF adviser.

TIP

Always make sure that a properly signed commercial lease is in place between the business and the SMSF for the rent of the commercial property. Sure, it's going to have the same signatures for the business owner leasing the property and the SMSF trustee who has put up the property for rent, but this is a legal requirement. The Australian Tax Office likes all i's dotted and t's crossed when it comes to SMSF administration, and having the document there in case you're audited is critical.

Borrowing to Invest in Property in SMSFs

Property has always been an appealing asset class for SMSFs. But, in the past, SMSFs had to have enough cash to purchase a property outright, or potentially purchase the property with another party. They would also need to then have some sort of funds left over to allow for diversification. For example, if a SMSF wanted to buy an 'average' Australian property for around $650,000, it would need in excess of $800,000 in order to both buy a property and still have enough cash left over to invest in other assets, including cash, fixed interest and shares, as well as liquidity to pay the usual bills.

But since 2007, SMSFs can purchase property without having to fund the entire cost with cash. Funds can, potentially, purchase property with a much smaller deposit. If they're going to borrow money from a commercial lender, they may only have to put up a minimum of between 20 and 40 per cent of the purchase price.

In the following sections, we cover the limited recourse arrangements that now apply to borrowings made within SMSFs, and provide some examples of the benefits of using gearing within these funds.

Limited recourse borrowing arrangements

One of the most important aspects of the rules for borrowing in SMSFs is that the loan itself must be limited recourse, which is where the unwieldy term limited recourse borrowing arrangement (LRBA) comes from. This means that the lender to the SMSF can only take a charge over the asset that the loan was made for.

So, if the borrower (the SMSF) is unable to repay the loan for whatever reason, the lender is only able to take possession of the property loaned against in order to try to repay the money loaned. They can't go after the other assets of the super fund.

WARNING

The LRBA rule has been partly avoided by commercial lenders who have sought 'director's guarantees' for the loans, meaning the members, as directors of the corporate trustee of the SMSF, may be responsible to pay outstanding debts over and above the LRBA.

Here's an example of how LRBAs work. If a loan of $520,000 was made to buy a $650,000 property, the lender can only take that property as security. If the property fell in value to $500,000 and had to be sold, the lender would only receive $500,000 (less whatever other sale costs were owed).

This is important to understand because it is the reason that major lenders only lend up to about 80 per cent of the value of a residential property to a SMSF (see 'Regular lenders' later in this chapter).

This differs from investing in your personal name. Loans given to individuals outside of super are generally recourse loans. If the borrower fails to make repayments, lenders generally take hold of the asset to sell to recoup its money. However, they can then go after other assets held by the individual, including the home, other investment properties, shares and other assets, including motor vehicles.

Non-recourse loans — which limit the lender solely to the asset itself — are very rare in Australia but limit the lender to the mortgage asset only.

In super, LRBA arrangements sit inside a bare trust. They are regarded as 'limited recourse' loans because the lender can only take ownership of the property, which, for asset protection purposes, should be the only asset in the bare trust. However, if the bare trust inside the SMSF owns other assets at the time of the loan default, such as cash or other assets at the property, those assets could also be used to satisfy the loan. As a result, the bare trust should only hold property in the trust.

Using gearing to increase diversification and returns

With the ability to borrow, SMSFs with smaller balances can directly purchase residential investment property. SMSFs no longer need balances large enough to cover the full purchase price of a property and purchase costs, as well as investments in other asset classes to ensure adequate diversification. Combining the benefits of leveraging with the tax advantages of super funds allows SMSFs to boost returns, as the following example illustrates.

A SMSF with two members, both aged 50, has $400,000 of assets. The two members would like to use funds from the SMSF to purchase a property, and find a suitable option for $440,000. They find a bank that's prepared to lend the SMSF 70 per cent of the purchase price, or $308,000, on a 30-year loan. (See the section 'Working Out Who Can Lend to SMSFs', later in this chapter, for the sorts of institutions that lend to SMSFs.) Assuming 6 per cent of the purchase price is required to cover legal and stamp duty costs, the SMSF needs to contribute a total of $158,400 to purchase the property. This leaves the SMSF with a little more than $240,000 in assets for diversification.

The property is purchased and held for 15 years. By then, the two members are aged 65 and have started to draw a pension from their SMSF, and the property makes up part of their pension fund. The property is sold for $950,000 and the remaining loan balance is repaid. The SMSF has been able to use property gearing strategies to make a profit of $510,000 (not including deductible costs) that is now tax-free.

REMEMBER

In practice, the property in the preceding example would most likely be negatively geared for a period of the time it was held. But, because only 70 per cent of the purchase price was borrowed, the property would be neutrally geared and then positively geared for a portion also. (For more on negative, neutral and positive gearing, see Chapter 15.) The major advantage for a SMSF is that if the members are able to start taking a pension from their fund from age 60, any positive income from the property (assuming it was positively geared) would, along with the capital gain when the property is sold, also be tax-free.

WARNING

SMSFs aren't allowed to buy residential property from related parties — a no-exclusions ban applies. That means that if you, personally, or a related party to the fund (which includes, but is not limited to, spouses and business entities) own a residential property, you can't sell it or transfer it into your SMSF. This rule does not apply to commercial properties (refer to the section 'Owning Your Business Premises Inside Your SMSF', earlier in this chapter). Likewise, related parties cannot use the residential property.

Understanding Your Legal Requirements

SMSFs can use gearing to purchase property through an LRBA (refer to the section 'Limited recourse borrowing arrangements', earlier in this chapter, for more). In order to even consider entering into a LRBA with a SMSF, obviously you need to have a SMSF! And even if you have a SMSF, your existing SMSF trust deed (and the SMSF's 'investment strategy') may not allow you to enter into an LRBA. The governing rule for all SMSFs is the SMSF trust deed. And if your SMSF trust deed doesn't allow the trustee/s of the fund to enter into a gearing arrangement, then, simply, your SMSF can't do it.

In the following sections, we cover the legal requirements of establishing or upgrading a trust deed, and of bare trusts and LRBAs.

Trusting on a solid SMSF base

The governing document of a SMSF is a trust deed — it sets out the rules for the SMSF itself. Operating outside the rules of the trust deed is as much a legal problem for a trustee as operating outside the law, and big penalties can apply.

REMEMBER

While the rules of a SMSF can be somewhat flexible, they can't allow a super fund to do something that would be otherwise not allowed under the Superannuation Industry Supervision Act.

Starting with a new SMSF trust deed

The process for setting up SMSFs is not simply a case of grabbing your super and taking control of the investments. The trust deed needs to be purchased, a trustee (individuals or a company) need to be chosen, a bank account needs to be opened in the name of the trustees, an investment strategy must be written, the SMSF must apply for an Australian Business Number and Tax File Number, the trustees must make declarations and lodge elections to the Australian Tax Office, the trustees must nominate members . . . and these are just the start of the requirements. Setting up a SMSF is a complex process beyond the scope of this book. For more information on the process, see your financial adviser or accountant. Sometimes, the SMSF may also need to register for GST. This is applicable on the purchase of commercial assets, for example.

REMEMBER

The area of SMSFs is highly technical and advice should be sought from suitably experienced financial advisers and accountants before entering. And LRBAs are also highly technical and require considerable expertise. It is highly advised that you seek professional help if you are considering gearing inside a SMSF.

If you are considering an LRBA, a fundamental issue to check with your financial adviser is that your trust deed and investment strategy allows for the fund to enter into leveraged investing arrangements. Not all trust deeds allow this, although many modern deeds will.

TIP

Bruce would always recommend that new trustees setting up a SMSF for the first time choose a corporate trustee as the trustee of their SMSF, rather than themselves as individual trustees. A corporate trustee is a special company that acts as the trustee. While it costs a little extra to set up the company — and annually for company fees — it is generally a preferable structure for ease of management of the SMSF. In many cases, lenders will insist on corporate trustees being in place in any case.

Upgrading an existing SMSF

If you have an existing SMSF, you need to check whether your trust deed allows you to enter into LRBAs. If your existing trust deed doesn't allow for your super fund to borrow, you would be breaching your trust deed rules if you tried to enter into any sort of gearing arrangement.

Your existing SMSF trust deed needs to be read thoroughly to determine whether or not your trust is allowed to borrow to invest. If you don't know what you're looking for, or are unsure if the wording of your trust deed does specifically allow for borrowing arrangements, see a professional adviser or knowledgeable SMSF accountant.

TIP

All is not lost if your trust deed doesn't allow borrowing. Trust deeds can be amended, if allowed by the trust deed (which most do). If your trust deed doesn't allow the deed to be amended, your only option may be to open a second, separate, SMSF with a new trust deed and transfer the assets of the first super fund to the second. This is a complicated process and it is imperative you get financial advisers and accountants involved. The reality is that few trust deeds written before September 2007, when the borrowing rules were rewritten, allow for gearing. Many of those that are purchased today do allow it (but not all). The details of how a trust deed can be updated should be in the deed itself. If you're purchasing a new trust deed from a lawyer as an upgrade to your existing deed, that lawyer will most likely wish to check the existing deed to make sure it can be upgraded. Upgrading your trust deed is not something we recommend doing without professional advisers.

WARNING

The penalties for trustees who make serious errors with their super fund can be considerable. The ATO can impose expensive fines, and even prison terms. But for most, the biggest threat is that the ATO can declare your fund *non-compliant*. If a fund is declared non-compliant, the ATO may be able to tax up to 45 per cent of the entire fund. The average SMSF had assets of about $1,300,000 in 2020 — if the ATO taxed that fund at 45 per cent, the fund would lose nearly $585,000 to the ATO. It is important to keep this in mind when deciding on whether to save a few dollars by doing your trust deed yourself, or making sure it is done professionally.

TIP

Where an update or amendment to the deed has occurred, it is important to retain the original trust deed and all subsequent 'Deed of Variations' together as they will be read as a whole.

Borrowing through bare trusts

Having a SMSF trust deed that allows the fund to borrow is the first step. You can't enter into an LRBA without a friendly trust deed (refer to the preceding section for more on upgrading your existing trust deed).

But the LRBA rules state that a separate trust must hold the geared asset itself. That is, if your SMSF wants to purchase a property that will have a loan attached to it, the law states that it must be held in a separate trust on behalf of the super fund, until the final loan instalment is repaid. At that time, the trust holding the asset can transfer the asset to the SMSF.

The industry refers to these trusts most commonly as 'bare trusts'. Because it is a trust, the trust also needs to have a trustee. As with your SMSF trustee structure, Bruce recommends using a corporate trustee (refer to the section 'Starting with a new SMSF trust deed', earlier in this chapter) to be the trustee of the trust (and choosing a separate trustee to be the corporate trustee of the SMSF).

LRBA loan agreements

Just like a loan taken out from a major lender to buy a property in your own name, a loan agreement needs to be in place for the loan taken out by the SMSF.

If the loan is taken out through a major lender, the lender itself prepares the loan document, which will include the terms of the loan, such as the interest rate, the length of the loan and whether the loan is interest-only or principal and interest.

However, as is discussed in the following section, the trustees, as individuals, are potentially able to provide the loan to the SMSF. That doesn't get you out of a properly structured loan agreement between the lender (you) and the SMSF.

HOW LRBAs ARE STRUCTURED

When an LRBA loan is made, it's made to the SMSF, not the individuals within it. And many lenders will insist on the trustee of the bare trust being a corporate trustee.

So how does this all work? Say a couple, named John and Maria Bennett, have a SMSF called the Bennett Family Super Fund. And they also have a corporate trustee for that fund, which they have called Bennett Family Nominees Pty Ltd. So Bennett Family Nominees Pty Ltd acts as the trustee of the Bennett Family Super Fund.

The Bennetts have found a property they would like to buy within their SMSF and they want to do so with the aid of an LRBA. The property is situated at 25 Lakeview Drive, Nasherville. They set up a bare trust and call it Lakeview Drive Bare Trust. They also set up a corporate trustee for the bare trust, which they call Nasherville Pty Ltd. Then Nasherville Pty Ltd is the trustee of the Lakeview Drive Bare Trust.

Working Out Who Can Lend to SMSFs

For quite a period, very few lenders were prepared to lend to SMSFs, a situation that slowly changed over the years. Most of the major lending organisations — plus a few niche lenders — then reconsidered the new laws and started offering specialised loans for SMSFs.

But another important option should be considered — you as the lender.

Regular lenders

Any lender can, potentially, be the source of funds to be loaned to a SMSF under a LRBA. Most of the major banks joined the fray and started offering loans to SMSFs. However, in recent years, the major banks have largely withdrawn from offering LRBA loans, and loans in this area are now usually provided by smaller, niche lenders.

The advantages of using a specialist lender is that they source the funds for you, draw up loan agreements as part of the process and do most of the checks required to make sure the loan is being entered into legally. The downsides include that those lenders often charge a higher interest rate than you would normally be able to source if borrowing in your own name.

Importantly, because the loan must be limited recourse (refer to 'Limited recourse borrowing arrangements', earlier this chapter), with the lender only being able to seize the asset against which the loan was made, the lender will usually restrict the percentage of the cost of the property that they lend on. Most lenders restrict this to no more than 80 per cent for residential properties and 60 per cent for commercial properties.

You become the lender

Instead of accessing regular lenders for the loan amount (refer to preceding section) nothing is in place to stop you becoming the lender of the borrowed funds to your SMSF.

One reason you may consider this is that you have a surplus of cash in your personal name and you wish to receive a reasonable rate of return on interest for those savings. In more recent years, the ATO has given clearer guidance on individuals being the lender to their super fund, with notifications that the agreement between the SMSF and the lender (you) should be under similar conditions, including LVR and interest rates, to what a commercial lender would offer.

REMEMBER

Lending money into a SMSF is a tricky area and specialist advice is highly recommended. You can't just hand your super fund a wad of cash and call it a loan. The loan needs to be documented, and a fair interest rate needs to be paid for the loan by the SMSF (among other requirements). Essentially, the loan agreement needs to be made on an *arm's length basis* or meet what are called *safe harbour provisions*, as set by the ATO. If the interest rate is too low, the ATO might see it as the individual trying to make a contribution to the SMSF (which is allowed, but must count against a contribution limit; refer to the section 'Super: A low-tax environment', earlier in this chapter). If the interest rate is too high, it could be a breach of the sole purpose test, because the ATO sees this as the individual receiving a benefit prior to reaching the preservation age. If you're considering charging an interest rate that's not a commercial rate of interest, speak to a knowledgeable financial adviser.

Delving into Specific Tax Implications

The good news for SMSFs is that gearing, in many ways, works similarly inside super as it does outside super. We go into far more detail on gearing strategies (negative, neutral and positive gearing) in Chapter 15.

In most super funds, where no gearing is used, the super fund has income from a combination of cash, fixed interest, property and shares. Concessional contributions are also considered income to the fund. All of those are taxed at 15 per cent. If the super fund makes capital gains from assets that it has held for longer than a year, then it pays an effective tax rate of 10 per cent.

The main expenses of the fund are the administration costs and, if taken out, insurance for the members. But in most cases, for those funds in accumulation phase (that is, still accepting contributions), the income is positive and the fund will pay tax.

If your SMSF does enter into gearing arrangements, this brings with it certain tax implications, covered in the following sections. We also look at the taxation of contributions and capital gains within SMSFs, and how these may be lowered.

Negative gearing in super

Anytime a reasonable level of gearing is involved (say, more than 50 per cent of the value of the underlying asset), a possibility exists that the interest costs, when added to a property's other costs (see Chapter 9), will outweigh the income received. When that occurs, the property is considered to be *negatively geared*.

For example, say a $500,000 property was purchased in a SMSF many years ago with borrowings of $350,000 (70 per cent LVR) and an interest rate of 7.5 per cent interest-only. The interest costs on the loan are $26,250 a year, while the other costs (including insurance, rates, agent's fees and general maintenance) total another $6,000, meaning total costs are $32,250. The property is being rented out for $21,000 a year. In this example — ignoring other potential tax consequences — the property is negatively geared to the tune of $11,250 a year.

The laws surrounding bare trusts (refer to 'Borrowing through bare trusts', earlier in this chapter, for more) mean that the tax position of the bare trust flows through to the SMSF. So, the SMSF receives that negative income of $11,250.

The super fund itself, after putting in approximately $180,000 for initial equity and stamp duty for the loan purchase, still has approximately $300,000 in other investment assets. Let's assume those assets are earning an average income return of 4 per cent, or $12,000 a year.

Now, because the negative gearing of the bare trust passes through to the SMSF, the SMSF pays tax on earnings of just $750 ($12,000 minus $11,250), instead of paying tax on its other income of $12,000. On $750, it would pay income tax of just $112.50.

Prior to the acquisition, the super fund had an asset base of $480,000. But after the loan and purchase, the super fund has an asset base of $800,000, including the geared property. If the average capital increase across all assets classes was 5 per cent in a given year, the increase of a base of $480,000 would be $24,000, while the asset base increase on $800,000 would be $40,000.

REMEMBER

Negative gearing, whether inside a SMSF or in your personal name, means that negative income is being derived from the asset. This only ever makes sense if the overall value of the asset is increasing in value by more than the losses being incurred. This won't happen every year — shares and property, in particular, can go backwards in some years — but you should only purchase negatively geared assets where capital appreciation is likely to be reasonably strong. Always remember that negative gearing is most effective on higher tax rates, with the real wealth creation coming via capital growth in your assets over the years.

Eliminating contribution taxes using negative gearing

When a super fund receives *concessional contributions* (generally contributions made by an employer for an employee, or amounts salary sacrificed by the employee), it enters the fund as income. That means it's taxed at 15 per cent.

Here, we can use the same property as in the preceding section, which has produced a negative gearing return of –$12,000. However, for this example the asset base remaining for the SMSF after the purchase is just $200,000, on which 3.5 per cent income is earned, or $7,000. On top of this, one of the fund's members receives a concessional contribution of $7,000 from his employer, as part of the Superannuation Guarantee (SG) of 10.5 per cent paid on employee's wages.

In this example, the SMSF has negative gearing of $12,000 and total income of the fund of $14,000 ($7,000 in earnings from the fund's assets and $7,000 in SG payments). The fund now has income of only $2,000 on which 15 per cent income tax must be paid, for a total of $300.

Without the property as an asset, the fund would have had total assets of $380,000, potentially earning 3.5 per cent ($13,300), plus SG contributions of $7,000. That would be total income of $20,300 on which tax of $3,045 would be due.

How SMSFs pay low, or no, CGT on property

While reducing tax should be a happy by-product of negatively geared property investment, it should never be the sole reason to invest. In the two preceding sections, we describe how negatively geared property can lead to SMSFs reducing their tax bill — an advantage that's simply not available to other super funds that are regulated by APRA.

However, one of the biggest benefits of owning property in super comes on top of the tax benefits of the ongoing holding. And that's when you sell it.

When an entity makes a capital gain on the sale of an asset in Australia, it may need to pay what's known as *capital gains tax* (or CGT). This is essentially a profits tax. As explained earlier in this chapter, super funds are taxed at a lower rate than most other entities. Their maximum CGT rate (that is, for assets held longer than one year) is 10 per cent, versus the top CGT rate for individuals, which is essentially 22.50 per cent (or half of the gain at a marginal tax rate of 45 per cent). See Chapter 15 for more on making capital gains in an individual's name.

So, if a super fund in accumulation phase makes a $300,000 capital gain on the sale of a property, it pays tax of $30,000 ($300,000 × 10 per cent). If an individual on the top marginal tax rate (someone earning more than $180,000 a year) makes a gain of $300,000, the individual pays CGT of $67,500 ($300,000 × 0.5 × 45 per cent), plus potentially more for the Medicare Levy.

In most cases, therefore, a capital gain made in super is worth more after tax than a capital gain made in an individual's name.

TIP

On top of the benefits of tax paid for capital gains while a fund is in the accumulation phase, it can get even better. A super fund in pension phase pays no capital gains tax. So, if the SMSF had made a $300,000 gain on the sale of a property and has started to pay its trustees a pension, no tax would be paid. Not a cent.

A Warning on SMSFs: It's Complicated!

We have made warnings where appropriate through this chapter on the complexity of SMSFs and how they're not just a vehicle that you pick up off the shelf to use to buy property. While SMSFs (and super more broadly) are a generally very tax-efficient way to create wealth for retirement, SMSFs are complex vehicles.

TIP

Becoming the trustee of a SMSF brings with it considerable responsibilities. The Australian Tax Office's website (www.ato.gov.au) is a great source of information on what you need to know about how to run a SMSF.

WARNING

If you're a lover of real estate and are wondering if you might be able to benefit from owning property (geared or otherwise) through a SMSF, you're strongly advised to sit down with a financial adviser who is knowledgeable about SMSFs and property investing (and the number who are strong on both is limited, but includes QPIAs, so make sure you ask some questions of a prospective adviser first). The adviser should be able to tell you how property can work inside a SMSF, help you understand whether a SMSF is suitable for you and also outline the complexities involved in setting up the various structures required to establish a SMSF, and potentially a bare trust for a geared property.

Chapter **9**

The Ongoing Costs of Real Estate

U nlike almost any other asset class, direct property ownership is an invest-ment that the words 'set and forget' do not apply to. If you buy blue-chip shares, so the saying used to go, you can 'put the share certificate in the bottom draw and pull it out in 20 years to retire'. The holding time for property may be similar — real estate investment should be for the long haul — but a hands-off approach isn't possible in direct property investment. And one of the many reasons for that is that property, unlike other asset classes, has a large number of expenses and management issues that require ongoing consideration.

Ongoing costs are part and parcel of property investment. Although the income stream from property (rent) is usually fairly even, the expenses side of the equa-tion is less so. Some bills come monthly or quarterly. Some can be annual. But plenty of bills can come crashing down out of nowhere. And they simply must be paid. Taking the 'lumpy' nature of property costs into account when putting together your finances can save plenty of heartache down the track. From the mortgage to maintenance and body corporate fees, to ongoing property taxes, utility charges, agents' fees, property improvements and even insurance — this chapter tells you about the range of property costs that you need to budget for.

Budgeting for the Inevitable

Managing real estate investments is a slimmed-down version of managing your own business. If you've bought the property on your own or with your spouse (which is how most investment property is bought, although more and more people are investing when they are single or even independently from their partners), then your property is your business, and you need to be involved in making the decisions. Some of the decisions are small and can be left to people you employ, if you so wish, but some decisions are major, and you wouldn't want anyone else to make them for you.

Even if you've employed a property manager to do much of the work for you and an accountant to do some other parts of the work for you, they will always come back to you when the big decisions need to be made. The big decisions are inevitably about big costs — particularly where an item has given up the ghost and must be replaced.

In the following sections, we cover some of the expenses you need to budget for.

Mortgage interest — month in, month out

For most property investments, the single biggest ongoing expense is the interest on the mortgage, certainly in the first few years if most of the purchase price was financed with a loan. In many cases, this expense alone can soak up all the rent received and some of your personal income (for information on interest costs, if negative gearing applies to you, see Chapter 15). The good news is that interest paid on money borrowed is, in most cases, tax-deductible, meaning that it can be claimed against your income.

Interest costs are also one of the few costs that are likely to fluctuate significantly from year to year. Interest costs are linked to the interest rates set by the Reserve Bank of Australia (RBA). If the RBA is lifting rates because it's trying to control inflation or because the economy is picking up strength, interest costs can increase significantly. Conversely, if inflation is considered to be low or benign and the RBA is concerned about the economy slowing too much, rates can fall fairly quickly.

TECHNICAL STUFF

For all the media interest and focus on the issue, the RBA doesn't change interest rates all that often — unless significant global events are affecting the market dramatically. During the global financial crisis and the COVID19 pandemic, for example, cash rates dropped in rapid succession to protect national economies from the financial fallout as much as possible.

Over the course of any investment property loan held for longer than a year, interest rates will both rise and fall. Keep track of your account statements, because making sure you claim your legal entitlements to costs such as interest expenses is a considerable factor in determining the financial success of your investment property.

Financing unpredictable maintenance issues

Question: How can you plan for a heating or cooling system conking out? A toilet that now refuses to flush? Or for a keyhole rusting over? How about burst water pipes? **Answer:** You can't really. Whether you've previously lived in your parents' home, a rental property, or a home you bought and have lived in for some time, you probably have firsthand experience that property-maintenance issues are unpredictable at best and, at worst, perfectly timed to cause maximum financial distress.

If you have a large investment property with multiple residential tenants or a commercial property with a full-time manager, many potential issues can or will be caught as they arise or before they become a serious issue. But, usually, when looking after your first investment property, most maintenance issues aren't going to become obvious until they've actually gone beyond the 'maintenance' stage and are on to the 'repair or replace' stage. Some maintenance issues can be looked at semi-regularly — such as before each new tenant moves in or every few years with an ongoing tenant.

TIP

One way of finding out where some maintenance issues or structural problems may be hiding, especially before you buy a property, is to hire a professional builder to conduct a pre-purchase inspection report (for more information about property inspections, see Chapter 13). A building expert is able to point out major faults and potential structural-maintenance issues that could, or should, be looked at over the short term — one, two or three years. In some instances, the report may sway you against buying that property at all, or could give you leverage to negotiate the final purchase price. But even the experts can't predict the remaining life span of some of the bigger and important items.

When discussing financing regular property costs and 'lumpy' property costs, the biggest concern for a first-time property investor is 'How much do I need to have available for these sorts of emergencies?' Unfortunately, no simple answer is possible. However, you can use the following list to help figure out what you may need:

>> **Is the house old or new?** Older period-style houses are understandably likely to be more expensive to maintain, because more of the items in them are older and closer to getting to the end of their use-by date.

>> **Has the property been renovated recently?** Especially for older properties, does it look like the current owner has been doing work to update the property? If the house has things such as freshly polished floorboards, a new garden, or an updated bathroom, kitchen or laundry, it's possible they got a contractor to fix up a few other problems at the same time.

>> **Are the fixtures and fittings in the house old?** Have a look at items such as ovens, toilets, air conditioners, gas heaters, exhaust fans, hot-water systems and household taps to see how well they've been maintained or how recently they've been replaced.

One of the most important things you can do is ask questions. If you're buying the property to lease out to tenants immediately — that is, you're not buying the property to renovate or to knock it down and rebuild — ask the agent selling the property to find out when major structural work was last done or when things were last attended to. Not relevant for every property but, if necessary, ask about restumping, rewiring, reroofing and replumbing. When were these jobs done and by whom? If the agent can show you receipts, all the better (and retain copies of the receipts for depreciation purposes; for more information, see Chapter 15).

TIP

Here's a good standard for first-time property investors: Set aside or, at the very least, ensure you can easily access about $5,000 to fund small emergency maintenance or structural work.

WARNING

Be aware of tax implications that may also apply to maintaining your property. The Australian Taxation Office (ATO) has specific rules about what an investor can claim deductions for in the first year of ownership (as we explain in more detail in Chapter 15). The rules are designed to restrict obvious maintenance costs from effectively being passed on to the taxpayer. In some cases, early repairs and maintenance may need to be treated as a capital expense and depreciated over a number of years, rather than claimed as an up-front deduction.

Real estate agent management of maintenance costs

If a real estate agent is managing your property, be aware that most basic rental agreements usually give the agent the authority to approve urgent repairs up to a pre-determined limit. This arrangement is to cover most true emergencies that affect the ongoing enjoyment of the property by the tenant — hot-water systems breaking down, problems with heating or cooling systems and leaking pipes or toilets, for example. In most cases, the property manager uses a contractor, who bills the agent, and then the real estate agent bills you. If the work is less than the rent the agent collects for you each month, in most cases the agent will take the charge out of your next month's rent and pass on any remaining rent as normal.

Funding major maintenance issues

Bigger and more expensive maintenance work is not uncommon. If a particularly expensive problem emerges — such as the realisation that the roof really must be replaced immediately or the bathroom, kitchen or laundry needs to be renovated before leasing out to tenants — then it could be time to go to the bank to get funding.

PERIODICAL PROBLEMS

Bruce once bought an unloved period-style house after a court ordered its sale — and despite all its faults and a competitive auction that saw him pay a record price for the street, the house turned out to be a bargain! His pre-purchase inspection report showed that a significant number of long-term maintenance issues had not been attended to. Among thousands of dollars of work that had been recommended by the building inspector, the roof was leaking and probably should have been replaced ten years earlier, the downpipes and guttering were similarly past it and the house had a sub-floor ventilation problem, which was partially responsible for widespread rising damp. The bathroom had been half-completed 20 years earlier and had exposed asbestos on the floor. Then there were the inevitable cracks in the walls that had been plastered over immediately prior to sale, which didn't become obvious until the house had been lived in for a few months.

Some issues were unavoidable features of the age of the house. Cracks in the walls were endemic to the area because of the clay soil the house was built on and the lack of rainfall caused by the ongoing drought at the time. Plastering back over them when it came time for a repaint was the only real solution. The cracks would come back within months again, anyway.

But the leaking roof, the downpipes, the sub- floor ventilation and the rising damp weren't immediately obvious to an untrained eye. Knowing that the problems were there didn't make them go away, but did alert Bruce that he would have to address them and plan financially to have them fixed over the first few years of ownership.

Though the property had been bought for almost exactly the suburb's average price in 2001, when sold in 2010, the relatively inexpensive 'fixes' to the property allowed it to be sold for a price 13 per cent above the average price for the suburb.

Body corporate fees

Most apartments or units are governed by a *body corporate* or *owners corporation* (to an extent determined by the laws of the state in which the property is located), comprised of all owners of individual units within the block.

Several laws govern the existence of bodies corporate, designed to cover everything from blocks of several hundred apartments to a subdivided property with joint use of land. The main purpose of a body corporate is to take control of the maintenance of common property, usually the external areas of the buildings and shared grounds and facilities, and issues that affect many or all of the owners of properties that are adjoined or share a building lot. Some bodies corporate simply get together once a year to determine if any issues exist that require a vote. Legal requirements vary from state to state for the responsibilities of a body corporate but, normally, a body corporate must have a committee, hold committee meetings and an annual general meeting, and ensure that the public liability insurance for common areas is up to date.

One of the main duties of a body corporate is to look after joint maintenance issues — such as gardening, external painting and cleaning. These items are paid for through funds, via quarterly fees, raised from the owners of the properties. The day-to-day maintenance issues are usually covered by a body corporate administration fund. Most complexes also have a building or sinking fund for major capital works.

In most cases, both of these funds require regular contributions from owners so that enough money is available to deal with maintenance issues over time. Regular contributions are put aside so that major maintenance projects can be attended to when required or scheduled.

WARNING

Before you buy a property that may have a body corporate attached to it, make sure you find out the exact status of its finances. Also, make sure you read the body's governing document. Bodies corporate that have administration funds or building/sinking funds that are broke, that have trouble collecting dues from their owners or have a long list of items that look like they should have been attended to some time ago could be a warning to keep clear of the property. Before buying in, find out exactly what you'll be required to pay each quarter or each year, and any work that has been planned and costed that will require you to put your hand in your pocket. Some body corporate items still come out of the blue but, by doing your research, you may be able to reduce the impact of unexpected financial shocks.

Ongoing Property Taxes

Governments at all levels have their fingers all over real estate. A few big taxes are levied up-front, such as stamp duty to state governments (refer to Chapter 5) and the 10 per cent GST on property construction to the federal government. And, of course, you have annual income tax return commitments (to find out how a property is affected by income tax, see Chapter 15). But you'll also find a few other less well-known taxes that you may need to pay regularly and should be aware of.

Council rates

Rates are levied by individual local councils and shires across Australia to pay for services provided to residents, such as rubbish collection, the building of footpaths and bicycle tracks, street cleaning, parking management, tree trimming, the maintenance of public gardens and traffic maintenance (which are important to the upkeep of your house and your street). Rates can also contribute to local services and community organisations, such as parents' groups, senior citizens' groups, libraries and family care centres (all of which may be of interest to your tenants). Unlike stamp duty and land tax, discussed in the next section, at least you get something directly in return from ongoing council rates. In some states, councils or council-run bodies are also the providers of some utility services, including water, drainage and sewerage (for more information on these services, see 'Utility charges', later in this chapter).

Every council has its own method of determining the actual rate to be levied on individual properties. In most cases, the amount is worked out according to the value of the property — that is, higher value properties pay proportionately more in council rates than lower value properties.

WARNING

Rates are usually levied quarterly, half-yearly, or annually in advance. How those rates can be paid is determined by individual councils. A previous owner has likely paid council rates in advance, covering a proportion of the post-settlement period, requiring the new property owner to reimburse the previous owner for that expense. The amount owing is usually calculated during the conveyancing process and the payment made during the settlement process (for more information about conveyancing, see Chapter 12).

Land tax

Land tax is another charge levied by state governments and the Australian Capital Territory. At the time of writing, the Northern Territory doesn't have a land tax. Like stamp duty (refer to Chapter 5), no obvious or direct benefit flows on to the person being charged the tax. Land tax is a regressive wealth tax designed to target property investors specifically. To that end, land tax is usually not levied on a person's principal place of residence (the family home), but is levied on all other landholdings within a state.

Land tax is an annual tax that's charged differently in every state. In some states, it's not levied until a property owner has land valued above a specified amount. When that ceiling has been breached, land tax then becomes payable on the value of all remaining land held by the investor in that state. The land value under that limit is never taxed. And that's an important point. Land tax is levied on the value of the land held by the investor, not the value of the property (which includes buildings and capital improvements) itself.

TIP

For details of exactly how land tax is charged in your state or territory, contact your local state revenue office or department of treasury. The following list of website addresses can help you get started:

>> **Australian Capital Territory:** www.revenue.act.gov.au/land-tax

>> **New South Wales:** www.revenue.nsw.gov.au/taxes-duties-levies-royalties/land-tax

>> **Queensland:** www.treasury.qld.gov.au/budget-and-financial-management/revenue-and-taxation/

>> **South Australia:** www.revenuesa.sa.gov.au

>> **Tasmania:** www.sro.tas.gov.au/land-tax

>> **Victoria:** www.sro.vic.gov.au/land-tax

>> **Western Australia:** www.wa.gov.au/organisation/department-of-finance/land-tax

As an investor, you can't do a lot to escape land tax if you're investing in one state or territory and own a number of investment properties. With rising property prices around the nation, land tax can be many tens of thousands of dollars per year but it's important to understand that you do normally need a reasonably sized portfolio for land tax to kick in. That means that most investors — who generally own just one or two properties — may never have to pay much land tax or pay it at all. Owners of big commercial properties, however, may need to pay many tens of thousands of dollars a year. Big city office buildings might be slugged hundreds of thousands of dollars a year.

You can (at the time of writing, at least) escape paying land tax by buying property in different states. For example, if you own four small properties in Victoria, you may well end up breaching the state's threshold and have to pay land tax. However, if you own two properties in Victoria and two in New South Wales, you might not be caught under any land tax net.

In 2022, the Queensland Government passed legislation to take into account your total holdings across Australia when working out the land tax to be paid on your holdings in the Sunshine State. (Land tax was to be calculated on your total holdings, and then a percentage charged based on how much of this total was made up of holdings in Queensland.) Seen by many in the industry as a cash grab and even 'rent theft', industry associations such as Property Investment Professionals of Australia (PIPA) and the Real Estate Institute of Queensland (REIQ) campaigned against the controversial legislation. In September 2022, the Queensland Government shelved the changes — which isn't to say they might not emerge again in the future.

Other Costs to Be Aware Of

Investment properties incur a number of costs additional to the inevitable charges of mortgage interest, council rates, body corporate fees and taxes. You need to also budget for some utilities, the cost of managing the property, improvements to keep the market value growing, insurance and, in some instances, even garden maintenance.

Utility charges

The past two decades have seen much headway in transferring the costs associated with utility usage to the people responsible for the actual usage — tenants. In the 1990s, state governments began introducing legislation to encourage (or in some cases to make it compulsory) for landlords to install individual meters on most new properties (and some older developments) so that usage of water, electricity and gas could be measured by the individual unit forming part of a block. When that occurred and tenants had to start paying for their own usage instead of landlords paying, usage dropped dramatically.

Usage charges are, therefore, now largely paid by tenants; however, some caveats exist to this, depending on the location of the property. In circumstances where individual meters aren't installed, the landlord is still required to pay for those charges where they can't be separated. Where individual meters are connected, electricity, gas and water usage are charged directly by the utility company to the tenant. In some locations, the property also needs to be water-efficient for usage charges to be transferred to tenants.

The utility cost that's still usually levied to the property owner is non-usage charges for water. The provision of the water service, sewerage service and drainage is still generally levied to the landlord.

Agents' fees

One of the biggest ongoing fees associated with property investment is the cost of employing an agent. Agents in Australia tend to charge a percentage of the rent to manage your property. What you get for your monthly fee varies enormously, as does the quality of letting or leasing agents (for more information on hiring a property agent, refer to Chapter 4).

AGENTS' ECONOMIES OF SCALE

Although nothing is wrong with opting to manage your own property, we don't recommend you do so, especially if you're a first-time property investor, or you're an investor who owns only one or two properties. Here's why.

The average cost of employing a property manager for an Australian property is a small percentage of the total cost of owning of the property, generally anywhere from $2,000 to $4,000 annually, depending on the property's rent. For that price, you get a professional, or a team, who knows the many laws that govern running properties in your state. Usually, the agent knows what to do, has experience in doing it and has the systems in place to do it quickly. If a problem with a tenant arises, an agent can quickly organise the paperwork to get to the right tribunal to sort the matter, because it's something agents occasionally have to do. If an emergency occurs in the middle of the night or on a long weekend, agents know immediately which tradespeople will take the call. They also know a few strategies when it comes to getting tenants to pay outstanding rent (although they're certainly not perfect in that regard). Think of the time you might spend collecting rent and answering maintenance requests, even if you own only two properties in different parts of your city. Agents also have a good idea of what the local properties are renting for and how much your property is worth. Their fees are a small price to pay for peace of mind.

On the other hand, managing your own properties may make sense if you run a significant portfolio, own a block of apartments or have plenty of available time and the interest to become acquainted with the laws and processes you need to follow.

The base fee charged by agents is usually about 8 per cent of the rent (plus 10 per cent GST). Fees are usually higher for short-term rental properties, such as Airbnb, holiday homes and weekend rentals. For full-time tenanted properties, if your monthly rent is $2,400 (the equivalent of $600 a week), your agent may generally charge you about $211 (including GST) a month to look after your property. Most months, for most properties, all the agent has to do for that fee is ensure that the rent is being paid on time. The agent is also responsible for chasing up the rent if the tenant forgets to pay or has trouble paying (although the property owner also needs to keep an eye on the agent when things get patchy). When everything is going smoothly, the tenant is paying on time and the property is holding itself together, agents seem to be overpaid. But when something goes wrong, having an agent to organise repairs, deal with tenants and attend court can be the cheapest employment contract you've ever signed. For more information on the services agents provide and what they charge for those services, see Chapter 13.

REMEMBER

Some very good agents out there charge at the lower end of the scale and some very bad ones charge top dollar. Price isn't necessarily any indication of quality. The fees associated with agents are usually tax-deductible (for more information on tax deductions, see Chapter 15).

Property improvements

Properties require regular updating. Not every year and not for every tenant, but every now and then a property needs to be spruced up. If you want to get the best market rents, sometimes you need to splash on a coat of paint, modernise some of the fixtures and fittings, replace carpet and curtains or even give an entire room or two a new feel.

Although you can easily research what each of these items cost, what's important to know is how they're treated in relation to tax (for further information on deductible expenses versus depreciable capital works, see Chapter 15). Most of the other ongoing expenses covered in this chapter (including agents' fees, land tax, council rates, body corporate fees, utility charges, gardening and insurance) can be claimed in the same year that the expense occurred. That's not necessarily the case with physical improvements to the home.

Some improvements are seen as repairs and maintenance and some categorised as capital improvements. The difference is important, because it determines the speed with which you can claim the item's cost in your tax return. As a broad rule, big items need to be depreciated over many years, whereas small items can be claimed against the investor's income in the year the expense occurred. If you need to replace one venetian blind that costs a few hundred dollars, you may be able to claim that in tax in the year it's purchased (thereby getting a return according to your marginal tax rate). But a new dishwasher will probably have to be depreciated over a number of years.

Insurance

Don't consider starting out in real estate investment if you aren't prepared to be properly covered with insurance. Property assets are usually very big and expensive assets and having one burn down or devastated by a storm can set you back years (maybe decades) if the house isn't properly insured.

Being a property investor, you'd be foolish to go without various types of insurance (and this book devotes the whole of Chapter 14 to them). The first and most obvious is house and contents insurance — to ensure the building can be rebuilt if it's wiped out by the aforementioned disasters. Make sure the insurance covers the fixtures and fittings (so you don't end up short of money to carpet the place and put window furnishings in).

Several providers in Australia also offer landlord's insurance. This allows an investor to cover lost rent if the house becomes uninhabitable for various reasons or if you get the tenant from hell. Both house and contents insurance and landlord's insurance are options designed to protect the property itself and are fully tax-deductible.

Next up is the group of life insurance products that are more about insuring yourself and your family to make sure that the investment property strategy you're developing doesn't have to be cancelled should one of life's disasters happen to you. You want to consider four products — life insurance, total and permanent disablement insurance, trauma insurance and income-protection insurance. The first three pay a lump sum in the event of, respectively, your death, an injury that makes you no longer capable of working and a traumatic illness (such as heart attack, stroke or cancer). Income-protection insurance insures a portion of your income in case illness or an accident stops you from working for an extended period. These insurances are covered in more detail in Chapter 14.

Gardens

If your investment property is a house and you find a tenant who looks after the garden, you've found a rare tenant indeed. Tenants can be notoriously unreliable when it comes to looking after the outside of the house they're living in. Many, in fact, believe it's not their responsibility, even though their rental agreements usually state that they should be maintaining the garden, including weeding and watering (with a mind, of course, to local water restrictions). Unless you've got a long-term and gardening-inclined family living in your property, your tenants are unlikely to even own a lawnmower, whipper snipper or a pair of secateurs, and are even less likely to go out and buy some.

You have the option to do the gardening yourself, but you would need to come to some arrangement with the tenant. Strictly speaking, a property manager or owner must allow the peaceful enjoyment of a tenanted property, which means that tenants must be given proper warning of any visits (for more information about legal responsibilities of owners and managers, see Chapter 13). This requires you writing to them to give them advance notice every time you want to go around and pull out a few weeds.

The good news is that, if you can't convince your tenants to do their duty, hiring a gardener is also a tax deduction.

The responsibility for gardens at multi-unit developments is usually addressed by the property's body corporate. In some cases, tenants may wish to look after small patches themselves, but the general rule is that gardening expenses come out of funds levied by the body corporate (for more information, refer to 'Body corporate fees', earlier in this chapter).

3

Finding and Evaluating Properties

Find out everything you need to know about what, where and how to buy a rental property, including what to take into account if you're looking at opportunities outside major metropolitan areas, and what tenants want.

Understand how to value and evaluate real estate investment properties, and know what to be wary of when taking on a previous investor's lease.

Aim to make money when you buy the property by knowing how to source the information you need to reduce the chance you'll overpay.

Get the low-down on negotiating contracts, performing inspections and how the settlement process works.

IN THIS CHAPTER

» **Choosing your investment area**

» **Looking at what makes a good investment area**

» **Analysing opportunities for tenant appeal**

» **Understanding city living**

» **Checking out regional and rural property**

» **Weighing up community attributes**

» **Getting to know sellers' markets and buyers' markets**

» **Valuing the property and looking at existing leases and capital improvements**

Chapter **10**

Location, Location, Value

s the most well-known saying in real estate goes, 'The three most important factors to success in real estate are location, location, location!' A strong correlation *does* exist between the location of your real estate investments and your financial success. And we firmly agree that the location of your real estate investment is critical in determining your success as a real estate investor. But you also need to find good *value* for your investment dollar.

Merely owning real estate isn't the key to success in real estate investing; acquiring and owning the right real estate at the right price is how to build wealth. As you gain experience in property investment, you'll develop your own strategy, but to make any strategy succeed, you need to do your homework and diligently and fairly evaluate both the positive and negative aspects of your proposed real estate investment. That's where your expert team and your own education come in.

In this chapter, we cover the important aspects of what makes metropolitan, regional and rural demographics different, how to analyse the economy and which factors are most important to property investing. We also discuss barriers to entry and the supply–demand equation. Then we show you where to find this information and how to interpret the numbers to determine your local areas with the most potential. Finally, we discuss real estate cycles and timing, plus provide some pointers on how to begin the ultra-important process of putting a price on your property.

Deciding Where to Invest

If you're going to invest in real estate, you need to decide on a location. Most real estate investors initially used to look around their local communities, but their continued education over the past decade in particular means that many are looking much further afield than their own backyards. We certainly don't recommend that you acquire investment property in the suburb you call home, or an adjoining suburb, because that would lack diversification — that is, if your home suburb is performing poorly, then your investment property would be, too. This applies particularly to those living in the smaller cities and towns outside of Australia's major state capitals.

If you live in a state capital city, that's probably where you may like to begin your search for potential investments. Knowing what's happening on the other side of the state capital city where you live is easier than knowing what's happening interstate, though we do discuss the many benefits of owning property interstate later in this chapter.

REMEMBER

The vast majority of Australians live in the mainland state capitals of Melbourne, Sydney, Brisbane, Adelaide and Perth. The rest of Australia is pretty sparsely populated. And it's in those major cities — particularly Sydney, Melbourne, Brisbane and Adelaide — that more long-term stability and proven growth in property prices usually (but not always) occur. (See the section 'Australia's major property markets', later in this chapter, for more on this.)

TIP

Although virtually everyone lives in an area with opportunities for real estate investing, not everyone lives in an area where the prospects are good for real estate in general. That's why it's important to broaden your geographic investment horizon.

Even if you decide to invest in real estate in your own area, you still need to do lots of research to decide where and what to buy — these are extremely important decisions with long-term consequences. In the pages that follow, we explain what to look for in a city or town before you make that investment decision. Keep in mind, though, that you can spend the rest of your life looking for the perfect real estate investment, never find it, never invest, and miss out on lots of opportunities, profit and even fun. This is why we have seen such growth in the professional property investment advice sector — to help people actually achieve their real estate investment goals, rather than just going around in circles and doing nothing at all.

Evaluating a Region: The Big Picture

Though we usually advise you to consider your state capital, at least for your first property, unless you are opting to become a rentvester for a while, any decision about where to invest should start with an evaluation of the overall economic viability and trends for that city. If your state or territory capital isn't economically sound, the likelihood for successful investments within that area is diminished. To buy right, you need to understand how to evaluate important economic data so that you can invest in the areas that are poised for growth.

We define those regions as most areas in the state capitals of Australia — Sydney, Melbourne, Brisbane, Perth, Hobart and Adelaide. The two territory capitals, Canberra and Darwin, are generally very small markets, which can be overly affected by economic conditions or the decisions of governments.

TIP

Gathering and analysing the relevant economic data has never been easier courtesy of the plethora of information available online. The most important data for population growth, job growth, property statistics and economic trends is available online. From the federal government (the Australian Bureau of Statistics, at www.abs.gov.au, is a good source of this type of information), to state and local governments, to universities, business groups and specialised property data houses information on economic trends is readily available.

REMEMBER

When concentrating on state capitals, you're looking for a diverse economic base with strong employment prospects. In the following sections, we cover some of the more significant factors that can affect real estate demand and values.

Population growth

Population growth is one of the cornerstones upon which demand for real estate is based, but it is not the be-all-and-end-all when it comes to strategic property investment. An area with a steady growth in population is soon going to need more residential and commercial rental properties. More people mean more demand for housing, higher demand for retail shopping and increased demand for offices and service providers. In other words, people use real estate, so the demand for real estate is enhanced as the population increases.

Increases or decreases in population are the result of three activities: Births, deaths and people moving into or out of the area. In most areas, births just exceed deaths (partly because Australia's population base is living longer), and thus most areas experience moderate net growth. So, the real impact comes from a mobile society and other dynamic factors. Tremendous shifts in population have occurred from time to time — from the larger states of Victoria and New South Wales, for example, to higher growth states such as Queensland and Western Australia. Immigration has also been a major factor in many parts of the country over the past two decades due to the resources boom.

REMEMBER

How does population growth affect your real estate decisions? Simply put, economists theorise that a new household is needed for every increase in population of three people. Of course, these numbers can vary, based on average household size (which most recently was 2.5 people, according to the 2021 Census). However, if you're considering investments in rental homes or small apartment buildings in a certain area, the overall net population growth can be a factor in determining current and future demand for rental housing.

But knowing the increase in population for the entire region isn't enough, because population growth isn't evenly spread and can vary. As you get down to the next level in your research (see 'Investigating Your Intended Real Estate Market', later in this chapter), you need to determine the communities where the increased population will want to live, work and shop. Real estate developers, and their lenders, look closely at net population growth in specific submarkets to forecast the demand for their proposed developments, which can see a sharp increase in supply — and thus usually a dampening of property price growth.

Job growth and income levels

Job growth is another fundamental element in determining demand for real estate. One measure economists often use is a belief that a new household is needed for every 1.5 jobs created. So, if a new employer moves into the area and brings 150 new jobs, the local real estate housing market will need approximately 100 new dwelling units. Of course, these new jobs also positively affect the demand for commercial, industrial and retail properties.

TIP

The Australian Bureau of Statistics (ABS) compiles job growth and other economic data by state and region. This info is available at the ABS's website (www.abs.gov.au).

You also need to know about the types of jobs people in an area are employed in before you can estimate their effect on the demand for each type of real estate. Although job growth is critical, so are the following factors:

>> **Income levels:** Without stable, well-paying jobs, an area can stagnate. Even with positive growth in population and jobs, a low overall income level can stifle the demand for additional residential and commercial properties. Many areas of the country have plenty of jobs, but they're lower rather than higher paying jobs. Ideally, look to invest in real estate in communities that maintain diverse job bases, rather than one-industry locations.

>> **Level of employment diversification:** If the local economy is heavily reliant on jobs in a small number of industries, that dependence increases the risk of your real estate investments. Several large 'second cities', such as Geelong and Newcastle, are notable examples where the job market, and hence real estate market, was once tied to the rising and falling fortunes of, respectively, Ford and the steel-making industry. Canberra is another example — its property market is unduly affected by the government of the day and their belief in the ideal size of the public service.

>> **Industries represented:** Consider which industries are more heavily represented in the local economy. If most of the jobs come from slow-growing or shrinking employment sectors, such as farming, small retail and manufacturing, real estate prices are unlikely to rise quickly in the years ahead. On the other hand, areas with a greater preponderance of high-growth industries, such as technology or next-gen industries, may stand a greater chance of faster price appreciation.

>> **Types of jobs:** The specific types of jobs available can be important, depending on the target market for your property. If you're buying an office building in an urban area, look for statistics on current and future employment levels for professional employment. For example, owning an office building across the street from a new courthouse gives you a real advantage in attracting law firms and legal support firms. Of course, you also want to make sure that the area boasts a good mix of nearby retail and food services to complement and support the tenants in your building.

In addition to job growth, other good signs to look for include the following:

>> **Stable to increasing wages:** The demand for real estate is clearly correlated to income levels, so local jobs with strong underlying demand are key. With many jobs being outsourced to other parts of the country and around the world, it's important that the local jobs are not only secure, but also unlikely to see an erosion in purchasing power.

- **A recession-resistant employment base:** Traditionally, jobs that enjoy stability are in the fields of education, government and medical services. Even areas renowned for strong demand and limited supply of real estate can slow down if the economy is hit hard.

- **Employment that's highly unlikely to be outsourced:** Jobs can flow to another area of the country or overseas to the latest low-cost manufacturing base, so look for industries that are more likely to stay put due to required expertise.

- **Declining unemployment:** Examine how the jobless rate has changed over the years, and look out for industries that are no longer significant contributors to the economy. You wouldn't want to have invested your savings in a rental property located next to a large typewriter factory!

Investigating Your Intended Real Estate Market

With real estate investing, deciding where to invest is frequently more important than choosing the specific rental property. You can have a rental property that meets the needs of the market, but if it's located in a declining area where the demand is weak or in an area that has been overbuilt with an excess of available properties, then your investment won't perform financially. (These are the properties that perform the worst over time but are typically the types of properties highly touted by property seminar spruikers, who love to brag about how much real estate they control but rarely tell you about their long-term investment returns.)

Likewise, you need to determine the areas that may be too richly priced, because your cash flow and future appreciation will be hurt if you overpay for a property. Often, properties in the best neighbourhoods in town are so overpriced that they may fall considerably in the short term; thus, we advise you to seek other properties (unless you're content with low returns analogous to investing in safe, low-yielding bonds).

Australia's major property markets

Around 66 per cent of Australians live in the greater metropolitan areas of Australia's eight capital cities. So, it should go without saying that plenty of the real estate opportunities in this country are available in most of those cities.

Australia has only five cities with populations of more than one million; however, Sydney's population is now more than 5 million, with Melbourne not far behind. The population of Brisbane has soared over the past decade in particular, with about 2.5 million people living there at the time of writing. Major regional centres have also seen a big uptick in population, especially since the COVID-19 pandemic, as more and more people had the option of working from home.

REMEMBER

The importance of Australia's mainland capital cities in real estate markets outweighs just their weighting of the total population. They can be better real estate markets in which to invest because of their relative stability, but this isn't always the case. A case in point was the superior price growth recorded in major regional areas during 2021 and 2022 compared to capital cities. However, the economic factors we cover in the following section apply particularly to the five mainland capital cities.

The main reason that the mainland state capitals offer the most opportunities revolves around the diversification offered via the volume of industries and employers. Although Perth is highly susceptible to the health of the resources and mining sectors, for example, the West's capital has many other major industries that employ significant numbers of people.

TIP

Melbourne — and the other major state capitals — is large because significant headquarters for Australia's largest government, manufacturing, banking, telecommunications, health care, information technology, mining and resources, and utilities sectors are based there. Where the headquarters for these industries lie outside of metropolitan areas, they are often the major employer and bring major employer risk with them.

As opposed to the major state capitals, most of the smaller towns in rural and regional Australia have one or two large businesses that dominate employment in the town. If that employer went broke, or decided to relocate to another area, the impact on the town's economy could be devastating. This was certainly the case during the mining downturn that occurred during the 2010s, which saw prices stagnate or fall in many Queensland and Western Australian locations.

Later in this chapter, we delve further into the benefits and risks of metropolitan and non-metropolitan properties.

Supply and demand

The supply and demand for real estate in a given market has a direct impact on the financial performance of your investment property. And, although we firmly believe that the overall economic prospects of a city are vital, you must also find supply and demand information about the specific type of real estate that you plan to purchase.

Obviously, the best environment for investing in real estate is one with strong demand and limited supply. When the demand exceeds supply, shortages of available real estate occur.

Both sides of the equation — supply and demand — have indicators you want to evaluate in forming your consensus about the strength of the local market. Supply-side indicators include building permits, the rate at which new properties have been rented or absorbed into the market, and the availability of alternatives for similar real estate. Demand indicators include occupancy and rent levels.

Before we look at different types of indicators in detail, you need to know how they work together:

>> The overall relationship between supply and demand determines the market conditions for real estate. For example, a large number of pending or recently issued building permits, weak absorption, or rental, of new properties and an excess of rental-property listings that have been on the market for an extended time are all indicators that the supply of a specific product type is greater than the demand. Such market conditions will soon result in lower occupancy, lower rents and, occasionally, concessions like free rent — those seemingly attractive 'rent guarantees' or lower rental rates early in the lease, which mean lower cash flow and smaller capital appreciation potential. These aren't the markets you should be seeking.

>> When the demand for real estate is high, vacancies are few and property owners move to raise rents and remove any incentives, such as discounted rent, that were earlier offered to attract tenants. In commercial properties, landlords cut back on the building-improvement expenses and require the tenants to take the space as-is and make any upgrades or changes to the space at their own expense.

Building permits

Building permits are often the first tangible step outlining the intent of developers to build new real estate projects. Therefore, the number of building permits issued is an essential leading indicator to future supply of real estate.

TIP

The trend in the number of building permits tells you how the supply of real estate properties may soon change. A long and sustained rise in permits over several years can indicate that the supply of new property may dampen future price appreciation. Many areas in state capital cities experienced enormous increases in new building during the late 1990s and early 2000s, right before property prices peaked. Although oversupply can and does happen in all major cities, the impact of overbuilding was evident from the low apartment prices in inner-city Melbourne and Sydney after the end of their property booms in late 2003. In 2008, during the credit crisis, major banks drastically cut their lending to high-rise, inner-city apartments due to oversupply. And when banks cut the loan size that they're prepared to lend you on a property, which they do very infrequently, you can take this as a straight-shooting sign that they believe property prices for those types of properties in those areas are overpriced. As another example, we saw a significant increase in new residential developments being constructed in Sydney, Melbourne and Brisbane during the 2010s, which added to rental supply and kept rental growth under inflation for a number of years.

An excess of building creates supply-side problems that can cause lingering issues for both capital appreciation and rents in an area. For example, take the areas of Southbank and Docklands in Melbourne, where development opportunities seem almost unlimited — that is, supply of new properties to buy or rent is almost unlimited.

The supply equation is simple — new developments are going to be constantly popping up in inner-city areas for a very long time. If you're trying to resell (or let) a unit in one of these areas, attracting a buyer or renter is going to be much more difficult if, at around the same time, a new development is being marketed or sold. Given a choice between your three-year-old unit for $600 a week and a brand-new apartment for $600 a week, a tenant is understandably usually drawn to the newer unit (or one of several dozen new units in that new development). This situation leaves you with little option but to drop your asking rent, or potentially face an extended period without rent.

Availability of alternatives — renting versus buying

When the cost of buying is relatively low compared with the cost of renting, more renters can afford to purchase, thus increasing the number of home sales and lowering demand for rentals.

A key indicator you can use to gauge the market is the number of property listings, as follows:

>> **Increase in property listings:** Increasing numbers of property listings is an indication of future trouble for real estate price appreciation. As property prices reach high levels, some investors decide that they can make more money cashing in and investing elsewhere. When the market is flooded with listings, prospective buyers can be choosier, exerting downward pressure on prices.

>> **Decrease in property listings:** A sign of a healthy real estate market is a decreasing and low level of property listings, which indicates that the area's existing residents are content where they are and are not inclined to move or sell. At high prices (relative to the cost of renting), more prospective buyers elect to rent and the number of sales relative to listings drops.

Although these guidelines are true for all types of real estate, the best example is when low interest rates lead to record home purchases, as happened during the COVID19 pandemic. Agents surveying their departing residents routinely hear that their tenants are moving after purchasing a new home because lower interest rates made the option more affordable. However, a rise in interest rates can have a negative effect on house sales, with the average time on the market increasing significantly. That will mean an increase in the availability of purchase alternatives and lower demand for homes, while the demand for rental housing rises.

Vacancy rates

Vacancy rates are another way to gauge the supply and demand for a given property type in the local market. A vacancy rate for a particular type of property is the percentage of that type of property available for rent. For example, you may find data telling you that a local market has 2,312 rental properties in total, with 70 available for rent. That means a vacancy rate of 3 per cent (or an occupancy rate of 97 per cent). For commercial, industrial and retail properties, the occupancy level calculation is based on square metres.

TIP

Before you invest, determine the current occupancy levels for your proposed type of property. Simply ask a few local real estate agents two questions. First, how many properties do they manage? Second, how many are currently vacant? Most real estate agents boast about the number of properties they manage, and then may be reticent to say how many are vacant. However, a number of online property data sources track vacancy rates, such as SQM Research (sqmresearch.com. au), which you can access for free.

Rental levels

The trend in rental rates that renters are willing and able to pay over the years also gives a good indication as to the supply–demand relationship for property. When the demand for real estate just keeps up with the supply of housing and the local economy continues to grow, rents normally increase. This increase is a positive sign for continued capital appreciation.

Path of progress

Buying real estate in up-and-coming areas that have new developments or renovated properties greatly enhances the ease of finding and keeping good tenants, and can also lead to higher occupancy, lower turnover and higher rates of appreciation.

In virtually all major cities, some areas are experiencing new construction and growth — and have the reputation of being the area to live in. But by the time most people feel this way, you've lost an opportunity to get in when prices have more upside potential. So, here are a few indicators to use to stay ahead of the game:

>> **Follow the retailers:** You can often take a cue about where you should invest by looking for major retailers, which do extensive research before making a decision to open in a given suburb or town. For instance, maybe a new home-improvement store such as Bunnings or Spotlight is opening or anchoring the new shopping centre.

>> **Follow the highways:** One of the best and most obvious indicators of where new development is headed is transportation. But make sure that the roads or public transport projects actually are being built. With so many funding and environmental challenges today, investing in real estate based on proposed transport projects can be extremely risky. But, after they're built, you're sure to find real estate investment opportunities.

The path of progress isn't limited to new development. Many cities have areas that have seen better days, and local leaders are doing their best to revitalise these tired and even blighted sections of town via urban redevelopment programs. Often, these are suburbs on the fringe of a central business district that were occupied by manufacturing and heavy industry from the late 1800s and early 1900s. But, as the factories move to more-modern premises further out in the suburbs, these areas are ripe for redevelopment.

WARNING

Although redevelopment areas can be great opportunities, significant risk is associated with investing in areas that are dynamic and changing. As with transportation projects, sometimes the best intentions of local political or business leaders can hit a snag.

Considering barriers to entry

One trend to follow that can increase demand against limited supply is the creation of roadblocks to new development. These roadblocks can put severe limitations on the construction of additional buildings to meet the increasing demands for real estate, even from natural population growth.

For example, maybe your chosen area has inhabitants with strong anti-apartment sentiments or concerns about the environment. If you currently own or quickly invest in existing apartments in such areas, these factors can actually work to your benefit — because the addition of more housing units (competition) becomes more difficult.

TIP

We suggest that you look for markets where natural and even artificial barriers to entry exist.

The popular board game Monopoly taught many people at an early age about the importance of location and barriers to entry. When you control the playing field and prime properties, you dramatically improve your odds of successfully building wealth. In the real world, the prominent factors that limit the supply of real estate, but enhance cash flow and future appreciation if you own existing properties, are environmental issues, the shortage of buildable land and the restrictions brought about by pressure groups — although this last element is less of a factor than in days gone by, given we have such a strongly growing population in this country.

Environmental issues

Individuals and organisations expressing concern about the environment isn't a new trend, and is becoming more prevalent these days because of climate change. Environmental issues are now a key factor in the potential development of real estate projects.

Those concerned about the environment are expressing their disapproval of new and proposed projects with more authority and success because of laws requiring extensive reports on aspects of proposed land development. In some urban areas, it can be difficult to find land suitable for development that doesn't have some limitations or require remediation, such as the relocation or preservation of endangered animal or plant species. (Remediation can also include the clean-up and removal of contaminants.)

Many of these laws or guidelines find universal support — no-one wants to live in a concrete world or destroy the beautiful countryside. And nearly everyone wants clean air, clean water and the highest quality of living possible.

Shortage of buildable land

Economics 101 teaches that strong demand and a limited supply leads to rationing through higher pricing. Well, that's exactly what happens in many of Australia's major metropolitan areas as the supply of buildable land is exhausted.

This is good news for the current owners of properties in these areas. The steady influx of new residents, combined with new construction at levels significantly below the demand, usually leads to higher occupancies and upward pressure on rents.

The impact of governments on real estate

This country offers many examples of the importance of state and local governments to prospects for prosperity. The following are key governmental and quasi-governmental factors to consider when researching a prospective community in which to invest:

>> **Tax considerations:** For decades, Queensland's unbeatable combination of great weather and job growth has attracted residents and employers. But another factor also influenced decisions in the past. Both groups 'moved in', at least in part, because of lower state taxes, such as stamp duty, petrol excise and payroll tax. (Bear in mind this situation may change.)

>> **Economic development incentives:** At various stages of the economic cycle, state governments themselves go on the offensive and advertise in business publications and major newspapers to encourage employers to relocate, offering real estate incentives such as cheap land or lower taxes. Besides lucrative offers of real estate and tax incentives, as the global economy becomes ever more competitive, businesses are being lured to locations that can reduce their costs of labour, transport and energy.

>> **Community reputation:** Your state government, local chamber of commerce, tourism bureau and council all work very hard to establish the right reputation to attract the top employers. These organisations can have a real impact on the market environment for businesses and thus create more jobs in the long run, which leads to increased population and higher demand for all types of real estate.

>> **Business-friendly environment:** We can't underestimate the importance of a pro-business attitude among state and local governments to help create a vibrant economy where your real estate investments will prosper.

On the Block: Metropolitan Properties

Australia is a very large country with a relatively small population concentrated largely in metropolitan areas, the majority of which hug the edges of the continent. Many property-investment opportunities, therefore, are in the mainland state capital cities. That's not where all investment opportunities are, but it's where 66 per cent or so of Australians live, as discussed earlier in this chapter.

Dozens of investment strategies are touted by experts on where to invest — buy inner city, buy suburban, buy coastal. And this advice is often intertwined with, or led by, gearing strategies, promoting either positive cash flow or negative gearing. Although our general advice is to stick to large cities because they have an abundance of employment opportunities and aren't reliant on single large employers, as some regional towns are, money can be made from property everywhere — it's simply a matter of what risks you're prepared to take. The last 100 or so years has seen a concentration of population growth in cities globally, but our major regional areas with diverse economies, and especially those within manageable commutes to capital cities, can make equally sound property investment locations.

In the next few sections, we discuss the relative merits and risks associated with the different types of locations. We look at the different types of properties that you can find in each type of area, and give you an overview of the types of people who tend to live there.

Inner city

When we say *inner city*, we really mean within a small distance — up to 10 kilometres, depending on the size of the city — of the central business district (CBD) of the major Australian capitals: Adelaide, Brisbane, Melbourne, Perth and Sydney.

Although some states have very large regional cities (such as the Gold and Sunshine coasts in Queensland, Wollongong and Newcastle in New South Wales, and Geelong, Ballarat and Bendigo in Victoria), they're not the primary markets of their states, and they're often beholden to a small number of large employers. With their larger populations, mainland state capitals tend to have a larger spread of employers, plus the headquarters of the largest employers — governments. Each state capital has the advantage of being both the headquarters of state government bureaucracies, and the state-based headquarters of a large number of federal government departments.

Supply and demand dictate that inner-city properties will always be the most expensive, depending on a number of factors including dwelling type. On the supply side, for a start, fewer properties are available in the inner city. If you draw a circle on a map with a 5-kilometre radius from the CBD, the area is, obviously, more limited than the area in a circle drawn, say, 15 or 20 kilometres from the CBD. On the demand side, inner-city properties have what people are prepared to pay more for — they're closer to corporate head offices, entertainment venues, regular public transport, older private schools and universities. That is to say, those living in the inner city often choose to do so because it cuts their travel time to and from employment or schools to a minimum. The low-supply, high-demand equation causes inner-city properties to have higher prices; however, this is not necessarily the case if you purchase a cookie-cutter unit in one of the plethora of new residential high-rise apartments that have been built in the inner cities of most mainland capitals over the past decade.

Some other trends that separate what's available in the city, compared with further out in the suburbs, are

>> **Rents tend to be higher.** People who don't want to buy, or can't afford to, are often prepared to pay to rent a place in the inner suburbs for the same reason others buy — the proximity to major city employment opportunities and attractions.

>> **Properties tend to be smaller.** The higher rents are often for much smaller places. A small three-bedroom terrace house within a 20-minute walk to the CBD could cost twice as much per week to rent as a three-bedroom, free-standing home on a big block of land 40 kilometres out. Demand for space means that apartments are more common in the city and houses are more common in the suburbs.

Suburban

Not everyone can afford to live in the inner city. More importantly, not everyone wants to live in the inner city. Some don't like the unclean air. Some hate the noise. Or, perhaps it's the traffic, the congestion on the footpaths and the fact that finding grass to put beneath your feet may require you to first take a 20-minute walk. Safety aspects, for children, pets or yourself, also come into it. The buzz of a city doesn't attract everyone.

The fact is the suburbs are where many people happily choose to live. And that's something to remember when you buy an investment property (despite what some property experts say). In any state capital, a significant percentage of residents live outside a 5-kilometre radius of the CBD. In the outer suburbs, houses on larger blocks are more prolific than flats, and rents are normally cheaper than suburbs closer in. Plenty of jobs are located in the suburbs. Not everyone works in the city, and many of those who work in the suburbs want to live near work. Plus, increasingly, many people can now work from home — and want to have a bit more space around them when they do.

Of course, any metropolis also has its anomalies — glitzy suburbs that have properties with $2 million (or even $5 million-plus) price tags, which are usually exclusive to inner-city suburbs. These higher-priced suburbs may be beachside, bayside, riverside, in the hills or the mountains, or offer tremendous views.

The ripple effect

Throw a stone into a still pond or puddle and you'll see the ripple effect — everyone will have done it in their lifetime. A few circles of ripples start where the stone lands and the circles these create continue to grow from the epicentre to the edges of the pool. As the ripples move out, they get weaker and weaker.

When it comes to property, the ripple effect describes two things. The first is why very expensive suburbs are usually surrounded by other expensive suburbs. Suburbs, either inner-city or out of town, gain reputations that can stick with them for generations. An expensive suburb is popular because it usually has something special to offer, which can be most easily shared by the residents in immediately surrounding suburbs, so they become popular, too.

The second ripple effect is that price movements tend to have an impact on surrounding suburbs. If the price of one suburb jumps 20 per cent over the course of a year from $800,000 to $960,000, for example, that suburb may now be too expensive for some buyers who had been hoping to live there. Those buyers might, however, be interested in buying in the neighbouring suburbs, which have a lower average price of $750,000. People who were initially prepared to pay $800,000 to live in the first suburb are often willing to pay a little more than the average price to live in their second-choice suburb, pushing up its price also.

Seek and You Shall Find: The Sea, Ski or Tree Change

The turn-of-the-millennium ABC television show *SeaChange* can probably claim some of the credit for causing the shift by baby boomers to a lifestyle away from the cities. But, even if it can't, the show's name was certainly responsible for the coining of the phrase that's now a permanent part of Australian vocabulary.

The show certainly caught a trend in its infancy and succeeded in lifting the 'sea change' lifestyle — moving to the coast to escape a life you may not have been overly enjoying in the city — as an ideal for older Australians. It didn't take too long for a move to Australia's alpine regions to become known as a 'ski change' and a move to a rural or bush property to be called a 'tree change'.

The trend to move out of town isn't really new. It just has a catchy name now and a large number of Australians talking about it. Obviously, people were living in regional and rural areas long before baby boomers began their wind-down into retirement. But the impact of the baby boomers' shift can't be underestimated. Along with a generally wealthier population that values having a holiday home, it's caused house-price inflation in areas outside of state capitals, along Australia's immense coastline and in other 'greener pastures'.

The shift of boomers into retirement started more than two decades ago, with the first boomers turning 55 in 2001 and the last of them due to turn 65 in about 2026 (depending on whose version of the period you use). If they continue to make the move out of the city and away from their children and grandchildren to the relative peace and quiet of non-metropolitan areas, their impact on property prices will continue for some time. However, we also saw significant migration away from capital cities to regional areas throughout the COVID-19 pandemic. Time will tell whether these recent migration decisions wind up being temporary or permanent.

The sprawl of Australia's cities is nothing compared with what lies beyond them. Seaside, regional and rural real estate make up the bulk of Australia, and Australians' interest in investing in that property has increased.

Holiday homes — a general warning

When considering non-metropolitan properties, you need to be very clear that a holiday home is not necessarily an investment property. Many differences exist between a 'home' and an 'investment property' (refer to Chapter 2), not the least of which is tax treatment (see Chapter 15). But the differences are a little more blurred when you're talking about holiday homes and investment properties.

A holiday home is a home away from home — a place for the family to use on weekends and holidays. An investment property (even one by the sea, in the mountains or on the farm) is a place that's available for lease by full-time tenants or is permanently available for casual letting.

REMEMBER

You can have a property that's both holiday home and investment property — say, a coastal property that's let for part of the year and used for personal use for part of the year. But an important difference exists for tax purposes. If you use your investment property for part of the year for personal use, then for tax purposes your property will be considered a home for part of the year and an investment property for the remainder. When a property is considered a home, the owner cannot claim tax deductions. You need to be very careful when making tax claims in this area. Make sure you confer with your accountant.

Heading for the coast

Whether it's a shack or a mansion, owning a beachside house is a widely held dream in Australia. If it's a holiday home, the attraction probably has something to do with romantic views of the ocean, playing beach cricket with friends and family or memories of your favourite childhood summer holidays. If your beach house is an investment, it can be a canny way of making money from understanding others' inclination to pay people rent for short stays at the coast.

REMEMBER

An important point to keep in mind is that the majority of seaside properties across Australia are actually owned or rented by full-time residents. Some of these people have lived in the region their entire lives, some are 'newcomers' who showed up only a few decades ago or moved there when their sea-change moment dawned on them, sometimes in retirement and sometimes in their youth to bring up their families away from the big smoke.

The outcome of owning property beside the sea depends on what you're trying to achieve. If you're all about buying a holiday home for the family to enjoy on weekends and holidays, forget about it being an investment and enjoy. You can probably use the same sorts of criteria that you used to purchase your own home. That is, a place that fulfils your family's needs. If the purchase is about investment and making money, you need to consider more risks than with the purchase of a property in a major city.

When coastal property is in fashion, more often than not the general economy is strong, and people have spare money to indulge in their long-held dream to own a beachside place. But when the economy is weak — when corporations are culling jobs and the share market has taken an extended downturn — one of the first things to go during these tough times is the beach house. People can't afford two mortgages anymore and opt to keep their full-time home.

This sort of economic reality makes prices of seaside properties more likely to move at an exaggerated rate compared with those of other properties (see 'Timing real estate markets', later in this chapter). They're more likely to both way overshoot what could be considered fair value in good economic times and also fall well below fair value in bad times.

Short- and long-term rentals

Two types of rentals for properties exist in getaway-style locations, whether beachside or rural, which offer different benefits and rewards — short term and long term.

Short term

Short-term letting is about renting out your holiday home to a tenant for a night or two, a week or perhaps even a few weeks, often using a specialist platform such as Airbnb. With this option, some fixed costs usually remain the same or similar — whether the tenant is staying overnight or for several weeks. One cost is cleaners. Unless you live nearby, expect to pay $200 to $300 to get a cleaner to go through the property and have it sparkling and ready for the next tenant. You'll also probably need to pay a minimum fee or a fixed percentage of the rent to a local agent or the platform. And you'll need a gardening and mowing service if you don't live close enough to do this yourself.

For short-term tenants, the property owner has to wear the cost of water, electricity and gas usage. These costs can't be passed on to overnight or short-stay rentals and have to be built into the overnight or weekly price.

The shorter the stay, the more expensive the nightly cost of short-term rentals. Pricing is also determined by the time of year. The Christmas holiday period is the major family holiday time in Australia, as well as school holidays throughout the year, and houses let out in getaway locations can attract stunning prices for a week or two's rent. In fact, many owners of holiday-style properties that are permanently available for rent find that a considerable amount of the money they make for the year is made in the six or seven weeks of school holidays that make up the second half of December and the whole of January.

For example, a property may attract rents of $30,000 over the course of a year — an average of nearly $600 a week. In many cases, the property is fully let during the summer holiday period for $3,000 a week, raking in $18,000 (gross, before expenses) over the period. It may sit largely vacant for the rest of the year, picking up a week or two here and a few weekend bookings there. The income during these other parts of the year could be as little as $1000 for the occasional week, or perhaps $600 for a weekend booking over Friday and Saturday nights.

These sorts of short-term renting arrangements are used by those who want to still occasionally use the property as a holiday home themselves. (If that's your intention, make sure you're aware of the tax implications, discussed in more detail in Chapter 15.)

Long term

Clearly, with long-term rentals, you can't expect to be able to use the property on weekends. You may plan to use it once a year or every few years when a tenant moves out, or you may intend to have it fully rented for several years until your situation changes. If you're in the market to buy a holiday property with a view to renting it out long term, you need to do the same types of research that you'd do for any property you want to rent long term. That is, make sure it's the type of property that's in demand by local residents. Are schools and hospitals nearby? Do employment opportunities exist in the area? (For more information on sourcing a property, refer to the section 'Evaluating a Region: The Big Picture', earlier in this chapter.)

TIP

Spend time finding out who the best local agent is for your property. Find the agent locals go to when they want to find a place to rent, which isn't necessarily the same flashy agent out-of-towners go to for their holiday-letting requirements.

In regions where populations are small, demand may be limited, which means properties put up for rent can often be vacant for longer. You may find that your place is snapped up quickly, but you should probably leave a buffer in your finances to cover a longer period without rent. In this sort of situation, expect rental returns to be low. And remember, if you're going to rent the property out to a full-time tenant, you won't be able to get the high overnight or weekly rents that you charge short-term tenants (as we discuss in the preceding section).

Comparing Communities Come Investment Time

The reputation of particular communities can be based on many factors, but certain key or essential elements differentiate the neighbourhoods with good reputations and positive trends from the areas that are stagnant or trending in the wrong direction.

Employment opportunities

A major consideration for many tenants when deciding where to live is the property's proximity to job opportunities.

Although some people are prepared to travel long distances by car or on public transport every day to fulfil work commitments (commuting each day from the suburbs to the city and back), many people decide where to live based on limiting the amount of travel they have to undertake each day to get to work. These people choose to live in a suburb or region that offers good employment opportunities. For example, the local businesses in big shopping malls or shopping centres need employees, as do the local factories, schools and suburban offices, which enhances the reputation of the suburb or region.

Don't underestimate the importance of a nearby supply of employment opportunities. Employment growth is one of the major attractions for new tenants to an area.

Schools

If you don't have school-aged children, you may not initially be concerned about the reputation of local schools in a region. Think again. Whether you're investing in residential or commercial properties, schools matter. The demand for residential and commercial property (and the subsequent value of the property) is highly correlated to the quality of local schools.

Ask any real estate agent about the impact of schools on the demand and sales price for a home in a great school district. Likewise, employers use the quality of local schools to recruit personnel.

Public transport

Not everyone owns a car and many people who do don't want to drive to work. Some of the key reasons commuters choose public transport over taking their cars, particularly in metropolitan areas, include

>> **Car running costs:** Catching trains, buses and trams is usually cheaper when taking into account rising fuel prices and vehicle servicing costs.

>> **Parking:** Costs to park your car in the CBD or inner-city areas have risen considerably faster than inflation in recent years. And those who park on the street often risk parking fines or pay through the nose for the privilege.

>> **Stress:** Many people choose to take public transport rather than deal with the stress of traffic, and a long train journey may give them time to read, catch up on work, or simply zone out for a while.

The closer a suburb is to the heart of the city, the better the public transport network tends to be. Population density plays a huge role here, but the point we want to make is this: Inner-city residents who take public transport get access to more regular services, which allows them to get around with ease. This factor enhances a community.

People who don't own cars rely on public transport — unless they can walk or ride everywhere. They need to live in an area that provides public transport so they can get from A to B. Many university students, for example, don't own cars and base their decision on where to rent on how quickly they can catch public transport to or from campus. Similarly, the clincher that gets them to sign a lease may be a train, tram or bus service running conveniently past their door, even if the property is located some distance from their university.

Amenities

Amenities are important to the vast majority of tenants. These include the availability of reasonable shopping precincts, hospitals and government services. Some suburbs have been overlooked by governments over the years, for one reason or another, and provide minimal services and, therefore, fewer incentives for people to live in the area. Often those that are in 'safe' government or opposition seats miss out on political pork-barrelling that sees new services introduced to suburbs where votes are seeking to be 'bought'.

Federal, state and local government amenities include services for families and the elderly, such as public libraries, maternal and child health services, childcare, schools, hospitals, government-sponsored employment services and sporting facilities — including parks, football ovals and swimming pools. All these facilities not only provide much-needed services for local communities, but also create a source of employment for locals.

The availability of a shopping district is just as important. Everyone needs to shop regularly for food and essentials. A rental property with limited access to a shopping precinct will struggle to attract a tenant who rates these amenities as important. For example, is a home in a new suburb without decent public transport and that involves a 15-minute drive to the local supermarket going to appeal to a single-parent family or a senior citizen without a car?

Restaurants can also be a big drawcard. The modern Australian lifestyle includes eating out more often — not only for the food but also for socialising. Having restaurants nearby is a plus for many residents.

Crime rates

Crime can have a significant and sobering effect on the demand and desirability of all types of properties. No-one wants to live in a high-crime area, and commercial tenants and their customers will neither work at nor patronise unsafe businesses. No areas are going to be crime-free, but you don't want to find out after settlement that you've purchased a rental property at the epicentre of the local drug trade. Before you make your investment decision, consider consulting these sources:

>> **Local police:** Contact the state police or local station to obtain the latest and historical crime statistics and compare them to a relatively 'safe' area.

>> **Local newspapers:** Newspapers often have a crime-watch section that provides information on major and even petty crimes in a community.

Pride of ownership

Pride of ownership is an intangible attitude that has tangible results. Pride of ownership also has no economic boundaries — even modest-income areas can really look sharp.

TIP

Look for investment properties in communities that reflect pride of ownership — well-kept, litter-free grounds, trimmed plants, beautiful flowers, fresh paint and so on. This is the kerb appeal that helps you attract and retain your tenants.

Although everyone may have a different perception of exactly what constitutes a well-maintained property, pride of ownership is readily apparent, and the effort made by business owners and homeowners to keep their properties looking sharp is important to real estate values.

You may find that some of the more aesthetically pleasing areas look that way for a reason: Bodies corporate and business parks typically routinely inspect their properties as well as review and restrict improvements to meet certain standards.

You can control the appearance, condition and maintenance of your own property, but your options are limited if the properties surrounding yours fall into disrepair. Your purchase of a renovator's delight and the investment of time, money and sweat won't be properly rewarded financially if the surrounding properties are in a state of neglect.

TIP

Inner-city suburbs that have slid substantially can be good candidates for the 'next big thing' — where, if *gentrification* (smartening up a rundown area) takes hold, property prices head upwards. Suburbs that are prime candidates for being gentrified include those with a low proportion of renters, where local transport networks provide good access to employment opportunities, and with existing public assets such as schools and hospitals. Gentrification also often occurs when architectural elements are strong in the local properties, the housing stock itself is relatively affordable, and a more wealthy demographic of residents starts to move into the area.

Role play: What attracts you to the property?

One of the best ways to evaluate the prospects of a particular neighbourhood is to play the role of a residential tenant looking for the best place to call home. Go back in time to when you made the decision to live at your current address. What were the primary criteria you used to make that determination? You're probably typical of many of your potential tenants. Use that knowledge or inquisitiveness to investigate the area you're considering investing in. As we mention in earlier sections of this chapter, tenants prefer rental properties in close proximity to employment centres, public transport, schools, childcare, shopping, recreation, entertainment and medical facilities. Keep a property knowledge sheet to record these details (see Figure 10-1).

Property knowledge sheets

Although we don't recommend managing your property yourself, one of the best ways to have the answers to the questions that may be raised by your rental prospects is to prepare a property knowledge sheet for each of your rental property locations. A property knowledge sheet contains all the basic information about your rental property, such as the size and type of the property, plus the age, type of construction and other important details.

TIP

As well as specific details of the property, a thorough property knowledge sheet also contains important information about the local neighbourhood and general area. Like a tourist information centre, you want to be able to answer questions about the area. Rental prospects are usually interested in knowing about employment, public transport, local schools, childcare, shopping and medical facilities.

Much of the required information about the local area of the property you're considering is readily available online — meaning you can access it without having to leave your home. Many real estate sites tell you how close the nearest schools are, how many restaurants are in the local area, and where the local shopping precinct and supermarkets are.

TIP

If you're looking to do research from home on a property or an area, find nearby properties for rent online through the major real estate listing portals and agency websites. These sites can also often give you ratings guides on the pluses and minuses of renting in the area, directly from local residents, which can be invaluable information.

With all this vital information from your property knowledge sheet at your fingertips, you can start to clarify whether the property is a possible investment option.

Check out Figure 10-1 for an example of a property knowledge sheet.

Property Knowledge Sheet

Address: _____

No. of bedrooms: _____

No. of bathrooms: _____

Security deposit: _____

Type of dwelling: house townhouse unit flat

Facilities: _____

Laundry: _____

Pets allowed: Y/N

Heating/cooling type: _____

Special features: _____

Floor-covering type: _____

Community information

Creche/childcare: _____

Preschools/kindergartens: _____

Primary schools: _____

High schools: _____

Universities: _____

TAFE/other colleges: _____

Places of worship: _____

Police station: _____

Fire station: _____

Ambulance: _____

Hospital: _____

Pharmacy: _____

Vet: _____

Supermarkets: _____ km _____ km

Electricity: Y/N

Gas: Y/N

Cable/satellite TV: Y/N

Libraries: _____

Post office: _____

Public transport: _____

Restaurants: _____

Other advantages of this property:

_____

_____

FIGURE 10-1:
Property knowledge sheet.

Mastering Sellers' Markets and Buyers' Markets

Some real estate investors make the mistake of not continuing to research the economics of their real estate markets after they've made their investments. Even if you plan to buy and hold, you need to pay attention to the market conditions. The criteria we advise you to consider in making decisions about which markets are the best for investing are dynamic — they fluctuate.

Savvy real estate investors monitor their markets and look for the telltale signs of real estate cycles. These cycles present opportunities for expansion of your real estate portfolio or repositioning from weaker markets to stronger markets, because not all areas experience peaks and troughs at the same time. That's why you need to know and track the timing of sellers' and buyers' markets.

Real estate cycles

Real estate is cyclical, and successful real estate investors always remain aware of the real estate cycles in their areas. But first, what are buyers' and sellers' markets?

>> A **buyers' market** occurs when the current owners of property are unable to sell their properties quickly and they must be more flexible on the price and terms.

>> A **sellers' market** is almost like the classic definition of inflation — too much money chasing too few goods. In this case, the goods are real estate properties, which are in high demand, with buyers lining up for the chance to purchase them. When sellers are receiving multiple offers within 24 to 48 hours of a listing or you see properties selling for more than the asking price, you're in a strong sellers' market.

Real estate traditionally experiences cycles as the demand for property leads to a shortage of supply and higher rents and appreciation. That leads to the building of additional properties, which, along with changes in demand due to economic cycles, usually results in overbuilding and a decline in rents and property valuations.

However, not everyone agrees that real estate cycles are relevant to residential real estate investors. Some property spruikers claim investing in homes and apartments is recession-proof because people always need a place to live. Although that's partly true, we think that the economic base of the community where you invest does have a direct impact on all aspects of your operations — occupancy, turnover, rental rates and even quality of tenants.

For example, when times are tough, residential tenants will improvise with some taking in housemates in order to save money. Some renters are even willing to move back in with Mum and Dad or another relative when their personal budgets don't allow them to have their own place.

Can real estate investors who track these real estate cycles make investment decisions based on this information? Absolutely. Timing the real estate market is how many successful and knowledgeable real estate investors can increase their real estate investment returns. Read on.

Timing real estate markets

Although the length and depth of real estate cycles vary, they do have clear highs and lows that real estate investors need to consider — the skill, of course, is knowing before anyone else does, which is not easy for the beginner, or even experienced, investor.

Regardless of the market conditions at the time, one of the tried-and-true techniques that savvy investors use is to identify those markets with excellent economic fundamentals, where prices have remained low, and invest there. The concept is similar to the 'buy low, sell high' concept for stocks, except you sell in overpriced markets and reinvest in the lower priced markets. Such markets do exist, but the question is whether the properties in the lower priced markets are going to provide the same or better investment returns in the long run versus alternative markets.

WARNING

Unlike the stock market, real estate transactions entail significant transaction costs (as a percentage of the market value of the property). That's why selling and buying property too frequently undermines your returns.

Our contention is that, even in the few markets where such 'bargains' exist, they aren't really great opportunities. We're reminded of the consumer concept that in the long run you usually get what you pay for! The projected rent and the selling price aren't the only things to consider. Without going into a detailed analysis of property condition, expenses and other invaluable criteria, simply think about whether these areas will pass muster after you perform the proper economic analysis (refer to the sections 'Evaluating a Region: The Big Picture' and 'Investigating Your Intended Real Estate Market', earlier in this chapter). Probably not.

Risk and return are related. That is, the lower the risk you take, the lower your expected return. (That's why short-term government-backed bonds usually offer nominal rates of interest or return on investment, and investments with higher risk, such as real estate, demand higher rates of return.)

So, the real question is: What are the risk-adjusted returns like for investing in areas of the country with record-high prices versus the risk-adjusted returns available in other lower priced real estate markets? At the end of the day, you may find that your lower-priced market with all of those 'bargains' provides you with minimal cash flow and marginal appreciation.

Knowing when to sell and when to buy real estate is easier said than done. But, if you follow the fundamentals of economic analysis, and remember that 'location, location, location' is the key to successful real estate investing, you can do well.

If you study particular markets over periods of years — both cities, major centres and individual suburbs — you can get a good feel for when the good times to both buy and sell properties are. In a broad sense, Bruce is a strong believer in two signs that indicate property markets are overpriced and, because of this, indicate a bad time to buy in a timing sense. The first is general media hype. The more headlines start screaming about how 'unaffordable' property prices are, the closer to a peak of a boom the market usually is. The second indicator is the talk around the barbecue or the dinner party table, and the same general rule applies — if everyone is talking about how easy it is to make money in property, the better the chances that the smart money is about to move on. From a timing sense, it's not the time to be buying.

The same applies in reverse. When the media headlines are negative and none of your friends are talking about property, this is a good indicator that property may be bottoming out — as appeared to be the case in mid-2012 and 2022 in many property markets — and the ability to 'buy low' has just presented itself.

Understanding Value

What you pay for the property and the cash flow it generates makes a significant difference to the success of your investment. In Australia, the majority of residential investment properties are usually 'vacant at possession' (when settlement occurs). But this isn't always the case: Most commercial properties will be leased and, occasionally, residential properties will be occupied by tenants when ownership changes hands, particularly if you're buying a block of apartments.

When researching potential properties, understanding basic valuation concepts and how leases, particularly existing leases, influence value is important. Also important is accurately estimating (as much as is possible) the cost of required capital improvements.

Understanding the principles of valuation

Valuing a property is part art, part science. And for novice property investors, it can be a fascinating part of purchasing your first property (or first few properties).

Knowing certain economic principles can be useful when evaluating the current and future value of potential real estate investments. Closely watching property price sales data in your chosen area is one way of getting an understanding of the 'true' value of a property. But that can only go so far.

A residential property in Australia can be broken down into two parts — the building itself and land on which the building sits. For example, what is the cost of a square metre of land in your chosen suburb? And how much would it cost to rebuild a similar home in that area?

The main cheap sources of information on this come from recent sales data and from local real estate agents. However, the best source is usually a qualified property valuer.

Hiring a valuer

Valuing a property isn't a simple process. Understanding how to value land itself plus the buildings that go on top of it involves significant complexity, and covering these complexities is beyond the scope of this book. For an untrained investor, trying to arrive at a valuation for a potential property can soak up dozens of hours of your time — and you're likely to still get a price estimate that isn't particularly accurate.

While a reasonable indication of the potential value of a property is easy to obtain nowadays by checking online and by tracking recent sales in the area in which you have chosen to invest, working with a qualified valuer to help you with the process of deciding what to pay for a property can be a considerable time saving.

Qualified valuers have access to databases that track sales in your area going back a considerable time. Given the basics of your intended property target, a valuer can give you a good indication of the property's true worth. The valuer's fee could be a bargain if it stops you from overpaying for a property, or highlights a significantly undervalued property in your price range.

Evaluating existing leases

A lease is a contractual obligation between a lessor (landlord) and a lessee (tenant) to transfer the right to exclusive possession and use of certain real property for a defined period for an agreed consideration (money).

In Australia, the majority of residential tenancy leases used are standard forms, usually provided by state-based authorities, including the local real estate institutes. They cover the majority of potential issues that may arise during the course of a lease.

TIP

Regardless of the type of property you're considering as an investment, make sure the seller provides the full lease documents (if relevant). Don't accept just the first page or a summary of the lease — insist on the entire document along with any addendums or written modifications.

Lease transferability and analysis

Existing leases almost always run with the property upon transfer of ownership and thus are enforceable. As the new owner of a property, you can't simply renegotiate or void current leases you don't like. At a minimum, you have to give the proper notice period (which varies depending on whether the lease is fixed term or periodic) before making any changes to a lease. Because you're legally obligated to all terms and conditions of current leases when you buy a property, be sure you thoroughly understand all aspects of a property's current leases.

WARNING

A requirement that sellers be honest and disclose all material facts about the properties they're selling would be nice. But, in Australia, the onus is on the buyer to find out all the facts before purchasing a property. So, even though your real estate agent and members of your property team (refer to Chapter 4) may assist you with inspecting the property during the transaction, at the end of the day, you're the one who cares the most about your best interests.

Note the expiration dates of the leases and evaluate any lease that's about to expire, based on current market conditions. Future leases may not be at the same rent level, and you must consider the concessions or tenant improvements that may be necessary to get the lease renewed. Remember that, in down economic times, residential lease renewals may require rent to be discounted or possibly a perk for the tenants to be added, such as installing air conditioners.

Factor any costs required at the lease renewal into your analysis, because renewing a tenant, even with the associated costs, is typically much more cost-effective than the turnover of a tenant, particularly if the likely result is an extended period without a tenant.

Comprehending residential leases

The analysis of current leases for residential properties is usually fairly straightforward, but that doesn't mean you shouldn't do your homework! Review every residential lease (and, if you're buying a block of flats, that means reviewing each and every lease) to make sure that no hidden surprises await you, such as limits to rent increases or promises of new carpet.

When you're looking for finance for residential properties, banks normally want some form of proof of the rent to be received. This proof may be a copy of the lease or, in the case of an owner-occupier, a written statement by a local agent of the rental price that's likely to be achieved for the property.

Making sense of commercial leases

Residential leases tend to be straightforward; however, evaluating commercial property leases is a whole different ballgame and beyond the scope of this book. If you're considering a commercial property, you're well advised to employ a commercial property lawyer who has experience with the type of property that you're looking to purchase to run an eye over the terms and conditions in the lease, in the same way you would get a solicitor to check the sale documents on a residential property.

Commercial leases are much more complicated than residential ones and, therefore, real estate investors must have a thorough understanding of the contractual obligations and duties of the lessor (landlord) and lessee (tenant), particularly as to who pays for what property expenses. Many of a commercial property's expenses are usually paid by the tenant but the breakdown of these is usually negotiated through the lease document. You need a lawyer to do this for you — unless you have considerable experience in this area, do not try to do this yourself.

Making capital improvements

In developing estimates for the value of a property, many investors neglect to account for, or seriously underestimate the need for, capital improvements to the property. Capital improvements are the replacement of major building components or systems such as the roof, driveways, heating and cooling systems, windows, appliances, lifts and floor coverings. Real estate investing requires planning and the allocation of funds to protect and preserve the asset in the long run.

Often sellers indicate that the property has been fully renovated and imply that the purchaser won't incur any capital-improvement costs for many years to come. But buildings age and things break — especially in rental properties, where you can be assured that tenants break things and don't necessarily tell you! Just as bodies corporate need to put aside funds each year in a reserve account for capital improvements, you should allocate a portion of your income to reflect the fact that certain components of your property will deteriorate over time and will need replacement.

And that should influence the amount you're willing to pay for a property. Otherwise, you may find that your roof needs to be replaced and you don't have the funds to cover the expense.

REMEMBER

Capital improvements are also an essential component of the repositioning or renovation plans that can lead to improved financial performance for investment real estate. As an investor, always look for properties that owners have neglected to properly maintain and upgrade. These properties are one of the best target markets for investing, and your projections for income and expenses should contain a realistic capital-improvement budget.

Always make sure that you do your final walk through of a property in the week before settlement occurs to make sure that significant problems with a property haven't occurred prior to sale. You may consider involving the leasing agent you're intending to have on your team, or someone knowledgeable about competitive properties in the market, to help you with this important final inspection. Ask this person to compile a prioritised list of needed work and cost-effective upgrades that is most likely to position your property to outperform the rental market and that can be done very quickly once you take possession of the property.

The reserve of money you hold for capital improvements or replacements will vary based on the age, location and condition of the property, as well as the tenant profile. The higher the turnover of tenants and the less the prior owner has invested in properly maintaining the property over the years, the higher the capital expenses you need to plan for. Climate can also be a factor in the lifespan of building components. Properties located near seawater require more frequent painting and replacement of items affected by moisture and salt.

TIP

Capital expense calculations are a very subjective part of any plan. Our advice is to estimate towards the high side of any range. If you don't have to spend the funds, your real estate investment results will be enhanced. But you don't want to plan on scrimping by not addressing needed repairs and replacements. Deferred maintenance will be more costly to address in the future, plus you'll ultimately experience a negative impact on your income if your property doesn't attract financially strong and stable tenants.

Chapter **11**

Preparing to Bid or Make an Offer

You're likely to log many hours locating and assessing potential property purchases. Then comes the moment when you must decide whether you want to try to buy a property or keep looking for a more attractive opportunity. In this chapter, we discuss how to use your property assessment to determine your top buying price, and negotiate a deal that meets your needs, as well as considering those of the seller. Next, we cover the all-important details of real estate investment contracts. Finally, we look at the importance of ownership — before you sign on the dotted line.

Valuation: Working Out How Much to Pay

Throughout this book, we strongly recommend using an expert team to help you during your property investment journey. Professionals such as buyers' agents, qualified property investment advisers (QPIAs) and valuers can come up with a valuation figure for a potential property that's likely to be far more accurate than your own approach to property pricing and potentially save you a heap of time — and money. But it also helps to understand the three basic methods that valuers use to determine a property's value, so in the following sections we explain these methods.

Usually, each method arrives at a slightly different estimate of value. You or the valuer needs to weigh up which one makes the most sense for the particular property — it won't always be the one that arrives at the lowest value. But lenders require valuations to protect their position — that is, to make sure that if they're suddenly forced to take possession of the property and sell, they're less likely to suffer a loss.

REMEMBER

Property valuation isn't an exact science. Although property valuers apply their skill and experience to determine a precise market value on a property, it is accepted that variances, to some degree, will occur between two different valuers. That said, the variations should not be extreme if both valuers applied the same principals when conducting their assessments.

Market data (sales-comparison) approach

The *market data* (or sales-comparison) approach applies the economic concept of substitution to real estate — essentially, that the value of a given property should be approximately the same as a comparable property that provides similar benefits.

You've probably seen this concept before. You'd expect two similar homes built by the same builder at the same time on comparable lots to sell for analogous prices. (Of course, no two homes are identical, and you inevitably need to adjust for small changes.)

REMEMBER

The accuracy of the market data valuation approach relies on sourcing sufficient recent sales of comparable properties. This approach is primarily used for houses, apartments, units, townhouses and small apartment buildings, because sales are typically more plentiful.

If completed sales are insufficient to arrive at a reasonable valuation, valuers may consider current listings and pending sales, but they usually discount such potential transactions because they're not finalised and many things can happen before a sale.

Typically, valuers look for at least three comparable properties in close proximity to the subject property. Of course, the usage and type of real estate should be the same or similar — a good comparison should be similar in age, size, amenities and condition of property. How recently the sale occurred is also very important.

Valuers strive to find several comparable properties, but the reality is that every property is unique, so absolutely identical comparable sales or listings are unlikely. So, appraisers need to make either positive or negative adjustments to account for the differences. They factor all of these variances into an adjustment to the price and then calculate an indicated value for the subject property.

For example, say you want to purchase a house that you can rent out as an investment property. You see a property listed for $705,000 that's 400 square metres with a three-bedroom, two-bathroom house on it. The property is about ten years old, in good condition and has a great location on a corner lot. Using the sales-comparison method, you want to know the value of this property, so you contact a local agent and gather the recent sales data for comparable houses that have recently sold in the same suburb. Table 11-1 contains the information you've collected for recent sales of houses.

TABLE 11-1   ## Market Data Summary

Category	Proposed Acquisition	Property A	Property B	Property C
Price	$705,000	$665,000	$700,000	$720,000
Age	10 years	9 years	14 years	New
Location	Corner lot	Mid-block	Corner lot	Mid-block
Condition	Good	Fair	Good	Excellent
Features	Air conditioning	N/A	N/A	Air conditioning
Sale date	On market	10 months ago	Last week	Last month

Because the properties are different, you need to make some adjustments to formulate a price for the proposed property. The adjustments are made for features that typical buyers and sellers in that area feel have a material impact on value, either positively or negatively. For example, in many parts of Australia, a rental property with air conditioning is more desirable than one without, and property condition is important in all markets.

After researching the local market to establish what factors are important to buyers and sellers, determine what adjustments should be made for the subject property based on its age, location and condition, and the fact that it has air conditioning (see Table 11-2):

>> **Property A** is comparable in age to the subject property but is clearly inferior — it doesn't have air conditioning or the corner lot and is only in fair condition. The property sold 10 months ago, and your research shows that prices for comparable properties in the suburb have risen 3 to 4 per cent since then. You make adjustments for the corner lot ($10,000), condition ($10,000), air conditioning ($5,000) and market timing ($15,000). So, overall,

you expect that, if this property was on a corner lot, was sold today in good condition and had air conditioning, it would've sold for approximately $40,000 more than the actual sale ten months ago, or an adjusted sale price of $705,000, to bring the property in line for comparison with the subject property.

>> **Property B** is a little older but, because it's been well maintained and is in good condition, no adjustment is necessary for that factor. The property is on a corner lot and also sold just last week, so no adjustments are necessary for these factors. However, it doesn't have air conditioning ($5,000). With air conditioning, this property would've likely sold for $705,000.

>> **Property C** is brand new, has air conditioning and sold only last month. The only disadvantage when compared with your proposed investment is this property's location in the middle of the block. Overall, your research indicates that the price difference for brand-new properties is $15,000 higher than a ten-year-old property like the subject property. But comparable properties located in the middle of the block sell for $5,000 less. (**Note:** While a corner block may add $10,000 to the price, being in the middle doesn't automatically take off $10,000. The amount depends on other factors in the block's position.) Therefore, you need to adjust the Property C price lower by $15,000 for age and higher by $5,000 for the inferior location, which is a net downward adjustment of $10,000 and leads you to an adjusted value of $710,000.

In reviewing the results of your analysis and adjustments in Table 11-2, you feel that the asking price is right in line with (if not slightly below) the current market price for comparable properties in the neighbourhood. You decide that, if you can purchase the property for $705,000 or less, you'll have a good investment.

TABLE 11-2   **Adjusting Sales Price to Determine Value**

	Proposed Property	Property A	Property B	Property C
Price	$705,000	$665,000	$700,000	$720,000
Adjustment	0	$40,000	$5,000	($10,000)
Value	$705,000	$705,000	$705,000	$710,000

Cost approach

The cost approach to real estate valuation also relies on the concept of substitution, whereby an informed buyer wouldn't pay more for a property than the cost of building a comparable property. This approach to real estate valuation can be used when data on comparable sales is unavailable, but it's more commonly used — and even the preferred method — for proposed construction or brand-new properties.

REMEMBER

The replacement cost of a property often can be an indicator of barriers to entry that exist in the market (refer to Chapter 10). Owning real estate in high demand with high barriers to entry for competing properties is one of the best ways to ensure the success of your real estate investments.

In determining valuation using the cost approach, the property is divided between the land and improvements (buildings) and each segment is valued separately. Here are the steps a valuer may follow in applying the cost approach:

1. **Estimate the value of the land if vacant and being used in its highest and best use.**

   The valuer looks for sales of comparable vacant land in the area.

2. **Estimate the current cost to reproduce the existing building as new, before depreciation.**

3. **Estimate all forms of accrued depreciation and deduct that amount from the calculation in Step 2 to arrive at the approximate cost to reproduce the building in its current condition.**

4. **Combine the value of the land and the value of the depreciated improvements to arrive at the total value of the property.**

Accrued depreciation can be caused by three factors:

>> **Physical deterioration:** Normal wear and tear that occurs from use over time, such as a 12-year-old roof that can normally be expected to last 20 years.

>> **Functional obsolescence:** Decline in the usefulness of a property due to changes in preferences by consumers — for example, a rental home with three bedrooms and only one bathroom.

>> **External obsolescence:** Loss in value resulting from external forces, such as the major employer in town closing down, with longer travel times to comparable jobs.

Using the house example from the previous section, you determine that the cost of a comparable vacant lot would be $430,000. Checking with local builders in your market indicates that the cost to build a new house would be $2,200 per square metre; however, because the building is ten years old, some wear and tear is inevitable. You, therefore, estimate that the cost to rebuild the property in its current condition is \$1,950 per square metre (it isn't an exact science). The property is 140 square metres, so the total value of the depreciated improvements is \$273,000.

Adding the land value of \$430,000 to the \$273,000 value for the depreciated improvements gives an overall value of the property of \$703,000 using the cost method of valuation.

Calculating a yield-based return

An important tool when deciding on which property to purchase can be the income return of a subject property, in relation to other properties in the area. Determining the yield of a property can be a far more important source of information for an investor, particularly first-time investors, or investors in their early years of ownership.

The yield of a property is the annual income return that the property is promising, which can help determine whether you can afford the property or not.

The yield of a property is calculated by finding out what the weekly or monthly rent of the property is (or is expected to be, which you may be able to find out via local real estate agents), annualising that figure and then dividing it by the property's purchase price. This then allows you to compare it to other similar properties available on the market at a given time.

TIP

When annualising a rent figure, don't just multiply the weekly or monthly rent by 52 weeks or 12 months. As a property investor, you have to plan for the fact that your property is likely to spend some time vacant. More often than not, renters are short-term tenants who may only rent the property for one year or two. So, the property is likely to go through times of vacancy between when old tenants move out and new tenants can be found. To be conservative, you should probably allow for your property to be vacant for certain periods each year — in metropolitan areas, factor in at least two weeks of vacancy in a year and allow for perhaps three to four weeks a year in non-metropolitan areas. So, when you get a tenant that stays for five years, you have a rare tenant indeed — five years with a fully leased property is wonderfully consistent cash flow. Hold on to those tenants.

Allowing for average vacancy rates, the annual rental of a property that rents for \$600 a week is, therefore, \$30,000 — \$600 × 50 weeks (rather than 52 weeks). If you're likely to pay \$660,000 for the property, the annual yield is \$40,000/ \$660,000, which is 4.5 per cent. If the property is only being leased for \$570 a week, the yield is \$28,500/\$660,000, or 4.31 per cent.

This reasonably simple calculation allows you to compare one property to the next, if you can get reasonable estimates on what the property might sell and lease for.

REMEMBER

Annualising your rent figure gives you your gross yield. You have plenty of costs, which can often suck up all of that yield and more. But finding out the gross yield percentage is important for first-time investors, because lower yielding properties generally mean that you have to find more money from your own pocket to support the property until rents rise.

All some investors want from a property is yield, or income. They may be at a stage of their life where they don't feel they need capital growth anymore, but do need income from the property to support their retirement or to reduce their working hours. That's completely understandable.

WARNING

High yields aren't everything. Higher yielding properties can have their own drawbacks, or be typical of certain styles of properties (flats, for instance) that may not produce the capital gain that you seek from your property. Although higher yields mean the less money you have to find from other sources on a monthly basis, yield isn't everything.

Understand that yield and growth — in all investments, not just property — are a trade-off. A very general rule is that the highest yielding investments tend to be the lowest growth. It's not a hard and fast rule, but it's an important rule that also applies to property investment.

Finding properties where you can add value

Finding properties that are offering a lower yield or rental return can be profitable. You want to buy when you determine that the property has a strong likelihood of producing future increases in rent. So you should look for properties where your analysis shows that the income for the property can be increased simply and cheaply.

However, certain clues when putting your value on a property can indicate whether a property really has rents that are below market. Properties that are constantly occupied with little vacancy time are prime candidates. Other telltale signs are properties that have low turnover and then have multiple applicants for those rare vacancies. Economics 101 says that, if demand exceeds supply, the price is too low.

TIP

A common question asked is, 'How do I find underpriced properties?' Our experience indicates you're more likely to find characteristics of underpricing of investment properties (such as below-market rents) with owners who are older, have no mortgage and typically have exhausted the advantages of depreciation deductions on their tax return.

Look for properties where you can increase value over the first few years of ownership. These value-added properties are those that allow you to increase rents with comparatively little effort or expense. As we point out in the preceding section, the value of a property increases with an increase in rent.

Negotiating Basics

An important concept to grasp is this: You make money in property when you buy. If you purchase a well-located and physically sound property below market value and replacement cost, the property can provide you with excellent returns for many years. Superior knowledge combined with superior negotiating leads to superior returns. The following sections explain how to be a champion negotiator.

Selecting negotiating styles

A lot of forces are at work — and a lot of vested interests — when it comes to the negotiation of a final sales price of a given property. The buyer is seeking the lowest price to maximise future returns. The vendor wants the highest price to maximise the return she's about to crystallise. And the agent . . . well, in reality, the agent doesn't care what price it sells for, as long as it sells! The way that properties are usually sold means that agents are primarily remunerated only if they make a sale. Of secondary concern to an agent is the actual sales price.

Some people argue that ethics and morals have a place in purchasing property. We certainly don't condone shonky business practices (and you need to watch out for some agent practices that are, in fact, illegal), but morals and ethics mean different things to different people. Sometimes you'll do better out of a transaction as a buyer than the seller did. That's your aim as a property buyer — to get property for prices below the market value. But, even when the buyer believes she got a steal, the vendor could still be ecstatic with the price she received in return. Surely, you'd think, only one of them is right. Sometimes, they're both understandably happy with the final price.

Along with conditioning (see the nearby sidebar), another potential concern for vendors is when offers come from parties related to the selling agent. An agent who introduces a buyer who is a personal friend has a clear conflict of interest. While it's obviously okay for investors to develop working relationships with agents, it's a morally murky area if the agent helps an investor friend to buy a property off one of his clients when it's possible that the agent may not be working to get the client the highest price possible.

CONDITIONING VENDOR EXPECTATIONS

When it comes to dodgy selling practices, 'conditioning' tops the list, as far as we're concerned. Conditioning is a process whereby agents tell a prospective vendor that they believe the property can achieve a certain price (say, $550,000). Then, close to the auction, or as offers start coming in, the agent tries to get the vendor to lower her expectations for a sales price (to, say, $520,000). This is done to ensure that a sale occurs, because most agents don't get paid unless an actual sale of the property takes place. Some agents quote high to win the business from the vendor in the first place, and then try to cut the vendor's expectations — and it happens particularly regularly in markets with little price growth or few sales occurring.

Nicola had the experience of selling one of her properties in 2021 with the sales agent using every known tactic in his playbook in an attempt to condition her to take a lower sales price. Unfortunately for him, Nicola used to be responsible for running sales success conferences when she was the head of corporate affairs at the Real Estate Institute of Queensland (REIQ), so she had heard it all before. The agent tried very hard to get her to accept $499,000 for her property — when she had been very clear from the outset that she would not sell it for less than $550,000. In fact, she told him she would just withdraw it from sale and put it back on the rental market if she didn't achieve this figure. The hard pressure tactics continued for the next week, to no avail.

When the agent, clearly quite frustrated that his techniques weren't working on her, managed to extract an offer of $540,000 from a buyer, Nicola negotiated to pay him less commission if she accepted the deal, which he did. It seems she may have been the better negotiator than the agent appointed to act on her behalf!

The fuzzy concept of morals in purchasing property is difficult to reconcile with the intent of property investment, which is to make money. The old saying that 'you make your money when you buy' means that buying a property below market price — and the lower the better — gives you more money when you sell. If a vendor isn't properly informed, who's to blame? Certainly not the potential buyer!

In all fields of investment, information is queen. If one player has superior knowledge to another player, she has an advantage. Those who do the most research are in the best position to profit.

Desperate vendors, uneducated vendors and foolish vendors are always going to be around. And some vendors really don't know enough to be playing in a particular market. But those who refuse to seek proper advice from trustworthy professionals have only themselves to blame.

Although it's true that real estate agents are a close-knit community of professionals who network — and getting on the wrong side of agents in an area that you're looking to buy in can hamper your success — they're also salespeople with a product to sell, the price of which is (usually) negotiable. Being a bit hard-nosed, without agents finding your demeanour offensive, is almost expected. In fact, not having a bit of toughness about your offers leaves you, as the buyer, open to being manipulated.

Here are some of the necessary negotiating tactics that show strength, without being off-putting:

>> **Setting a time limit:** If you're making an offer in a private sale, particularly in a weak market with few buyers and many potential sellers, put a sunset clause on your offer. It's not quite the 'my way or the highway' style, but it puts a little pressure back on the vendor (whose agents are expert at putting pressure on buyers). If you've made a reasonable offer that's at about the market price, even if a little on the low side, give the vendor 24 or 48 hours. If you call her on a Thursday, give her until close-of-business Friday. Don't let the vendor have the weekend, giving her another 48 hours to canvas more offers.

>> **Lowballing:** If a house has been on the market for a long time in any market, you never know just how desperate vendors have become. They may have knocked back a reasonable offer a month ago in the belief that someone would offer more soon. But, if no further offers were forthcoming, they may now be getting desperate. Talk to the agent. Find out what offers have been rejected before.

>> **Keeping your cards close to your chest:** Don't tell the agent financial details that she doesn't need to know, or that could be used against you. Agents don't need to know what your budget is — knowing your upper limit for a purchase could certainly be used against you. The correct answer to questions about the size of your wallet is, 'It depends on the property.' But being rude to agents is unnecessary, and allowing them to show you properties that are definitely out of your price range is a waste of your time and theirs.

TIP

While a property remains unsold, its agents are still waiting to receive their commission. Getting them onside with a property they are sick of the sight of — perhaps because the vendor knocked back reasonable offers or because one too many bids have fallen through — may even get them to become your ally in trying to get a below-market sale through.

WARNING

The problem with many aggressive negotiating techniques is that you can get so wrapped up in just 'making the deal' that you forget what you're doing. You can make some serious mistakes and buy properties you should've eliminated during your pre-offer due diligence. Don't get emotionally involved in any potential property — or negotiation process. You're buying an investment, not your dream house. You simply want someone else paying rent and making your mortgage repayments so you can build wealth and cash flow.

Building your knowledge base

The most important negotiating tool in an investment property purchase is superior knowledge. You need to know more about your proposed property acquisition than anyone else, especially the seller. You need to know about the property, nearby properties and the economic data that could point to this property being in the path of progress (refer to Chapter 10). Knowledge of local and state laws is often helpful as well. You need to set a maximum price you can pay and still receive a solid return on your investment in light of the associated risks.

Do your homework

We don't suggest that you mislead anyone, but it's amazing how many current owners of property just don't pay attention to even the most basic publicly available information. Your research with the local council may give you the vision to upgrade and renovate a property to achieve its full value because you've discovered that a major new employer is moving into the area and demand is highly likely to dramatically increase for half-vacant and tired commercial properties or properties to house incoming executives — like the one you're considering for purchase.

With property investing, you're likely to be more successful in negotiating great real estate deals if you not only have a good real estate investment team, but also know the important factors that affect supply and demand in the local market.

Maybe you're seeing local companies growing rapidly and hiring lots of new workers. You know that, because of a local housing shortage, many new families moving into the area will be unable to afford a new home and will need to rent instead. That's a good sign that rents will increase, and the demand will be high for nice three- or four-bedroom rental houses located in quiet cul-de-sacs near good schools. Clearly, you can use this information to properly negotiate the purchase of prime rental homes in such a market.

The reason that negotiating is so important to being successful with your real estate investments is this: You want to pay the seller only for the current value of the property as-is and not the future potential that your skill and expertise will create. Patience, vision and perseverance are also great virtues when it comes to making the best real estate deals. If you're unwilling to do the homework necessary to justify the right price, you're more likely to overpay for real estate.

Although an occasional seller dramatically underestimates the true market value of a property, the vast majority of properties you see offered for sale are overpriced.

Determine the current supply and demand in the marketplace so you know whether it's a buyer's or seller's market. You can still make some great investments, but you need to be realistic. Buying in a seller's market at prices above replacement cost is dangerous.

As the potential purchaser, discover as much as you can about the property (and the owner) before making an offer. How long has the property been on the market? What are its flaws? Why is the owner selling? The more you know about the property you want to buy and about the seller's motivations, the better your ability to make an acceptable offer.

Figure out the seller's motivations

Some agents love to talk and will tell you the life history of the seller. Encourage this free flow of information. The goal for you is to get the agent to reveal helpful information (without you sharing too much pertinent information about yourself). Always seek the answer to the most important question: 'Why is the vendor selling?' The answer can tell you a lot about the seller's motivation and may give you a reason to either move on or be calm and patient with your negotiations.

Also, if you know enough about the seller's motivation, you can avoid wasting your time negotiating with someone who isn't really motivated to sell. Some vendors are really just testing the market or are willing to sell only if they can get a price well over the market value.

Figure out how to spot these fake vendors early on. Look for the warning signs, such as unexplained delays in responding to offers or questions, a reluctance to answer questions or give you access to the property, and an uncooperative attitude across the board. If you see these signs, you don't even want to make an offer on the property.

We can't say this often enough: Don't give out any information about your motivations that give the seller added negotiating leverage. The less you say about how much you like the property or your reasons for making the offer, the better. For example, many vendors are able to stick to their full-price terms and as-is condition of the property if they know the buyer has a big enough budget at her disposal or has tight time restrictions. A buyer wanting to wrap up a sale before heading back home interstate may suddenly be agreeable to many reasonable conditions requested by a seller.

GET-RICH-QUICK SPRUIKERS' STRATEGIES DON'T PAN OUT

We hate to be the bearers of bad news, but all of those get-rich-quick property spruikers don't tell the full story when they and their testimonials say how easy it was for them to start with nothing and suddenly own vast real estate holdings that all seem magically to be worth millions and provide great cash flow. If it were really that easy, the gurus wouldn't be telling you about it — they'd be busy making great deals just for themselves.

There *are* times when you buy just before the market takes off and you can't lose. But the worst spruikers, when it comes to giving unrealistic expectations to potential property owners, are usually just the best salespeople.

The old adage 'If it sounds too good to be true, it is too good to be true' applies to real estate — and particularly the thought that the best real estate is available to the average person at unbelievably favourable terms. So much capital is available to owners of real estate that even truly desperate sellers usually have the ability to borrow more money. The interest rates and terms may be horrendous, but money is almost always available for any property that isn't a toxic waste dump — an owner doesn't need to give a property away unless it has no equity. Remember, there's no such thing as a free lunch — you usually get what you pay for.

The most frightening pitches for real estate have been made by spruikers trying to flog property in the 'next big place' that will cash in on a seemingly history-making industry boom in usually small regional locations. Pitches involving a small town where 'a large mining company is about to get approval for a mine that will last for 25 years' have become an all-too-easy way for developers to flog off properties in remote locations, claiming that the mine sites will need dozens, if not hundreds, of houses to satisfy the needs of mine workers. History shows us that many unwary investors who bought into this hype have ended up with properties not worth what they paid for them, as well as ones that they often can't even rent out.

Be *extremely* wary of buying properties promoted as sure things. In far too many cases, people have signed on the dotted line . . . and then found out that the mine has not been approved or would never have been approved, or the company has changed its mind because the project is no longer viable — and they are left with a worthless investment. Also make sure you are working with bona fide experts, especially when it comes to property investment advice, instead of blindly following the sales pitch of people who are just trying to line their own pockets.

Bring your data to the table

Bring facts that back up your argument to the bargaining table. Collect comparable sales data to support your price. Too often, investors pick a number out of the air when they make an offer. If you were the seller, would you be persuaded to lower your asking price? Pointing to recent and comparable property sales to justify your offer strengthens your case. Sellers often don't select properly comparable properties — preferring to creatively use just those prior sales that provide for the highest possible asking price. The heart of negotiating is information.

WARNING

If the property needs repairs, never rely on quotes provided by the seller. You must independently verify the numbers with licensed contractors. You can also use these written quotes to support your position regarding the true cost to make needed repairs rather than just making verbal representations that a prudent buyer would treat sceptically. However, you should always leave yourself wriggle room. We've found that, even with the most comprehensive quotes from the top industry professionals, any significant renovation or remodelling project is likely to take longer and cost more than is estimated.

Assembling attractive and realistic offers

We don't want to just tell you what not to do, so here are some examples of realistic and creative ways to negotiate and structure a real estate offer that accurately reflects the value of the property and also provides you with a reasonable return on your investment.

Factoring in fix-up costs

Say you come across an opportunity to buy a great three-bedroom, two-bathroom house. You've spent some time investigating and you know the area is terrific. The house would be an ideal rental because it's two blocks from a new school. You estimate that the property will rent for $2,750 per month, and the market indicates strong demand for rental homes. The seller is asking $730,000, which appears to be its market value — based on the home seeming to have no deferred maintenance. But all rental properties have some deferred maintenance, so you call your home-inspection contractor. Her report indicates that, overall, the property is in decent condition and the big-ticket items of appliances and flooring have recently been replaced. But she also has some bad news: The roof needs to be replaced in the next few years. You contact three reputable roofing contractors, and the best value quote for a roof replacement that'll last 20 years is $25,000. You also estimate that you'll need about $8,000 in minor repairs and upgrades to the landscaping and the irrigation system.

What should you pay? If you said $697,000, you aren't necessarily wrong, but you're not providing any room for contingencies — or any compensation or reimbursement for your time and the risk involved in overseeing and coordinating this work. We suggest you take your actual conservative estimates for all repairs and add at least 50 per cent. Cover those surprises that are likely to occur and compensate yourself for the time, effort and risk associated with renovations. Contractors and other professionals always allow for contingencies, overheads and profit when they present their quotes, so why should you as a real estate investor who invests your efforts using your own DIY or contracting skills not be equally compensated? This mistake is one of the biggest that novice real estate investors make — and can avoid.

Creatively meeting the seller's price

Price is only one of several negotiable items, but it's the first clause the seller reviews in a purchase offer. Because many sellers are fixated on the price they'll receive for the property (perhaps they're set on beating what the Joneses got last year for their house a few doors down), you can offer the full price, but seek other concessions in order to reduce the effective cost of buying the property.

One way to reduce the cost is to get the seller to pay for certain repairs or improvements. The buyer should consider asking the seller to correct all health and safety items before settlement. But other items can also be negotiated. For example, rather than have the seller patch that 30-year-old roof that you'll be replacing anyway, ask to take the cost of the repairs off the purchase price. This is obviously easier to request in a buyer's market, when sellers don't have numerous offers on the table. In a seller's market, where the seller is entertaining multiple offers, they may stop discussions with you if you make the negotiations too difficult.

TIP

The time that you need to settle on your purchase is also a bargaining chip. Some sellers need cash soon and may concede other points if you can settle quickly — in, say, 30 days instead of 60, or 60 days instead of 90.

Finally, don't fall in love with a property. Keep searching for other properties even when you make an offer — you may be negotiating with an unmotivated vendor.

Making Your Offer

The purchase and sale of real estate is always done in writing. The most critical document in any transaction is the purchase agreement, which is usually referred to as the contract of sale. After you've found a property that meets your investment goals, you need to pick up the seller's contract and get your solicitor or conveyancer to look over the contract for irregularities prior to making your offer.

Understanding the basics of contracts

A real estate contract is a legally binding written agreement between two or more persons regarding an exchange of some sort. These contracts are legally enforceable sets of promises that must be performed and that rely on the basics of contract law. (Contracts may also be oral but, as we discuss in this section, oral contracts should be avoided.)

A legally binding contract must include consideration (usually money) passing between the parties, an intention from all parties to be bound to the contract, a meeting of the minds of the parties as to the contents of the contract and an element of clarity so the terms of the contract may be interpreted, understood and enforced by a court, if necessary. Such a contract is valid because it contains all of the necessary elements that make it legally enforceable. In the following list, we outline the basic elements of a legally binding and enforceable real estate contract. The terms may sound a bit technical, but you need to be familiar with them:

>> **Legally competent parties:** Every party to the transaction must have legal capacity, which is defined as being of legal age (usually 18 in Australia) and having the mental capacity to understand the consequences of their actions. Convicted criminals and certain mentally ill persons may not have legal capacity. Be careful when dealing with older persons if they seem to have any difficulty understanding or communicating. Politely enquire if they have anyone who is acting on their behalf in a representative capacity.

>> **An offer:** An offer to purchase property is a written communication to the owner of the buyer's willingness to purchase the property on the terms indicated. Unless an expiration clause is included, the seller may accept an offer at any time before it's rescinded by the buyer.

Most offers should have a specific expiration time. ('This offer is valid until Friday, 19 June, at 5 pm AEST only.') Back up that time limit to prevent the seller from using the offer as a negotiating tool with other interested parties, shopping your offer around, trying to entice other buyers to raise their offer. Also, if the offer is open-ended, the buyer has to actively withdraw the offer, which is more work and trouble than simply having the offer expire after some passage of time.

>> **Acceptance:** Acceptance is a positive written response in a timely manner to the exact terms of an offer. A legal requirement to have acceptance is that the buyer must be given legal notice of the acceptance. Often, the seller won't accept the offer as presented, but will propose changes in the terms or conditions — which is a counteroffer.

>> **Counteroffer:** Legally a new offer, where the original offer is rejected and is void. Counteroffers can go back and forth until both buyer and seller have

agreed and the final accepted offer becomes the binding agreement between the parties. Just like offers, counteroffers should be in writing and can also be rescinded at any time prior to acceptance.

>> **Consideration:** Payment of money or something of value, which is typically offered by the buyer to the seller in exchange for the seller entering into the contract for purchase of real estate. A real estate contract isn't binding if each party doesn't offer at least some consideration to the other party.

>> **Clearly and uniquely identified property:** A requirement so no uncertainty exists about precisely which property is being sold and transferred to the buyer. Typically, a legal description of the property is used.

>> **Legal purpose:** The real estate contract must be for a legal purpose and can't be for an illegal act. An example of a potential transaction in which a buyer would want to cancel the purchase is if she is purchasing a house with the intent to run her company there but discovers during the settlement process that such use violates local prohibitions against operating a business in a residentially zoned area.

>> **Written contract:** A written contract is required for all enforceable transfers of real estate. All terms and conditions of the purchase agreement or sales contract must be set out in writing, even for minor items that may seem inconsequential. The written contract helps ensure no confusion exists about what's included in the sale. For example, if you want to make sure that the supplies in the maintenance shop for a commercial or apartment building are included and not taken before the sale, you must specify it in the contract. Remember that if something isn't in writing, you're unlikely to prevail.

WARNING

Agreements for the sale of real estate must be in writing or they're unenforceable. Never make an oral agreement of any type regarding real estate, no matter how convenient, expedient or reasonable it may seem at the time. Have your solicitor read all contracts of sale before you sign.

Besides all the legal elements, real estate sales contracts specify the sale price and the terms and conditions (see the section 'Using conditions effectively', later in this chapter).

Completing the contract of sale

The contract of sale (some states may have different names for the contract itself) is the legal document that outlines the details of the transaction for your proposed purchase of the property.

Victorian real estate agents also have a document known as a *contract note* — described in some quarters as little more than a way for agents to get around the contract of sale itself (in Victoria known as a 'Vendor's Statement' or a 'Section 32') — which may include sale conditions. If you have conditions on the sale written into the contract, the contract note may nullify those conditions. Never sign a contract note without getting the okay from your legal rep, after she has had a chance to read the actual contract of sale. The contract note becomes binding on its own.

Always include in the contract note, if one is offered to you, any conditions you want on the sale — no matter what the seller's agent says — before you sign it. If you want the sale to be dependent on acceptable finance or satisfactory building reports, put it in writing on the contract note itself.

No matter what it's called, the sales contract is the most important document in the sale of real estate. It indicates how much you pay, when you pay, the terms and conditions that must be met to close the transaction, and the conditions under which the agreement can be cancelled and the buyer's deposit returned. It starts out with the basics of the names of the sellers and buyers, a description of the property and the proposed financing terms.

Get your solicitor to go over the form in detail and carefully consider the terms that you'll offer in each paragraph (if that's appropriate). Don't leave any blank spaces and have your solicitor mark through any clauses you feel aren't appropriate. Just because a certain clause is pre-printed doesn't mean that you can't cross it out or modify the language to suit your needs. Just make sure that you clearly initial any changes you make and require the other party to also initial every single change and the bottom of each page to ensure that you've agreed on the specific terms.

Some terms are at your discretion, but your solicitor can advise you as to the local practice concerning issues such as the standard for deposits or the length of settlement periods. Your solicitor, in conjunction with the seller's solicitor, can also inform you about local standards for settlement costs.

The remainder of this section covers other key provisions you need to carefully evaluate, because you'll be making many decisions about your offer before the purchase agreement is ready for your signature.

Paying the deposit

The standard deposit paid on signing a real estate contract in Australia used to be 10 per cent, but it really can be whatever figure you can get away with and is usually negotiable. Some savvy property investors like to use a deposit as small as possible, to protect their own cash, or perhaps even a deposit that reflects the selling agent's likely commission — and no more. Your deposit is held in trust by the seller's agent and is usually paid by direct deposit into the trust account.

WARNING

Another way to pay the deposit is through a deposit bond (which is not always accepted by sellers). A deposit bond is a note usually issued through an insurer who promises to pay the deposit at settlement. The cost of a deposit bond — which rose to prominence during the property booms in Victoria and New South Wales in the early 2000s — can often be less than the cost of interest (particularly for longer settlements), but they're often mistrusted, or not accepted, by sellers or developers if buying off-the-plan.

Leaving the buy-and-flip door open

Even though we're not ardent promoters of the buy-and-flip strategy, the ability to assign or transfer your purchase agreement to another investor gives you the opportunity to realise a profit without ever having to close on the deal yourself. When the real estate market is appreciating rapidly, some real estate investors find that the property increases in value so significantly that they can onsell their contractual position before settlement. If you ever intend to do this, make sure your solicitor is in the loop, so that she can properly advise you when required. High rates of stamp duty in Australia make buy-and-flip positions usually fairly marginal.

WARNING

Never enter a property deal with the expectation that you're going to find a buyer for your flip, because one may not materialise when you need to sell. Make sure you have other strategies in place, such as proper financing, in case you're left with having to complete the deal.

In really hot housing markets, some property investors (they should really be called speculators) go to new housing estates or multi-storey developments and sign contracts with builders — up to a year or more before the property is built, known as buying *off the plan*. If, during the extended building or contract period, the value of the property being built goes up, the buyer can merely transfer the contractual rights to buy the property to another buyer, but at a new price and terms. Importantly, the price paid to the builder remains the same as recorded in the original contract, so the original buyer makes a profit.

Setting the settlement date

An important term of your purchase offer is the proposed settlement date. The length of the settlement period is a matter of negotiation between the buyer and seller, with consideration given to the length of time needed to complete the sale. Settlements can be any length of time, but are typically requested by sellers at 30, 60 or 90 days. Longer is okay, if it's agreeable to both parties.

Sellers are often interested in closing the property as soon as possible but, in most transactions, particularly where the premises are being occupied by the seller, the actual date depends on a number of factors, including the completion of other property transactions. Investment property buyers usually want longer periods to allow some flexibility in case something goes wrong with financing. Buyers may also occasionally want the right to close the transaction earlier if they've completed their work.

Ultimately, the terms you agree on in the purchase agreement are legally binding. In some cases, the settlement date is really just an estimated date, as a close of sale can involve many moving parts. But the date should be met unless both parties agree to an extension via a written addendum (see 'Ironing out other issues', later in this chapter).

Using conditions effectively

A *condition* in a real estate purchase agreement is simply a contingency that must be fulfilled or an event that may or may not happen before a contract becomes firm and binding. Conditions can be for the benefit of either the seller or the buyer. The seller of an estate property, for example, may put a condition that a court grants probate — the legal registering or acceptance of a deceased person's last will — before the sale is approved. Buyers often have conditions for financing, physical inspections, building and pest inspections, and other items.

Conditions are escape clauses that can protect buyers from purchasing a property that doesn't meet their needs. Purchasing properties without conditions can be extremely risky. Without conditions, buyers would need to be sure, before making an offer, that they have all of the financing in place, that the property is in an acceptable condition and meets their needs, and that the terms are acceptable. Buyers may be unwilling to meet these requirements prior to having some sort of agreement on price in a contract, or they'd discount their offer to account for the additional risk of buying a property without some protection of conditions.

WARNING

Don't forget that you can't set conditions if you buy a property at auction. Auctions are final and, therefore, require buyers to have done all their due diligence before attending and making a bid. Due diligence includes building and pest inspections, securing financing and any other conditions you may normally consider putting on a property bought through private treaty. (Refer to Chapter 3 for details of each type of sale.)

Conditions can allow a prospective buyer the exclusive opportunity to buy the property during a limited time frame but not obligate her to complete the transaction if any issues arise that can't be satisfactorily resolved within the time limits. Naturally, sellers attempt to eliminate unreasonable conditions.

The terms of most sales contracts provide that, by certain defined dates, all of the conditions must be resolved one way or another by the party who stands to gain from the condition. Once in place, a condition can have one of three outcomes:

» **Conditions can be satisfied.** When conditions are met, the pending sale is no longer subject to cancellation or modification for that particular item. For example, the buyer could comply with the financing contingency upon receiving a written loan commitment at acceptable terms.

» **The beneficiary of the condition can unilaterally agree to waive or remove the contingency.** For example, the seller may have asked for the sale to be conditional on the timing of the settlement of an unrelated property transaction, but no longer needs that condition to be met.

» **A condition can be rejected or fail.** The beneficiary of the condition is then no longer obligated to perform under the contract. For example, buyers may receive a termite-inspection report indicating extensive damage and infestation and then decide that they are no longer interested in completing the purchase. Under this scenario, the buyers typically receive the return of their deposit and are glad that they diligently conducted a physical inspection.

TIP

Although the list will vary depending on the property type, size and location, following are condition clauses that we recommend you consider:

» **Financing:** When buying, be as vague as possible. Use a term similar to 'subject to suitable financing with XYZ Bank', for example, unless the seller insists on you outlining what suitable financing means. In this case, outline the specific terms (type of loan and maximum acceptable interest rate) of a new loan that you require in order to complete the purchase.

» **Valuation:** This condition demands that an independent valuer of the property arrives at a value equal to or greater than the proposed purchase price. This valuation could be a function of the financing or simply because you don't want to overpay for the property.

» **Physical inspection:** Most contracts for a property sold through private sale treaty include an inspection clause that mandates that the buyer has access to the property for a certain amount of time to inspect its interior and exterior. Engage a qualified building inspector and, for larger purchases, include specialists in key areas such as roofing, plumbing and electrical systems to conduct a thorough inspection of the entire property. The results of the inspection can be used to negotiate with the seller by giving them the opportunity to make the necessary repairs, adjust the purchase price or simply terminate the purchase agreement.

>> **Books and records inspection:** Another important condition if you're purchasing a large residential or commercial property is the opportunity to review and inspect the income and expense statements and the leases. Verify rents with tenants. Check the lease documents.

Ironing out other issues

You also need to be sure that your purchase agreement clearly indicates what chattels are included. Chattels can be a significant factor in apartment buildings because they can include the appliances and window coverings, plus common-area furnishings and fixtures.

Particularly for larger residential and commercial properties, and depending on your plans for the property, you may want the property conveyed with or without tenants. If the tenants aren't on valid and enforceable long-term leases, and the property value can be increased by renovation and gaining new tenants, require the seller to deliver the property vacant.

Determining How to Hold Title

One last thing you need to consider before you sign on the dotted line relates to ownership: Who, or what, is going to own the title to the property?

This question might sound silly, with 'I will!' being the possibly all-too-obvious answer. But, although holding the property yourself may be the right option, putting it in your own name may be a costly mistake that could haunt you from day one, or come back to bite you on the backside in years to come.

WARNING

Making sure you get the property's ownership right before you sign the sale contract is incredibly important from a tax perspective. The wrong ownership structure may see you unnecessarily paying too much tax, while the right structure for the right property may reduce your tax liabilities to zero (in the case of income) or reduce them substantially (in the case of capital gains). And trying to change the ownership after purchase can be costly and involve paying further taxes and duties.

TIP

If you and your partner (if that's applicable) are looking to build a portfolio of many properties over time, consider placing the properties in differing titles (that is, some in one person's name, some in the other person's name and perhaps some in joint names). If you need to sell a property later on to either raise cash or reduce debt, you're then able to choose which property to sell in order to maximise the cash you raise, or minimise the capital gains tax paid, based on each individual's circumstances at the time you need to sell.

No single right answer exists as to the question of how to hold title, because each real estate investor has different perspectives and needs. The legal forms of ownership vary from state to state, so check your options with your solicitor and/or accountant before you sign.

In the following sections, we review some of the basics of each form of ownership — including taxation considerations — so you can build a working understanding of the pros and cons of each of the main alternatives available.

Sole ownership

Being a sole owner is certainly the easiest and cheapest form of ownership and requires no special prerequisites. Simply have title to the property vested in the name of an individual person on the deed and you have a sole proprietor. Owning a property in one name saves on not having to pay the ongoing cost of more complicated structures (for business-based or superannuation options mentioned later), such as accounting and legal fees.

Other advantages include

>> **Exclusive rights of ownership:** You have sole discretion over the use of the property, and the right to sell, bequeath or encumber the property any way you see fit.

>> **Simple record keeping:** Be grateful for the simplicity of financial records as a sole owner, but you still need to be disciplined.

REMEMBER

For those individuals in a committed relationship, two obvious options for 'sole ownership' are available in a household — either person could hold the title individually (we deal with joint ownership next). Depending on your individual circumstances, holding the property in only one of your names may make sense. If one isn't working or is in a much lower tax bracket than the other, consider placing ownership of positively geared investment real estate in that person's name. A negatively geared property, on the other hand, may be better in the hands of the higher income earner, because the tax deductions create a larger return, which then aids cash flow.

TECHNICAL
STUFF

Here's an example of how income tax brackets affect returns: Assume a property with rent of $30,000 has expenses (including interest, insurance, agents' fees and depreciation) of $42,000. The property is negatively geared to the tune of $12,000. Taking into account Australia's tiered marginal tax rate (MTR) structure for incomes at the time of writing, the following shows the impact that income tax has on the returns made by a property that is negatively geared by $12,000:

>> **MTR of 45 per cent:** The investor gets a tax return of $5,400, reducing the net loss to $6,600.

>> **MTR of 37 per cent:** The investor gets a tax return of $4,400, reducing the net loss to $7,560.

>> **MTR 32.5 per cent:** The investor gets a tax return of $3,900, reducing the net loss to $8,100.

>> **MTR 19 per cent:** The investor gets a tax return of $2,280, reducing the net loss to $9,720.

>> **MTR 0 per cent:** The investor wouldn't gain any tax benefit, meaning the cost would be the entire loss of $12,000.

Note: This list does not include the Medicare levy for the MTR ranges.

The reverse of this scenario is also true. If a property is positively geared to the tune of $12,000, the table is reversed and the tax return becomes the amount of tax paid, while the net loss becomes the net gain.

What this calculation shows is that, when an option exists, the person with the higher income should hold the negatively geared property. In a household with two incomes, you can make significant tax savings by structuring your ownership to keep in mind the tax implications of ownership.

Don't forget that rents rising over time eventually make almost all properties turn from negatively geared to positively geared.

Joint tenancy

Joint tenancy is a way in which two or more individuals may hold title to a property together when they own equal shares of the property. Joint tenancy is only available to individuals (not legal corporate entities), because a unique feature of holding title in a joint tenancy is the *right of survivorship*. Upon the death of one of the joint tenants, the entire ownership automatically vests in equal shares to the surviving individual or individuals without going through the probate process to ratify a will.

From a tax perspective, joint tenancy works best for two individuals, or a couple, where they're on similar tax rates and are likely to remain that way for the foreseeable future.

Joint tenancy requires unity of time, title, interest and possession, and that each joint tenant owns an equal interest or percentage of the property — so for two joint tenants, they each own 50 per cent, whereas four joint tenants would each own 25 per cent of the entire property.

Income and expenses from operating the property are reported on each individual's tax return in equal parts.

Tenants in common

A common form of co-ownership is *tenants in common* (also known as *tenancy in common*). In this ownership structure, several owners each own a stated portion or share of the entire property.

Unlike joint tenancy, in a tenants-in-common structure, owners can own a different percentage, can take title at any time and can sell their interest at any time, too. Another distinguishing characteristic is that owners have complete control over their portion of the property and can sell, bequeath or mortgage their interest as they personally decide, without any feedback from or recourse for the other owners. Further, upon their death, their share becomes part of their estate and can be willed as they see fit.

This ownership option has become more common in Australia, particularly during periods when property prices rise over an extended period. Non-couples often use tenancy in common as a way to make the purchase of property, usually as a home, affordable. Commonly, tenancy in common allows siblings to get together to help each other, parents to help their children into the market or friends to pool together.

WARNING

Tenancy in common is a popular way to hold title for real estate investors but can be problematic unless clear understandings are in place, preferably in writing, as to who is ultimately responsible for the asset and property-management decisions (including how much money is to be spent on maintenance and when, who's in charge of ensuring bills are paid on time and managing the property, or who's in charge of hiring management for the property). But, even then, problems and challenges are possible:

>> **Death of an owner:** You may find that a co-owner has left her interest in a property you partially own to someone you don't get along with.

>> **Sale by an owner:** Because each owner has equal rights of control over the property, serious conflicts may arise when one owner wants to sell or borrow against the property. Or an owner may decide to sell to an individual or entity, which disrupts the spirit of cooperation among the various owners.

>> **Financial problems of an owner:** You're financially tied to your co-owners for better or worse, even in their activities other than the jointly owned property. A judgement against one of the co-owners could lead to the creditor foreclosing on that co-owner's interest in the property to satisfy a monetary judgement. Or a bankruptcy by one co-owner could lead to the court ordering a forced sale of the property to satisfy the bankruptcy creditors, unless the other co-owners are willing to pay off the creditors and buy out the financially challenged co-owner.

>> **Different plans:** Each co-owner may have a different plan for the property or the way it should be managed. With tenants in common, majority rule does not operate, and no simple way exists to arbitrate differences in opinions and goals, except through a written governing document.

Self-managed super funds

Recent decades have seen a phenomenal rise in the number of self-managed super funds (SMSFs), as people take control of their investment future and escape the often-considerable management fees associated with traditional superannuation investments. (Refer to Chapter 8 for a full chapter on SMSFs.)

CREATING AN OPPORTUNITY TO BUY

Nicola bought her first property back in 2007 with her younger brother. At the time, as a single woman earning a modest income, she didn't qualify for enough funds to purchase anything with solid investment fundamentals in Brisbane. However, by joining forces with her brother, that situation changed.

They purchased a townhouse in a middle-ring suburb of the city, and decided to own it as tenants in common — with an ownership split of 70/30 between Nicola and her brother. At the outset, they agreed on the terms going forward, which were that if either of them wanted to sell their share, the other person had the first opportunity to buy the share.

They lived in that property together for a number of happy years and, when her brother wanted to sell, Nicola offered to buy him out, which he accepted. A year later, Nicola turned that property into an investment and it became the cornerstone of her portfolio — with her being able to extract equity from it twice to purchase additional investment properties.

Self-managed super funds can hold direct investment property, and many SMSFs are set up for this purpose alone. And since September 2007, a previously big drawback for SMSFs and property has been removed, in that super funds could borrow money to purchase real estate.

The trustees of an SMSF can buy property on behalf of the fund and the fund can operate the property. An SMSF can be the perfect place for high-yielding properties, with little tax paid on income during the accumulation phase. SMSFs can own either residential or commercial properties, although limitations exist on how SMSFs can acquire property.

WARNING

Transferring a property into your SMSF when it's no longer geared seems an attractive proposition. However, the only property you can transfer into an SMSF after you've already purchased it is business real property, which is property used solely for running a business. Residential investment property can be bought within an SMSF, but you can't transfer residential property into a super fund after you've bought it.

WARNING

The administration of superannuation, including SMSFs, is a very complex area and requires accountants, auditors and, often, financial advisers. These professionals don't necessarily come cheap. Depending on the fee structure and how much work you intend to do yourself, the consensus is that you should have at least $200,000 in a super fund in order to make the fees and charges worthwhile. The cost of property means that you're going to need significantly more than that to purchase a property. However, the changes to the borrowing rules for SMSFs (refer to Chapter 8) mean that many more SMSFs may find the idea of purchasing property inside super, with the help of borrowed funds, more appealing.

Partnerships and companies

Some particularly large property deals require investors to consider investment vehicles that can deal with considerable extra complexity. When deals involve sums of millions of dollars and/or have more than a handful of investors, you may want to consider setting up a more structured business relationship, which could take the form of a partnership or company.

Partnerships

A real estate partnership is a businesslike structure in which two or more persons join together to pool their capital and talent to purchase, manage and ultimately sell real estate. Investors in a real estate partnership don't have actual title or ownership interest directly in the property, but own an interest in the partnership.

Although a partnership interest technically is transferable, partners seeking to sell will find few, if any, ready buyers and will likely have to severely discount their asking price below its intrinsic value. The best option is to negotiate a buy/sell agreement (simultaneously offering one person the right to buy and another to sell) in which the terms are thoroughly discussed, and each partner has the ability to leave at any time, based on predetermined criteria. Often, such agreements call for the other partners to purchase the outgoing partner's share.

Partnerships have been a common and successful way for individuals to work together to purchase larger real estate investment properties. Often, they bring together individuals with complementary resources and skills. For example, a good partnership could include a real estate broker, a property manager, a real estate financial analyst and a real estate lender. The complementary skills of this partnership offer insight into each phase of the investment. Often, one of the partners doesn't have any real estate expertise or acumen, but instead provides a significant portion of the investment capital.

The main concern with partnerships is that they have unlimited liability for the partners themselves. All partners are responsible for any act by one partner. Potentially, one decision by one partner, which the other partners may not even know has been made, could send all partners into bankruptcy.

General partners have unlimited liabilities. But it is also possible for limited partners to exist within a partnership. Limited partners have an economic interest but are usually passive investors with limited liability.

Partnerships require substantial advice from both legal and accounting professionals before establishment (or at the point when it becomes obvious that a partnership has evolved).

Companies

Often referred to as corporations, companies are structures that are owned by shareholders and are responsible to the directors and the board. A company allows shareholders to have limited liability for their company's actions — that is, their financial responsibility effectively stops at the value of the shares. If a share becomes worthless, investors lose their entire investment, but are not liable for any further losses the company has incurred. A company in Australia can own property.

In order to become a company, the entity must become incorporated under the Corporations Act 2001 and be registered with the Australian Securities and Investments Commission (ASIC). A company requires its own tax file number (TFN) and Australian Business Number (ABN).

WARNING

Companies are usually the most expensive form of ownership, because of regulatory requirements. You'd really only consider setting up a company for larger deals or property holdings. You need the services of lawyers and accounting professionals to help you with its establishment and its ongoing operation.

Trusts

Trusts are legal entities in which assets are held by a trustee on behalf of a beneficiary (or beneficiaries). The trustee (an individual or a company) is the legal owner, but the asset or assets are held with the intention that the benefits are passed on to others (also individuals or entities). Trusts can be highly complex vehicles that require the professional help of lawyers and accountants to ensure they run smoothly and according to the trust's governing document, known as the *trust deed.* The powers of the trust deed determine the success or failure of the trust, and it's here that lawyers and accountants are most valuable.

TIP

One of the most common uses of trusts in Australia is for asset protection — ensuring that the value of an asset is not lost to third parties. Trusts can be used in myriad ways for property investment, and for myriad reasons. But the idea of protecting the asset for the ultimate beneficiary is pivotal.

A trust is able to pass on the benefits of the trust's assets (income, capital repayments or even the assets themselves) to the beneficiaries, who are then taxed according to their normal marginal tax rate when they become 'presently entitled' to the distribution of income or capital. If tax has been paid by the trust, the beneficiary is entitled to a credit for tax already paid.

Those who invest in listed and unlisted property trusts are using one form of a trust structure in which the income and capital gains are passed through and taxed at the hands of the ultimate investors.

Chapter **12**

Signing the Contract, Inspecting the Property and Settling

B y the time you're ready to sign on the dotted line of a contract, most of your investigative work — also known as *due diligence* — will be complete. Make sure you've done all your homework to double-check you're not making a mistake.

If you bought a residential investment property at auction, the time for backing out finished when you raised your paddle and your final bid was accepted. If you negotiated a private sale, you can now put conditions on the contract. But you'll sorely test the vendor's patience if you push the boundaries too far with terms and conditions.

In Chapter 11, we cover what you need to do prior to making your offer, which is essential in weeding out properties that clearly fail to meet your investment goals. But you need to do many things between the time you sign the contract and the time you take control of the property. The period prior to settlement is the time to prepare for your ownership of the property, verify material facts you couldn't confirm earlier and finalise your checks of the physical condition of the purchase.

In this chapter, we track the progress of your purchase from signing the contract, through the days leading up to settlement, to the transfer of the property's title into your hands.

Offer Accepted!

For your first few property purchases, the time that you sign on the dotted line is probably one part exhilaration, one part fear. Owning a property is a huge commitment, probably the biggest financial one you've made in your life to date. When you sign the contract, you set in motion a chain of events that, in a short period (usually 30, 60 or 90 days, but it can really be any length of time agreed between the parties), will see the transfer of the property into your name or other ownership structure (with a mortgage to your bank).

At the same time that you sign the contract, you'll also usually be required to pay the agreed deposit into the selling agent's trust account. Standards for deposits differ around the country (and between estate agents), but will regularly be requested as 5 or 10 per cent of the purchase price. If you've agreed to pay $700,000 for the property, you may need to pay a deposit of $35,000 or even $70,000. However, some agents may seek a deposit of as little as $1,000. Obviously, you need to have that money available yourself or have set up a facility with a bank to do so. Don't think you can sign the contract and tell them you'll pay the deposit next week! That won't go down well.

Setting a settlement date

You've signed for the property, so when do you get your hands on it? That's generally up for negotiation between the buyer and the vendor and depends on your competing interests.

With auctions, the terms of the sale often dictate roughly when the seller wants the exchange to take place. Settlement is often advertised as 30, 60 or 90 days from the day of the auction. But, unless you've spoken to the agent before the auction and got approval for a certain period, the actual date is usually agreed at the time of signing the contract. The topic is normally addressed quite casually, such as, 'Is August 13 okay with you for settlement?'

If you're buying a residential investment property from an *owner-occupier* — that is, the vendor lives in the house — as is often the case, the seller may have a rigid timetable over which they have little control. The timing of the settlement probably depends on the changeover of another property that the vendor is intending to move into. You may find negotiating in this position a little difficult.

TIP

For the seller, particularly if he's moving home, settlement day is likely to be more stressful than it is for an investor. Within reason, try to be flexible. Then, when your ownership is settled, you can get the place tenanted as soon as possible.

TIP

While trying to be flexible, you may want to flex some muscle when considering which month settlement will take place, rather than the number of days. The timing may be particularly important if you sign a contract in mid-November and settlement is negotiable — you probably won't want to take ownership in 30 days, or just before Christmas. Not too many people look for places to rent around Christmas time, and students who've rented for the year often end their leases and move home. A flood of properties usually come onto the market at the end of November and through December. The rental market may not pick up again until mid- to late-January, when students (and, to a lesser extent, teachers) come back to town. This isn't to say that you'll necessarily let to students, or families with students, but students are a big influence on the market on the supply side in November and December and a big factor on the demand side in late January and February.

TIP

As for a day of the week for settlement, our preference is for a Tuesday or a Wednesday. That gives you a couple of days to have a thorough look around the property yourself after settlement. You can also organise contractors (cleaners, locksmiths, painters and so on) to do their work during those two or three days before the weekend.

Avoid Fridays for settling. If anything does go wrong with a property settlement in the middle of the week, things only get delayed by about 24 hours. But, on a Friday, 24 hours becomes Monday morning, which is five days before the weekend peak viewing time for prospective tenants (meaning your property could be vacant and not earning rent for an extra week). In most real estate transactions, you won't have a problem. But when solicitors or conveyancers, or owners, can't get their act together, little can be done.

Hi ho, off to the lawyers you go

In legal terms, the transferral of property is called *conveyancing*. Depending on which state you live in, either a solicitor or a specialist conveyancing firm can do the conveyancing. And, although specialist conveyancers are not lawyers, they do perform a legal function. When it comes to property transferral, a large number of boxes need to be ticked, forms need to be filled in and government entities need to be communicated with.

When you've signed a contract, one of the first things you need to do is give the details of your solicitor or conveyancing firm to the vendor's agent. The agent usually emails the required documents to the buyer's and seller's solicitors in the next few business days and your solicitor contacts you when information is required.

You can hire a conveyancer (either a solicitor or conveyancing specialist) at short notice, but it's best to have one in place before you either bid at auction or make an offer in a private treaty sale (refer to Chapter 4 for getting this part of your team in place). Unless you're an expert on property title issues, have your conveyancing firm look over the pre-sale documentation to ensure no hidden surprises are in the contract.

Conveyancing can be performed by buyers and sellers in Australia. However, we don't recommend it. Conveyancing costs are normally between $1000 and $2,000 and the dangers of getting it wrong far outweigh this relatively small cost. Use professionals who are experienced in the field (and make sure they have professional indemnity insurance).

Conveyancers' duties

Send the final contract to your conveyancer within a few days of signing. The conveyancer's duty is to conduct the necessary title searches (usually for set fees), coordinate the various payments to government departments and the vendor, and ensure that title has been transferred properly by the agreed settlement date.

The conveyancer's duty includes checking the current legal title owner of the property and any mortgage held, unpaid taxes and judgements, or other recorded encumbrances against the property. These searches also show any easements or third-party interests that will limit your use of the property, such as covenants and restrictions.

Removing conditions

As we discuss in Chapter 11, the purchase contract can contain a number of conditions (when the property is bought through private treaty sale) that allow the buyer and seller to cancel the transaction if certain items or actions aren't satisfactory. One of three things happens with conditions: They can be approved or satisfied, unilaterally removed or waived by the beneficiary of the condition, or rejected or fail.

Conditions create a get-out clause and can be critical elements that make or break a transaction. The purchase agreement usually contains deadlines — the parties have certain rights pertaining to conditions for a limited period. For example, conditions relating to getting a satisfactory building and pest inspection may provide only ten days to make the inspection; after that, the condition is considered approved (or satisfied).

REMEMBER

The person making the condition should notify his own solicitor and the other party's agent immediately if a condition is rejected or fails. Agents aren't responsible for attempting to negotiate or mediate a resolution of any rejected condition or other deal-threatening issues that arise, but they'll often try to broker a solution.

Conducting Formal Due Diligence

With residential investment property, formal *due diligence* (checking the bona fides of the property as an investment) should really be conducted before bidding starts or the first offer is made. However, with larger commercial properties, you may have an opportunity to conduct formal due diligence.

REMEMBER

Performing your due diligence is the time to ask the tough questions. Don't be shy. Talk to the tenants, the neighbours, the contractors or suppliers to the property, and be sure you know what you're getting. Communicate regularly and work closely with the vendor and his representatives. Value information provided in writing more highly than that provided in conversation. This period may be your best or only opportunity to seek adjustments, if important issues have been misrepresented. After the property sale is completed, it's too late to negotiate on the leaky roof.

Practical examples of due diligence include verifying the accuracy of the financial information and leases presented by the seller and conducting a thorough physical inspection of the property by a licensed builder. Although you may have completed some of these financial checks before making your initial offer (refer to Chapter 11 for details on crunching the numbers), some of the information may become apparent only from a review of the seller's books.

REMEMBER

Don't underestimate the importance of reviewing the records — this review, along with the physical inspection, reveals the actual operations of the property and allows you to determine whether the property is suitable, fairly priced and meets your financial goals. The due-diligence period is your chance to decide whether you should complete the transaction or get your money back and search for a new possible acquisition. Move quickly, but thoroughly, so you don't unnecessarily hold up either yourself or the vendor in completing a sale.

Reviewing the records

Although savvy real estate investors conduct pre-offer due diligence and often receive a copy of a pro-forma operating statement for larger property deals, you likely won't have an opportunity to review the actual records until you have the opportunity to conduct due diligence.

When you do get that opportunity, ask the vendor or property manager for all the financial data. If they are not prepared to give you everything, get what you can from them and start the process of verifying it all. The sort of information you may try to get from the vendor, especially for commercial properties or apartment blocks (and, therefore, have to verify), includes:

>> **Income and expense statements for the past 12 months:** The actual income and expense history should reveal any surprises that may not have been obvious from more general statements previously received from the seller. This history may show the property has a serious problem with collection of rents or unexplained out-of-control expenses that should be passed back to tenants. This examination can also give you a good idea of where to look for opportunities to improve the financial performance of the property.

>> **An accurate rent roll of tenants:** A rent roll is a list of all tenants and their important details, including move-in date, lease-expiration date, current rents, and the security deposit or bond (lodged with appropriate authorities).

>> **A list of all tenant bonds:** When buying a new rental property, follow state laws in properly handling the tenant's security deposit. Make sure the vendor or property manager provides you detailed information on how much bond is held for each tenant and where (it should be with a state government body in cases of residential rents).

>> **Copies of the entire tenant file of each current tenant:** Make sure you have the rental application, current and past leases or rental agreements, all legal notices, maintenance work orders and correspondence for every tenant. Also ask that the seller or property manager advise you in writing about any pending legal action involving your tenants' occupancy (and make sure your solicitor is aware of any issues).

>> **Copies of every service agreement or contract:** Review all current contractors and service providers the current owner or property manager uses (maintenance, landscaping, pest control and so on).

>> **A comprehensive list of all chattels included in the purchase:** The list may include appliances, equipment and supplies owned by the current property owner. *Remember:* Don't assume anything is included in the sale unless you have it in writing.

>> **Copies of the latest utility bills:** Most tenants have to pay their own outgoings on utility usage; however, common-property utilities, if applicable to your property, will be your responsibility. Regardless, you should get as much detail on utility bills as possible, covering electricity, gas, water — including whether the property is water efficient — sewerage, garbage collection, telephone, and internet or NBN access.

REMEMBER

When you receive information, verify the accuracy of all records that you can. Most sellers are honest and don't intentionally withhold information or fail to disclose important facts; but the old adage 'buyer beware' is particularly true in the purchase of rental real estate. Questions and issues that are resolved at this time can eliminate unpleasant and contentious disagreements with your tenants in the future. The takeover of your new rental property can be chaotic, but don't fall into the trap of just verbally verifying the facts. Verify all information in writing and set up a detailed filing system for your new property. Ultimately, the best proof of the expenses is to insist on receiving copies of last year's invoices.

TIP

With experience, you'll be able to evaluate a property with surprising accuracy just by looking at the actual income and expenses, usually provided by the property manager. Look for discrepancies between the pro-forma operating statement given to you during pre-offer due diligence and the actual income and expense numbers provided.

Inspecting the property

If you've signed a private treaty sale contract, you can make the sale conditional on certain reasonable events occurring, such as suitable financing (refer to Chapter 11 for information on contracts). A satisfactory building report is a must. If you haven't received a building report prior to signing the contract, make such a report a condition of your signing. The wording of 'satisfactory' shouldn't be abused, but it is vague enough so that it's up to you to be happy with the report's findings.

The real reason for making a property sale conditional on a satisfactory building report is in case you uncover unexpected nasties. All homes have faults. Older homes are more likely to have more significant faults or maintenance issues, as a factor of their age. Younger homes, however, can still have significant problems. But a building and pest-inspection report that comes back with fundamental flaws that weren't obvious to your untrained eye could provide the wriggle room to get out of the contract, or give you the ammunition to negotiate down the price initially agreed to.

If you intend to develop a portfolio of properties, getting a well-credentialed builder on your team will help (for advice on building your team, refer to Chapter 4).

You can't put conditions on a sale when a property has been bought at auction. Building and pest-inspection reports must be done prior to auction day. Organising these reports for every property can become expensive if you continually miss out on the bidding. So, don't order these reports until the potential purchase has jumped a few other hurdles.

The condition of a property directly affects its value. The prudent real estate investor always insists on a thorough physical inspection before purchasing an investment property, even if the property is brand new. Do a walk-through at least a few times prior to making your offer. You usually also get an opportunity to make a final inspection of your property in the week before settlement.

Your new investment property may look good on paper and your pre-offer due diligence may reveal no financial issues or concerns. But your investment can be troubled by a weak link, and a physically troubled property is never a good investment (unless you're planning to demolish).

You're probably making one of the biggest financial purchases and commitments of your life. Though real estate investors by nature tend to be frugal in terms of spending for maintenance on their investments, never try to save money by forgoing a proper building inspection. (Refer to Chapter 4 for how to organise building and pest inspections.)

Our experience shows that an inspection usually pays for itself. In many cases, you're going to find items that the seller needs to correct that are greater in value or cost to repair than the nominal sum you spend on the inspection. Inspections are serious matters and not just a way to squeeze more from the seller.

The best result is if the inspection reveals no problems. Although you've spent money, knowing that your property is in good condition (at least at the time of inspection) is a great relief. That doesn't mean you won't find items in the future, possibly the very near future, that need attention.

Although you can usually cancel a transaction without major penalty or loss of the deposit if your physical inspection shows the property isn't satisfactory, more often than not, an unsatisfactory report leads to additional negotiations between you and the seller. A competently prepared written inspection report provides the information you need and can serve as the basis to ask the seller to fix the problems or reduce the property's purchase price (see 'Balancing at settlement', later in this chapter).

A good building inspector has a trained eye to pick up both the obvious and not-so-obvious problems in a property. If the offer is made and accepted, the professional inspection is to identify any deal-killer problems with the property or any items that warrant renegotiation. Essentially two types of defects commonly occur:

>> **Patent defects:** Defects readily visible by simply looking at the property. Patent defects could be a broken window or a leaking tap.

>> **Latent defects:** Hidden or not readily visible defects that require intrusive or even destructive testing. Examples include corroding copper pipes underneath the slab, or ceiling or window leaks that the owner has cosmetically repaired through patching and painting to hide from potential buyers.

Caveat emptor

Latin for 'Let the buyer beware', *caveat emptor* is the general rule of law for the sale of real estate in Australia. A vendor doesn't have to disclose the property's faults — it's your responsibility to know exactly what you're buying.

WARNING

Some problems won't be obvious to the naked eye. The most expensive ones usually won't stick out like the proverbial sore thumb. Electrical wiring and plumbing problems are usually hidden. Problems with the roof often won't be obvious from the ground (or inside the house). That's why buying property without having a professional spend time looking it over can be downright dangerous.

Types of inspections

Conduct your own physical inspection before making your offer. This initial overview doesn't cost anything other than your time and will keep you from wasting further time on properties that can't even pass your smell test. But it's no substitute for a professional building inspection.

TIP

Don't rush the inspection process. During the pre-offer inspection (especially for auctions), the seller must give you unfettered access to the property. If they won't make the time or they dodge making an appointment, that should serve as a warning. Don't agree to any unreasonable time or access limitations. We've seen sneaky sellers who unrealistically limit access to the property, particularly if it's occupied. Make sure that the tenants have been properly notified, as required by law and/or their lease agreements, with a liberal access period so you can thoroughly conduct all of your inspections without interference or interruptions.

Two types of professional inspections are usually performed either before offer (for auctions) or straight after the offer (for private treaty sales): Building inspections, and pest control and damage inspections.

Building inspections

Naturally, you, as the buyer, want to have all the physical aspects of the structures on your property inspected.

Areas that you want to hire people to help you inspect include

>> Doorways, walls and windows

>> Electrical systems, including all service panels and ground-fault circuit-breakers

>> Foundation, basements, sub-floor ventilation and decking

>> Heating and air conditioning

>> Illegal construction or additions and zoning violations

>> Landscaping, irrigation and drainage

>> Moisture intrusion (rising damp)

>> Overall condition of the property

>> Plumbing systems, including fixtures, supply lines, drains and heating devices

>> Roof and attic

>> Seismic, land movement or subsidence and flood risk

>> Structural integrity

WARNING

Some specific telltale signs indicate the property may have serious structural issues and require further investigation:

>> **Cracks:** Look at the entire property, including foundations, walls, ceilings, window and door frames, chimney and any retaining walls, for cracks. Don't let the seller or the agent tell you these cracks are merely settlement cracks; let your qualified property inspector or other qualified professional make that determination. A few isolated hairline cracks may be naturally occurring settlement of the structure over time, but if you can stick a screwdriver into the crack, something else may be going on.

>> **Uneven floors:** As you walk through the property, pay attention to any slant or sloping of the floors. Also watch for any soft spots in the flooring.

>> **Misaligned structure:** Your builder will look for floors, walls and ceilings that are uneven or out of plumb. A simple sign you can check yourself is when doors or windows stick and don't open or close easily.

>> **Grounds:** Excess groundwater, poor drainage or cracked or bulging retaining walls or concrete can be signs of soil issues such as slope failure or ground subsidence that require further inspection by an engineer. Be sure that the property drains properly and that all drains are properly installed and maintained.

>> **Moisture problems:** Look for current and historical indications of leaks such as discolouration and stains on ceilings, walls and particularly around window and door frames. Rising damp and musty odours or the smell of mould may be merely stale air or poor housekeeping; or they could indicate ongoing moisture issues. *Sump pumps* (which collect excess water and pump it away from the house) anywhere on the property are a red flag that should be explored in detail.

>> **Plumbing leaks:** Have a qualified plumbing contractor or other expert check all possible sources of leaks or moisture — under sinks, supply lines for taps, toilets, dishwashers and washing machines, plus roofs, windows, sprinklers and drainage away from the building.

Pest control and property damage

Pest-control firms are the natural choice for this type of inspection, but what they inspect is actually more than just infestations by termites and other wood-destroying insects. A thorough pest control and property damage inspection also looks at property damage caused by organisms that infect and incessantly break down and destroy wood and other building materials.

TECHNICAL STUFF

These conditions are commonly referred to as *dry rot* but, ironically they're actually caused by a fungus that requires moisture to flourish.

The report you receive from your pest control and property damage inspector usually includes a simple diagram of the property with notations as to the location of certain conditions noted. Some require attention immediately; others are simply areas to watch in the future.

Termites have the sort of reputation normally associated with viruses. But you usually don't need to panic if a pest-inspection report shows their existence. Ask the right questions of your inspector. Find out how much repairing any damage is likely to cost — you may get a pleasant surprise on how little the repairs cost, and it could be a great negotiating tool with the seller.

Environmental issues

Although environmental inspections aren't commonly required in Australia, buyers should be extremely careful if possible environmental issues affect their properties.

WARNING

When purchasing commercial, retail and industrial properties, particularly if they have certain types of tenants, such as drycleaners and any industrial tenants that use petroleum solvents, you may want to have an environmental engineer give you some guidance. Watch out for any property, and especially vacant spaces, sporting big oil drums.

Have an environmental engineer check drains that connect to the stormwater system or sewer to ensure that toxic or hazardous materials haven't been disposed of through your proposed property. If the local Environmental Protection Agency later determines that the source of the contaminants was your property, you could face a considerable clean-up bill.

Qualifying the inspectors

Inspect the property inspectors before you hire one. As with other service professionals, interview a few inspectors before making your selection. You may find that they don't all share the same experience, qualifications and professional standards. For example, don't hire an inspector who hesitates or refuses to allow you to accompany them during the inspection.

TIP

The inspection is actually a unique opportunity for most property owners and, because you're paying, we strongly recommend that you join the inspector while they are assessing your proposed purchase. What you learn can be invaluable and may pay dividends throughout your entire ownership. When an unscrupulous contractor later tries to tell you that you need to completely replumb your property, you can tell them to get lost if your property inspection revealed only isolated problems that you can resolve inexpensively.

Many firms can do both property and pest inspections for you, but you need to make sure of their qualifications to do one or both before you engage them. Find out what the inspectors' strengths and weaknesses are. A general builder's licence and certification as a property inspector are important, but ask if they have any specialised training in areas such as roofing, electrical systems or plumbing. These specialties can be particularly important if your proposed property has evidence of potential problems in any of these areas. For example, if a property has a history of roofing issues or mould or damp problems, an inspector who's a general contractor and a roofer is a plus.

The inspection report must be written. To avoid surprises, request a sample of one of their recent inspection reports prepared for a comparable property. This simple request may eliminate several potential inspectors but is essential to see whether an inspector is qualified and how detailed a report will be prepare for you. A simple check-the-box form may suffice for a house or apartment but, for larger properties, the more detail the better.

TIP

The advent of digital photography was a boon to property inspectors and made their sometimes mundane and difficult-to-understand reports come to life. Select a technologically adept inspector and require them to electronically send you the report, including digital photos documenting all of the conditions noted.

Although the cost of the inspection should be set and determined in advance, the price should be a secondary concern, because inspection fees often pay for themselves. Just like many other professional services, a direct correlation exists between the pricing of your inspection and the amount of time the inspector takes to conduct the inspection and prepare the report. If the inspector spends only 20 minutes at your new apartment, whatever you pay them is too much.

Using the Settlement Period Wisely

Most contracts require the seller to deliver the property in good physical condition with all basic systems in operational order, unless otherwise indicated. But the inspection process often reveals deficiencies that need to be corrected. For example, the physical and structural inspection by the property inspector may indicate the need to repair a defective electrical system.

So, with your inspection reports in hand, preferably with photographic evidence, you're prepared to contact the vendor's agent and arrange for the seller to correct the noted items at his expense. In some states, if the property is relatively new, you may be able to get the seller to have the problem fixed under builders' warranty insurance. And be aware that the seller isn't expected to fix all problems with the property, because the property is being sold as-is. The seller may be required, however, to fix any structural problems and, in most states, ensure electrical safety switches, smoke alarms and pool fences are installed and working. The seller must also attend to any breakdowns that have occurred since you agreed to buy the property (for example, a water leak has occurred, a fence has fallen over, or appliances have broken down).

TIP

If the property has problems not required to be fixed by the seller, such as cosmetic cracks in plaster or peeling paint, you may want to renovate as soon as possible, before the place is tenanted. As a buyer, use the period before settlement to your advantage and obtain all of your contractors' quotes so you're ready to begin as soon as the property settles, being wary that, until you actually own the property, you're beholden to the current owner giving you permission to get access. It may also help, if you can organise it, to have several contractors come to provide quotes at the one time, so that you're not constantly requesting access. We recommend you work out what renovations need to be done and speak to local real estate agents about getting the property leased in advance. But be wary of signing contracts to either begin construction work or give leasing permission to an agent before taking control of the property.

Taking control at settlement

Settlement is the consummation of the real estate transaction — the goal of the buyer, seller, agents and all the other professionals who were part of the effort. It's the culmination of numerous individual acts and sometimes constant negotiation right up until the last moment. The point at which a property settles occurs only when all conditions, if any, are fulfilled, including the funding of the loan. Quite a few details must be resolved before the conveyancers (either solicitors or specialist conveyancers) can actually close the transaction.

The process or formalities of settlement are handled in different ways throughout the country. But these days the buyer and the seller usually don't need to be present. Your solicitor or conveyancer will be at the centre of activity as the essential elements come together to make your goal of purchasing an investment property a reality.

TIP

Even if your solicitor or conveyancer is handling most of the details, a few fundamental items and details still need to be addressed as you move towards settlement and before you can call the property your own. Snags are still possible, so keep an eye out for the following:

>> **Lender requests:** You or mortgage broker need to make sure you're in contact with your lender to avoid any last-minute snags. Lenders are notorious for needing just one more signature or asking questions at the last minute about the source of your deposit or verifying your equity in other properties. These questions aren't as random as they may seem and are usually brought up by managers who must sign off on your loan.

>> **Document errors:** Don't assume the documents are correct. Read them as thoroughly as you would any contract you need to sign.

>> **Availability of parties and busy periods:** You need to be available to review and sign the loan documents, so let the lender or your mortgage broker know if you're planning any trips around closing time. But, during certain times of the year, things just take a lot longer. The Christmas holidays are the worst, but periods around all school holidays and long weekends can also be times when personnel plan their time off.

TIP

Most settlements occur without event, but 11th-hour issues often arise, so don't leave important details to the last minute or you may have your back to the wall, particularly if the contract contains a penalty clause to extend settlement. Documents can get lost and other unexplained communication breakdowns can occur any time when you have so many moving parts. Anticipate logistical delays and allow time for anything and everything to take twice as long as it should.

Insuring the property

Once you've signed a contract — and long before you've settled — you have an insurable interest in the property. You may not own it for three months, but if the house burns down in the meantime and the vendor doesn't have insurance, where would you be? As soon as you possibly can after signing the contract, call a reputable insurance company and organise appropriate temporary insurance, which gives you insurance for two weeks (or thereabouts) while you firm up exactly how much you need to insure the property for. Organise to pay for your insurance as soon as you can.

Banks will inevitably ask whether you've insured the property prior to settlement and will probably even insist on seeing proof if you're taking a mortgage with them.

The basic insurances you want in place from day one include insuring the cost of rebuilding the home and replacing the contents (see Chapter 14 for a fuller discussion on the different types of insurance). When a tenant moves in, also consider taking out insurance against tenant rental default or damage via specialist landlord insurance policies. And cover yourself with public liability insurance in case an accident occurs on your land.

Preparing for tenants

Although you may not be able to get into the property at will before you own it, you can start preparing the property for rent-paying tenants straightaway. Draw yourself up a list of what needs to be done in the first few days of owning the property. You may find some small jobs for contractors to do; you may want to have a contract cleaner in the house or get the carpets steam-cleaned (particularly if it was owner-occupied). You may want to get started on other more significant items ASAP.

TIP

The weeks prior to settlement are also the time to interview and choose the real estate agent you'll use to manage your property. In some cases, using the agent who listed the property for sale for the vendor can be an advantage, but it always pays to assess the best property manager for the property — rather than just using the one who has been managing it.

EASILY TAKING POSSESSION? DON'T BET ON IT!

Bruce has never settled on a property bought from an owner-occupier that could be considered 'clean and tidy' at settlement, with at least a half or a full day's work involved in just getting rid of the stuff the previous owner was too lazy to remove. Old paint tins, car tyres, stained offcuts of carpet, bits of scrap metal, busted electrical items, half-full boxes of rubbish and even collections of pornography have required trips to the tip or filling trailers and skip bins. This amount of rubbish may sound a little unusual, but Bruce swears that tenants usually vacate the properties in a cleaner state than most owner-occupiers.

Nicola, on the other hand, has been relatively lucky when it comes to issues at settlement — well, apart from the time a large branch went through a window the day before she legally owned the property (more on that soon). But one thing she always does is make sure she completes an inspection just prior to settlement to double-check everything is in order.

When she made an offer on her first property with her brother (as tenants in common — refer to the previous chapter), it had an existing lease in place that was due to finish in two months. Of course, the term of the lease was legally binding unless both parties agreed for it to be terminated early. Because Nicola and her brother would be shifting into the property as their home, they had a decision to make. Should they take on the existing lease and tenants for a few months, or should they have a longer settlement? After getting expert legal advice, they decided on the latter, because it removed any potential problems with the tenancy that they may have inherited for a few months. Negotiating for settlement to be on a day after the lease had ended turned out to be a much better outcome for them.

When Nicola bought an Art Deco unit in Brisbane in 2014 after being a rentvester for a while, a huge summer storm hit the area the day before settlement. She was renting a property just down the road at the time, so she was well aware of how damaging the storm had been. Very early the next morning, she walked to what was going to be her new home only to find that a large branch from a tree in the courtyard had smashed through some of the ornate windows of her stairwell.

She quickly called the agent and her legal representative and, within a few hours, had a formal written agreement in place that outlined how and when the damage would be repaired. Settlement was able to proceed as planned — although Nicola did have to put up with plastic garbage bags on the windows for a few weeks.

Balancing at settlement

When the transaction is complete and settlement has occurred, you receive a closing statement from your solicitor. Besides the actual purchase price, several expenses are incurred in the process of purchasing real estate that must be worked out. For example, the seller may have paid the council rates for the balance of the year and the buyer must reimburse the seller pro-rata.

The buyer also needs to pay expenses such as title-search fees. Table 12-1 contains some of the common expenses that are typical in the purchase of investment properties.

TABLE 12-1 ## Typical Allocation of Expenses

Item	Paid by Seller	Paid by Buyer
Agent's commission	X	
Mortgage discharge fee (seller's mortgage)	X	
New mortgage fee (buyer's mortgage)		X
Conveyancing	X	X
Title-transfer fee		X
Council rates		X
Stamp duty		X
Lenders' mortgage insurance		X
Loan-application fee		X
Loan-approval fee		X

In addition to the allocation of expenses between the buyer and seller, the final settlement statement provided to the buyer by the solicitor or conveyancer should contain a thorough breakdown of how the final bills have been settled. The statement the buyer receives should note the final sales price (if it differs from the contract), the amount of the deposit, the starting size of the buyer's new loan, the loan fees and other fees paid in the final settling of accounts.

TIP

Be sure to keep a copy of the closing statement, because this document will be used to establish your initial cost basis when you go to sell the property and need to determine your capital gain. Also, some of the expenses paid at settlement may be deductible on your tax return, such as loan fees, property taxes and insurance.

Pre-settlement inspections

A vital part of every property purchase is the *pre-settlement inspection* — more commonly known as the *final inspection*. This inspection usually occurs within three days of the final settlement date, and far too many buyers don't make the most of this opportunity to walk through the property one last time.

REMEMBER

These inspections are an opportunity to double-check that the property remains in the same condition it was in on the day you signed the contract of sale, and that none of the agreed fixtures or fittings have been removed. You will only have yourself to blame if the property condition has changed during the settlement period — for example, the property has been damaged, or plumbing or electricals have failed — and you were unaware of it until after the property had become legally yours.

Your conveyancer will be able to manage this inspection for you with the selling agent.

Taking ownership

After you receive word that settlement has occurred and you're the new owner, you should get moving immediately so you can get your property leased as fast as possible. As soon as you can:

>> Conduct another walk-through to make sure that the property hasn't been damaged during the moving process and prior to you taking control.

>> Verify that all items indicated on the personal property inventory list are present.

>> Make sure you've received all keys (you can change locks as an added precaution, if necessary).

>> Check the utility meters. Call the utility service providers to make sure the utility company has switched the billing, so you don't get billed for the former owner's usage.

Congratulations! You're now ready to begin your property investment journey!

4

Operating the Property

Gain the knowledge, training and experience needed to oversee your property investment, and a thorough understanding of property and tenancy laws — because ignorance is no excuse.

Work out what you need to know to attract and retain good tenants so you can build an effective relationship with your property manager and boost the value of your property.

Understand how to protect the investments you're making — and your their ability to continue with your wealth-creation plans should the unexpected or unfortunate occur.

Know how to reduce your tax bill (legally, of course) when it comes time to sell.

Take advantage of time — plus the powers of compounding and leverage — to help you build a properly diversified property portfolio.

IN THIS CHAPTER

» **Deciding how to manage the property**

» **Understanding how to fill vacancies**

» **Dealing with leases, contracts and money collection**

» **Getting on with tenants**

» **Staying on the right side of the law**

Chapter **13**

Property Management 101

By the time you settle on buying a rental property, you've probably already put in dozens, perhaps hundreds, of hours if undertaking the challenge yourself. Now, however, the real work begins. First, you need to decide whether to manage the property yourself (which we don't advise is wise, especially for first-time investors) or pay for professional property management. Then, to maximise the value of your investment, you've got to attract and retain excellent tenants, keep your eyes open for ways to cost-effectively improve your property, and oversee money flowing in and going out. You also need to understand the requirements of your tenants and act fairly, both to them and in the eyes of the law.

Managing Yourself or Hiring Experts?

A property owner is always required to make the major decisions over such things as expenditure on capital works and other major maintenance issues. But whoever manages your rental property — you or a property manager you appoint — needs to take responsibility for the ongoing management issues. These include advertising, tenant selection and rent collection, as well as maintenance and repairs.

Ignorance is no excuse

If you're buying your first investment property, you probably don't have a lot of recent experience with rental properties. In fact, your only first-hand knowledge may be as a tenant yourself. You need to know many, many laws and regulations. And ignorance of the law is no excuse when you need to front a tenancy tribunal.

You need to draw on varied sources of information if you're intending to manage your own property portfolio — and the sort of information you need to be aware of is covered throughout this chapter. However, we don't recommend that most landlords manage their own property. The cost of having a manager run your residential investment property is usually up to 8 per cent, excluding GST, of your rent plus some additional charges. That is, if your property rents for $2,400 a month, the cost is approximately $192 a month (if the fee is 8 per cent). The fee is also a tax deduction.

The argument against managing your own single investment property is this: You need to know the same number of laws whether you own one investment property or ten. If you own one property, managing it yourself saves you about $192 a month. If you own ten properties, doing it yourself may then save you $1,920 a month. Managing your own properties may make more sense when you have more than a few to manage, as long as you have the time to devote to the task and know you are as good as professional property managers who do it for a living, not just in their spare time.

If you're intending to fill the management position yourself, you have to possess a variety of skills to do so within the bounds of the relevant state-based legislation. Although you don't need a degree or years of experience to get started, adopting a trial-and-error method is potentially dangerous. If you decide to manage the property yourself — again, which we don't think is advisable — make sure you do plenty of reading on the laws themselves that affect tenancy in your state, as well as others' experience of them.

Assessing your skills as a property manager

Use the following questions to examine your own personality and skills to see if you're cut out to be your own property manager:

>> **Are you a people person?** Serving as a property manager is largely about managing people. You must enjoy people and solving problems — while often being unappreciated yourself.

>> **Do you have the temperament to handle problems?** Responding to complaints and service requests in a positive and rational manner is key.

- >> **Can you tackle basic accounting tasks?** Are you comfortable with numbers and meticulous with accounting tasks?

- >> **Do you have maintenance and repair abilities?** Being able to work effectively and efficiently with your hands goes a long way, because hiring contractors to cover all of your odd-job requirements can be costly.

- >> **Are you willing to work and take phone calls in the evenings and on weekends?** Who needs a weekend, right? Sadly, that's when things tend to blow up, break down and fall over.

- >> **Do you have sales and negotiation skills?** You need to sell the space.

- >> **Are you willing to commit the time and effort?** All these important tasks take time, and others, such as determining the right rent and becoming familiar with property-management laws, take even more time.

WARNING

If you're impatient or easily manipulated, you aren't suited to being a property manager. You need to convey a professional demeanour to your tenants. They must see you as someone who is going to take responsibility for the condition of the property. You must also insist that tenants live up to their part of the bargain, pay their rent regularly and refrain from causing unreasonable damage to your property.

A rental property manager must be fair, firm and friendly to all rental prospects and tenants. You need to treat everyone impartially and remain patient and calm under stress. You must be determined and unemotional in enforcing rent collection, as well as your policies and rules. And you must maintain a positive attitude through it all. Not as simple as it looks, is it?

REMEMBER

When you manage a rental property, you don't have to deal with just your current tenants. You also have to interact with potential renters, tradespeople, suppliers, neighbours and body corporate managers. People, not the property, create most rental-management problems. Be prepared to be flexible and learn from your property-management experiences. The best property managers may have credentials, but they have also graduated from the school of hard knocks. Practice makes perfect.

Hiring professional management

Most real estate agencies have a rental property management arm, and property management–specific real estate agencies are also available. Property managers take on the responsibility for all ongoing operations of the property (or as much or as little as you're prepared to cede to them). The right agent can make a big difference to the cash flow your rental property generates by finding good replacement tenants quickly or making sure maintenance and repairs are done quickly and efficiently. (Agents usually have a list of qualified contractors who charge a standard fee for their agency's clients.) Find property managers familiar with your kind of investment property as well as its location. With a little research, you can find the right fit for your property.

A poor management company cuts into your profits, not only with its fees, but also by providing improper maintenance and leasing to poor-quality tenants who run your property into the ground.

Researching local property managers

Research property managers working in the local area and spend time interviewing them. Make a few extra phone calls to check references and don't sign a management appointment until you feel confident the agency you hire has a sound track record. Find out how long they've been a property manager and how many properties they're looking after.

REMEMBER

Rental property management companies have a notoriously high staff turnover. You may well find that, even if you like the agency, you're dealing with a different staff member each 6 to 12 months (it's happened to both of us too regularly). This may, or may not, be an issue for tenants, who aren't necessarily long term. It's more likely to be an issue for you. Sadly, good, long-term property managers can be a little hard to find. If you're not happy with what your manager is doing, you need to be prepared to give notice and find someone who is better at the job.

TIP

Make sure the agency you appoint manages sufficient properties in the area, so they are familiar with the local market. Although the largest rental agency in a suburb or town is no guarantee of the professionalism or good service of the agents working there, it does suggest that interested parties (property investors) believe that agency is where the traffic lies — and, when you've got an empty property, traffic is probably the most important element in getting your property tenanted again. Also be aware that running a rental management agency is a volume business and many real estate agencies only run rental businesses with the aim that the thin margins will possibly be made up later by obtaining the listing to sell the property or even sell off the rent roll at some point in the future.

Be sure to investigate these issues:

>> **Licences:** Make sure the agency has the appropriate state-based licences to manage rental properties.

>> **Credentials:** Also examine the property managers' credentials — make sure they're members of their state real estate institute.

>> **Insurance:** The company should carry professional indemnity and public liability insurances. The management company is your agent and will be collecting your rents and security bonds, so you want to be sure it's protected against rogue employees.

In most property management agreements, an emergency clause gives agencies the ability and right to perform emergency repairs without advance approval from the owner (usually up to a certain limit). This emergency clause allows the agent to take care of unexpected problems. The dollar limit should be commensurate with the type and size of the property.

TIP

When you're in the early stages of working with a new property manager, make sure you closely monitor the property's expenses. Even though the property manager may have the legal right to use funds up to a certain amount, they should always keep you informed.

Agency fees and charges

Typically, in Australia, management companies receive a percentage of the collected income for managing a property. Usually, the larger the rental property, the lower the management fee percentage. Management fees for houses and apartments run between 5.5 and 8.8 per cent and are occasionally higher. Fees for commercial properties have a similar scale.

Additional fees for leasing a vacant property are often justified, because the most time-intensive portion of property management is tenant turnover. When one tenant leaves, the rental property or the commercial, industrial or retail suite must be made rent-ready; then the property manager must show the property and screen the tenants. Additional leasing charges for residential rentals can vary but are usually in the vicinity of one to two weeks' rent. Leasing commissions for commercial, industrial or retail properties are usually a percentage of the gross rent, with a declining scale — the longer the lease, the lower the percentage in later years.

Renting Vacant Properties

Vacant properties don't generate rental income, so fill your vacancies with good, stable, rent-paying tenants quickly. Verifying information on prospective tenants' rental applications takes a while, and is done by your property manager, but is always time well spent. Relying on your instincts will largely be inaccurate, arbitrary and potentially illegal (particularly if it leads to discrimination).

If you use a property manager (as we recommend), a lot of the areas covered in the following sections will be taken care of by your manager — such as the tenant selection criteria, advertising, and taking and verifying applications. Even so, knowing the steps your manager should be taking can strengthen the conversations you have with them — and help you notice any red flags.

Establishing tenant-selection criteria

In order to increase your chances of finding a long-term, stable tenant, the tenant-selection criteria and screening process you and your property manager use should be clear, systematic and objective. Determine the minimum qualifications and adhere to them, applying them consistently and fairly to all rental applicants. You or your property manager also need to be aware of federal and state discrimination laws when determining who will be the successful tenant for your property.

WARNING

Setting up a systematic screening process is particularly critical if you own only one or two properties. Deadbeat tenants who go from property to property causing damage and not paying rent are experienced and shrewd. They know novice property owners are more likely to be fooled and that professional agents have screening procedures to verify every single item on their applications. If certain items don't check out, professional managers don't just trust their feelings on the prospective tenant.

REMEMBER

The vast majority of residential rental applicants will be good tenants, pay their rent on time, take good care of their homes and treat you and their neighbours with respect. You just need to carefully guard against those few bad apples; don't hesitate to deny prospects who can't meet your standards.

Determining lease length

The lease or rental agreement is the legal document that specifies the terms and conditions of the contract that's supposed to bind the property owner and the tenant, although tenancy tribunals are increasingly refusing to punish tenants who walk out on leases. A lease is a contract between the owner of the property and the tenant for the possession and use of the property in exchange for the payment of rent for either residential or commercial property for a specific term.

Lease lengths are influenced by the property type:

>> **Residential tenants:** Generally, no minimum or maximum term is set, but most residential leases are initially signed for six months or one year. Landlords can offer a further set period at the end of the initial agreement but, sometimes, the agreement reverts to a month-to-month or periodic

lease. Renters in this situation often stay on for many years, and landlords usually keep rent increases to a minimum in order to keep a good tenant on.

>> **Commercial tenants:** Commercial, industrial and retail investment property owners almost always use long-term leases. Fixed-term contracts obligate you and the tenant for a set period; some owners like the commitment required from the tenant and tenants have certainty to assist the development of their business. With such a lease, renegotiating aspects of the lease — including rents and tenancy length — can't be done until the lease expires, unless both parties agree, or the tenant doesn't pay the rent or violates another term of the lease.

Setting the rent

Setting the rent is about walking a fine line. If you set your rent too high, you won't get tenants. No tenant equals trouble with the mortgage repayments. And, if you set your rent too low, your income will suffer. Essentially, rents are set by market forces — supply and demand. If many properties are available for rent, tenants can be choosey. If a property shortage exists, landlords are in the box seat.

The best way to find out what your property's worth on the rental market is to either ask property managers in the area or do the legwork yourself and research 6 to 12 properties similar to yours in the area.

TIP

Setting the rent is particularly critical if you own a house or apartment or a small commercial property, because the rent loss from an extended vacancy or one bad tenant can seriously jeopardise your investment. Be realistic in setting your rents to attract good long-term tenants who pay on time. Using a realistic budget for your property that anticipates a slightly lower rent and at least two weeks' vacancy each year also helps to avoid nasty surprises.

REMEMBER

Setting your rents properly should be an independent decision based on current market conditions. The realities of the market will put limits on what rent you can reasonably charge for your property.

Evaluating the rental rates being charged for similar properties in comparable locations is a great way to gather information before setting your own rent. Make minor adjustments in your rent because of variations in the location, age, size and features of the properties you're comparing.

For example, if you own a residential investment property and one of your competitors has an available rental nearly identical to yours, your rent should be slightly higher if you also have air conditioning. Of course, make a reduction for aspects of your rental property that aren't as desirable.

Adding value through renovations and upgrades

For residential properties, almost every rental has the potential for some renovation or upgrade. Often, upgrades allow you to create the real value in rental properties: When you have a dated property, a cosmetic renovation can allow the rent to be increased. Pay particular attention to items that are quick, easy and inexpensive to replace but can really improve the overall look, such as cupboard doors and handles, a new letterbox and basic light fittings.

TIP

If you have an older investment property, renovating or making tenant improvements may be more difficult due to some of the hazardous materials used in the building's original construction. Asbestos and lead-based paint were commonly used in many properties (prior to the early 1980s for asbestos and about 1970 for lead paint), and these materials can be quite costly to remove. Often, you're better off just leaving them in place, as long as they haven't been disturbed. Consult with experts in these issues before doing any work.

Again, if your chosen investment properties are residential, keep in mind what features and strengths your prospective tenants will find in competitive rentals. For example, if most of your competition offers dishwashers but your property doesn't have one, you may want to install a dishwasher so you remain competitive.

Enhancing external appearances

Make sure that your prospective tenants' first impressions of your residential or commercial rental property are positive — because, if they aren't, they'll most likely never take the time to see the interior. Start at the street and carefully critique your property as if you were entering a contest for the best-looking property in your area. Your property manager will be able to advise you on this as well.

TIP

To attract tenants who will treat your property properly and stay for a long time, be sure that the grounds and exterior areas are sparkling clean, and the landscaping is well maintained. Renovating the grounds by removing rubbish and weeds is an inexpensive task.

Make sure the entry is clean, well kept, and well lit. The entry door should be cleaned or freshly painted. Buy a new welcome mat. Remove or replace a broken screen door.

Improving what's inside

The most qualified renters always have choices. You're in competition for these tenants and you need to ensure that your rental property stands out. The positive first impression of your rental property's exterior won't matter if the interior is poorly maintained.

TIP

Don't show your rental property until it's completely ready. Although you may lose a couple of potential showing days by taking the time to get everything ready, you'll benefit in the long run with a more conscientious tenant. Here's a list of things to check:

>> All plumbing and appliances are operating properly.

>> Counters, cabinets, doors, mouldings, thresholds and metal strips are clean and fully operational, presenting no hazards.

>> Cupboards and storage areas, cupboard doors, rods, hooks, shelves and lights are in good order, and floors and walls are clean.

>> Floor coverings are clean and in good condition.

>> Heating and air conditioning are operational. Be sure the thermostat, filters, vents and registers are all in working order.

>> Locks have been changed (although sometimes it may be unnecessary, you should always consider changing locks) and are operational. Pay attention to all latches and catches, doorknobs and pulls, doorstops and sliding doors.

>> Paint and/or wall coverings provide proper coverage, without holes, cuts, scratches or nails.

>> Patios, balconies and entries are clean and the railings secure.

>> Smoke detectors, all lighting and electrical outlets, including circuit-breakers or safety switches, are working properly.

>> The toilet, tub, shower, sink, mirrors and cabinets are thoroughly cleaned. If your budget allows or it's required, consider re-enamelling an old bathtub, replacing aged mirrors and installing a dual-flush cistern.

>> Windows, window locks, screens and window coverings are clean, secure and operating properly.

Using contractors

Particular maintenance and improvements are best handled by qualified, licensed tradespeople.

REMEMBER

Every day your residential rental property sits vacant is costing you income that you can never recover. Painting your own rental may take you six days working in the evenings and weekends to complete. If the rental market is strong and the daily rental rate is $100 per day, you're actually losing money if you could've had the property professionally touched up in one day, given the loss in rental income for the six days it took you to complete the job — and you've had to soak up your own valuable holidays or down time to do the work.

Regardless of how much work you choose to handle yourself, have on hand a list of competent and competitively priced service companies and suppliers for those times when you need a quick response. Of course, your property manager will be able to handle this for you as well. Also ensure contractors have the proper insurance in place before you allow them to commence work on your property.

Advertising for tenants

Advertising is how you let people know that you have a vacant rental property available. Money intelligently spent on advertising is money well spent. When done poorly, advertising can be another black hole for your precious resources.

Determine the most desirable features of your rental property for your target market. You can also ask people who look at your property — whether or not they agree to rent — what aspects of your property they found of interest. Incorporate these selling points into your marketing efforts, or work with your property manager to do so.

REMEMBER

One of the best advertisements for your rental property is street appeal — the exterior appearance. Properties that have well-kept grounds with green grass, trimmed shrubs, beautiful flowers and fresh paint are much more appealing to your rental prospects. A well-maintained property often attracts a tenant who'll pay more rent and treat your rental property with care. This also applies to apartment buildings, so work with your body corporate if necessary to ensure the exterior of the building and the gardens are well maintained.

TIP

These days, the vast majority of potential tenants first see the property they end up renting on a specialist property listing website.

One of the most time-consuming aspects of owning and managing rental property is the time spent filling vacancies. Real estate investors with commercial properties use professional leasing agents and so should residential property investors in our opinion, too. Although most residential property investors also use real estate agents to have their place leased initially, those who have the inclination to take on the management individually should be aware that it can be a huge time trap.

Efficiently scheduling showings

The most efficient approach to showing your residential rental is to hold an 'open for inspection', which enables you and your property manager to show your property to interested rental prospects within 15 minutes or half an hour. Work with your manager to select one or two periods for your open house that are convenient for most working people (preferably during daylight hours). Combining a weekday early evening open house with one on the weekend enables virtually all prospects to fit the rental showing into their busy schedules.

TIP

Often an online listing simply indicating the time of your 'open for inspection' is sufficient. If the place appeals and the advertised time is both short enough to create a sense of interest from those coming and going and long enough to allow those visiting property all over town to see your property, you may find that these opens for inspections are long enough to get a couple of qualified applicants.

If you're trying to lease a property in a depressed rental market, or if you find you need to fill a vacancy during the holidays, you may not be able to generate enough interest from an open house to get a sense of urgency among multiple prospects. If you have to schedule individual appointments and are managing the property yourself, keep these points in mind:

>> **Be prepared to show your property at night and on weekends for short, but reasonable, time frames, when most of your prospects are available.**

>> **If you've made appointments with individuals, call to verify the rental showing before making a special trip to the property.** By calling, you're also reassuring the prospect that you're going to be there and aren't going to be delayed.

Showing vacant versus occupied rentals

When showing a vacant residential rental when managing your property yourself, be a tour guide but don't be too controlling. Allow the prospects to view the rental in the manner that suits them. Some prospects go right to a certain room. If the prospects hesitate or are reluctant to tour on their own, casually guide them.

Most properties are typically shown vacant, although you may be able to obtain the cooperation of a vacating tenant to show prospects through the property while occupied. Because commercial tenants almost always require some specialised tenant improvements, working off drawings of the space, rather than conducting a physical tour, can be more useful. If you do show an occupied commercial space, just be sure not to disrupt the current tenant's business activities.

If the current residential tenants are at the end of their lease or have given notice to vacate, the owner or property manager is usually allowed to enter the property to show prospective new tenants. You and your manager must comply with state laws that require you to give tenants advance written notice of entry prior to showing the rental.

Cooperate with the current tenants when scheduling mutually convenient times to show the rental — and respect their privacy by avoiding excessive intrusions. Although the current tenant may be legally required to allow you, your manager and your prospects to enter the rental property for a showing, they don't have to make any efforts to ensure that the property is clean and neat.

Showing a vacant rental is usually much easier, but touring your prospects through an occupied rental property does have some advantages, particularly if your current tenants are friendly, cooperative and are leaving for understandable reasons (such as having bought a house or needing more room for a larger family). The rental prospects may want to ask the current tenant questions about their living experience at your property if they are home at the time of the inspection.

WARNING

If your current residential tenant is being evicted, isn't leaving on good terms or has an antagonistic attitude for any reason, don't show the rental until the property is vacated. Also consider this strategy if your current tenants haven't taken care of the rental property or if their lifestyle or furnishings may be objectionable to some rental prospects. Also bear in mind that, sometimes, showing a property while the current tenants are in the throes of moving can invite your prospective tenants into a nightmare of boxes, half-packed clothes and uncleaned walls and carpets. Use your own judgment here.

Communicating with prospective tenants

If managing your property yourself, tenants want to feel they can communicate with you if a problem arises. They also appreciate someone showing an interest in their lives. By showing an interest, you set yourself apart from other property managers. Some prospects will take a rental property that isn't exactly what they're looking for if they have a positive feeling about the property owner.

TIP

The goal at the end of the showing is to receive a commitment to rent from the prospect by having her complete a rental application. But don't forget that you (or your property manager) still need to thoroughly screen the prospect and confirm that she meets the rental criteria before you sign a lease or rental agreement.

Taking and verifying applications

Offer every interested prospect the opportunity to complete an application. Information provided on the application enables you or your property manager to begin the screening process and select the best tenant for your rental property.

Prior to accepting the rental application, you or your property manager should carefully review the entire form to make sure each prospective tenant has legibly provided all requested information. Pay particular attention to all names and addresses, employment information, driver's licence numbers and emergency contacts. Make sure that the prospect has signed the rental application authorising you (or your manager) to verify the provided information. Ask prospective tenants to show their current driver's licence or other photo ID so that you or the property manager can confirm their correct name and current address.

TIP

If a rental prospect dithers through the process, delays returning phone calls or insists on additional time, cutting your losses and moving on to the next prospect may be best.

Ask about any discrepancies between the application and the ID provided. Even if the explanation seems reasonable, be sure to write down the new information.

Rental history

When you or your property manager first contacts the rental applicant's current or former agent or owner, you or your manager needs to listen to her initial reaction and let her speak about the applicant. Some agents or landlords welcome the opportunity to give you information about your rental applicant, but others may be

>> **Dishonest:** An agent or landlord may be upset with the tenant for leaving the property or unwilling to say anything bad about a problem tenant so that she can get the tenant out of her property and into yours.

>> **Unforthcoming:** Some agents or landlords may hold back information because they're concerned that they'll cop liability if they provide any negative or subjective information.

If you're managing the property yourself, when current or prior agents or landlords aren't overly cooperative, try to gain their confidence by providing them with some information about yourself and your rental property. If you're still unable to build rapport, try to get them to at least answer the most important question of all: 'Would you rent to this applicant again?' They can simply give you a yes or a no without any details. Of course, silence can also tell you everything you need to know.

TIP

Written references are almost worthless without having them thoroughly backed up verbally by the author.

Employment and income

You or your manager need to independently verify the company information and phone number applicants put on their application if you have any doubts about its authenticity. Also request recent payslips. For prospective commercial tenants, a copy of the most recent tax return, or verified letter from their accountant, could be suitable.

Notifying applicants of your decision

Be sure to notify the successful applicant promptly (either directly or through your manager) when you make the decision. You may want to request a part-payment — one or two weeks' rent is common — as a holding deposit at this point. You could also notify any applicants who've failed to meet the criteria, because you won't be offering the property to them in any case.

REMEMBER

Don't notify the other qualified applicants that you've already rented out the property until all legal documents have been signed and all funds due upon move-in have been collected in full. This way, if your first-choice tenant can't take the property or was successful elsewhere, you haven't sent other qualified tenants out to continue their own searches.

Signing Leases and Collecting Money

Tenants, property managers and property owners alike are aware of all the legal paperwork involved in renting a property. And, although sifting through all that legalese isn't fun for anyone, it *is* important. Rental property owners and tenants each have specific legal rights and responsibilities that are outlined in these documents, and being aware of what you're agreeing to — and being sure your tenants know what they're agreeing to — is crucial.

Reviewing and signing documents

After you approve your selected tenant, you should have them sign the rental agreement as soon as is practical.

Be sure your tenant understands that when she signs your rental agreement she's entering into a contract that has significant rights and responsibilities for both parties. Be sure to have all approved occupants review and sign all documents — including any lease or rental agreement addendums — before taking possession of the rental property. Never enter oral agreements with tenants — it opens the door to much potential confusion.

Collecting the money

If managing the property yourself, be sure to collect the agreed rent in advance and the bond (usually four weeks' or one month's rent) before you give the tenants the keys. (If using a property manager, your manager will take care of this for you.) Make sure that you and the tenant are perfectly clear how rent will be paid for the remainder of the lease. Your preference should be for electronic transfer, which is most efficient for all concerned.

The rental, or security, bond is a deposit from the tenant on the property as a possible part-payment against the cost of potential damage and non-payment of rent. Landlords are not allowed to physically hold rental bonds paid by tenants in Australia. The bond, which is usually limited to one month's rent for residential properties depending on a few factors, is required to be made out to a government-run organisation. These agencies act as a trust and hold the bond on behalf of the landlord and tenant in case of dispute at the end of the tenancy. If a dispute arises, getting access to the money usually requires an application to a state tenancy tribunal.

Inspecting the property

When properly completed, the inspection form clearly documents the condition of the rental property upon move-in by the tenants and serves as a baseline for the entire tenancy. These are usually called *entry condition reports*. If the tenant withholds rent or tries to break the lease claiming the property needs substantial repairs, you may need to be able to prove the condition of the rental upon move-in. When the tenants move out, you and your manager will be able to clearly note the items that have been damaged or haven't been left clean by the vacating tenants.

You might want to consider completing the inspection form with the tenants prior to or at the time of move-in (or ask your manager to). Walk through the premises with the tenants and agree that all items are clean and undamaged, or note any pre-existing damage, before they move in. Note the condition of the floor coverings — one of the most common areas of dispute upon departure. Although tenants shouldn't be charged for ordinary wear and tear, if they destroy the carpet, they should pay for the damage. Most lease documents now stipulate that a tenant must steam-clean carpets before they hand in the keys at the end of the tenancy. Taking photos of the property to refresh the tenant's (or your own) memory at the end of the tenancy or to show in court will be helpful.

REMEMBER

Generally, property managers will provide the entry condition report for tenants to complete and return to them within a certain time frame at the start of the tenancy.

Working with Existing Tenants

Although most residential investment property in Australia is sold as 'vacant at possession', occasionally the rental property you've recently acquired has tenants already living there. Tenants are typically full of apprehension when the owner-ship of the property they're renting is changing, so beginning your relationship with your tenants on a positive note is extremely important.

Entering into a new rental agreement

Although you may want to make some changes to the lease terms or policies, when you acquire an occupied rental property, your legal and business relation-ship is already established by whatever agreement the tenants had with the former owner. Therefore, you need to wait until the expiration of the lease to change the terms — or provide the tenant with proper written notice of proposed changes as required by law.

New owners may attempt to convert existing tenants to their own lease or rental agreement as soon as possible. Keep the following in mind:

>> **Residential tenancies:** Implementing your own rental agreement as soon as legally allowed is relatively easy and can be done upon the expiration of the lease and normally with written notice if the tenant is on a month-to-month rental agreement. However, most rental agreements in Australia are fairly standard and rarely need to be significantly changed.

>> **Commercial properties:** The existing leases are valid and binding until their expiration, so you must wait to implement new leases until tenant lease renewal or turnover.

Increasing rents

When you acquire an investment property, part of your research is to establish the fair market rental value of your new property. If the tenant's current rent is below market value and they are on a month-to-month rental agreement, one of your toughest jobs is how to implement rent increases. As the new owner, you're likely to have much higher mortgage repayments and expenses to make necessary repairs and upgrades to the property than the last owner did. No tenant wants a rent increase, so you'll be able to do little to appease them.

TIP

The majority of tenants will reluctantly accept a rent increase as long as the rent isn't raised beyond the current market rent for a comparable place in the area and you're willing to make needed repairs or upgrades to their rental property or suites.

Avoiding Discrimination Complaints

Discriminating against tenants based on religion, sex, nationality, age, marital status or disability is illegal. Stiff penalties can be awarded against landlords who discriminate. Problems often arise because property owners are unaware that their policies or practices are discriminatory. Discrimination laws also impact on your advertising, tenant-screening, and selection process. This is another reason we advocate working with professional property managers.

Being fair to families and children

All residential rental properties must be available to all applicants, including those with children. However, because non-residential properties are less regulated, some commercial property owners may be within their legal rights to use their business judgement to refuse or discourage an applicant with plans to use the leased space for certain reasons — for example, as a day-care facility or other business that caters for children.

TIP

As a residential rental property owner, you should welcome renters with children. Families tend to be more stable, and they look for safe and low-crime environments in which to raise their kids. Along with responsible pet owners, who can have difficulty finding suitable rental properties, families with children can be excellent long-term renters. And, typically, the longer your tenants stay, the better your cash flow.

Dealing with tenants with disabilities

Federal and state laws stipulate that communities should be blind to (as in not notice or discriminate against) people's disabilities, including when it comes to financial matters. In Australia, not all houses, units or commercial properties are required to be accessible to people with disabilities. But some properties will naturally be more suitable to a tenant with a disability.

Governments and the courts are not in the practice of forcing private landlords with single houses to spend thousands of dollars putting in ramps and widening doorways to potentially cover tenants with disabilities; however, tenants with disabilities are increasingly offering to pay for these modifications at the start of the tenancy and *make good* at the end — that is, return the property to its pre-lease state — by agreement with the landlord.

If you have a multi-unit property, you may be required to

>> Make reasonable accommodations at your expense for tenants with disabilities, so they can enjoy the rental property on an equal basis.

>> Make reasonable adjustments to the rules, procedures or services, upon request. A common example would be providing a wider and more convenient parking space, if practical.

>> Allow tenants with a disability the right to modify their living space at their own expense, as long as

- The modifications only extend to what is necessary to make the space safe and comfortable and are considered minor.

- The tenant agrees to restore the property to its original condition upon vacating the property (when it's reasonably likely that the tenant *will* vacate).

- The tenant obtains your prior approval and ensures that the work is done in a professional manner, including using licensed tradespersons.

Animals that assist tenants with daily life activities (such as guide dogs) must be allowed in all rental properties, regardless of any no-pet policies.

Dealing with tenants and pets

Tenants and their pets are an issue that landlords come up against from time to time. Some tenants will be up-front about owning a pet when they seek to rent a property. Others may deliberately fail to disclose that they have pets when they fill out an application form. Some tenants acquire pets only after they move into the property.

REMEMBER

Most states and territories have amended residential tenancy legislation to ensure that tenants with pets are not discriminated against, including making it much more difficult for a landlord to refuse a reasonable application by a tenant with a pet.

Like renting to families, pet owners who find a suitable property can make good long-term tenants. And some landlords are pet lovers who aren't concerned about tenants with pets — if that's the case, you might even advertise as being a pet-friendly landlord. You're bound to be inundated with potential tenants.

Chapter **14**

Protecting Your Investment: Insurance and Risk Management

After years of accumulating resources, all investment property owners need to be concerned about protecting their assets through insurance and risk-management programs. You've worked and sacrificed to build your wealth through real estate, so you don't want to be careless and lose it.

The concept of risk management includes much more than simply having an insurance policy to cover the property itself burning down. You need to take care to practise proper maintenance and record keeping and require that others provide you with coverage for their activities. You also need to ensure that a personal disaster doesn't ruin the wealth-creation strategy that's meant to look after you and your family in the decades to come. Insuring yourself as an investment is just as important as insuring the bricks and mortar. In this chapter, we cover these risk-management and insurance issues.

Developing a Risk-Management Plan

Many people get into the world of property investment without knowing how much risk they're exposed to just by owning real estate. Investment property owners need to minimise risks because they can become targets of those who suffer a personal injury or whose property is damaged.

You can take steps to reduce and control your risk. Consider the following suggestions as preventative actions to minimise the potential of legal action:

>> **Inspect the property as part of a thorough maintenance program.** Ensure your property is regularly inspected by your property manager with issues correctly identified and remedied as soon as possible. Your property manager will complete an inspection checklist that should be shared with you as well as retained on your lessor file.

>> **Listen to and address tenant complaints.** Be open and responsive to feedback from your tenants and others expressing concern. A track record of a quick response to complaints is a solid defence in court. Make sure you're available to respond to your property manager's communications about any maintenance or repair request promptly.

>> **Transfer the risk to others.** Transferring risk from the owner and property manager to the vendor or supplier is sound policy for managing and minimising the risk. You can transfer risk in two ways. The first method is by using only licensed and qualified contractors and suppliers who provide their own insurance cover. Require them to provide evidence that they have proper insurance coverage in place. Second, you can pay insurance companies directly to take on certain types of risks, including fire, theft of property, tenant damage and rental default.

>> **Remove certain risks or never allow them in the first place.** For example, many owners of residential properties remove diving boards and pool slides. Commercial property owners often restrict access to the roofs of their buildings with emergency-door hardware.

REMEMBER

Although you can minimise your risks by taking some of these steps, you can't eliminate risk completely, and that's why you need proper insurance coverage. Insurance is an essential element in any risk-management program.

Getting the Property Insurance You Need

As the owner of investment real estate, insurance coverage is one of your best protections and an essential risk-management technique to ensure that you hold on to the wealth you create.

If you've ever sat down with a sharp and assertive insurance agent, you may know that some insurance companies can sell you coverage against any possible danger or loss in the world. Experienced insurance agents seem to have mastered the art of describing all sorts of horrible problems that could befall you. But you need to sift through the sales pitch and decide which cover is right for you — and make sure you're covered at a reasonable cost.

TIP

Your goal is to pay only for coverage for events and losses that could occur at your property. The right insurance coverage is worth a lot, but use resources wisely — cyclone insurance in Melbourne or Hobart may not be your best bet.

You need to be concerned, but not overly, about legal actions and having the proper insurance coverage to defend yourself and protect your assets. Insurance doesn't just provide protection against actual losses. Insurance is even more beneficial in that it provides a legal defence against the claims made against you as the owner of real estate. The expense of retaining competent legal counsel is what makes the threat of a lawsuit so devastating to most people.

WARNING

Don't assume that all potential losses are covered by your insurance coverage. Your best defences against losses are to ensure your properties are professionally managed and to assertively eliminate, transfer or control the inherent risks of owning and managing rental property.

Understanding insurance options

The proper insurance coverage can protect you from losses caused by many dangers, including fire, storms, theft and vandalism. A comprehensive policy also includes public liability insurance, covering injuries or losses suffered by others as a result of defective or dangerous conditions on the property. Public liability insurance may also cover the legal costs of defending personal injury lawsuits, a valuable feature because the legal defence costs of these cases are commonly much greater than the ultimate award of damages, if any.

General insurance brokers

If you've always done your own shopping around when it comes to getting general insurances — for your home, contents and cars, for example — then becoming a property investor may be the time to find yourself a general insurance broker. A variety of online platforms can also now do this for you.

Common coverage

The following list describes the general levels of coverage available, all of which should include public liability coverage. Many insurance companies and/or brokers offer competitive insurance packages especially designed to meet the needs of rental property owners, so remember to shop around. Consider these options:

>> **Basic coverage:** Most companies offer a basic coverage package that insures your investment property against loss from fire, lightning, explosion, windstorm or hail, smoke, aircraft or vehicles, riot or civil commotion, vandalism, sprinkler leakage and even volcanic action. Outside of major listed events, this style of cover often has exclusions for defined events. Insurance companies often have minimum policy premiums, so certain insurable items and acts aren't worth including because the potential for a claim is minimal and the costs are high.

>> **Mid-range coverage:** You get the basic package, plus protection against a list of other events, which may include losses relating to glass breakage, falling objects, weight of snow, flooding, water damage associated with plumbing problems and collapse from certain specific causes.

>> **Comprehensive coverage:** This cover is the broadest available and covers your property against most conceivable losses, except those specifically excluded from the policy. It offers the highest level of protection but is typically more expensive.

Insurance companies offer two types of cover:

>> **Indemnity value:** The coverage pays the cost of replacing property, less physical depreciation.

>> **Replacement value:** This coverage pays the cost of replacing the property without subtracting for physical depreciation. You may pay extra for replacement-cost coverage. We encourage you to purchase replacement-cost coverage.

TIP

As with homeowners' insurance policies, the location, age, type and quality of construction of your investment property are significant factors in determining your insurance premiums. Be sure to get an insurance estimate before you buy your property to avoid unpleasant surprises (older properties with wood shingles, located away from fire protection may not even be insurable, for example) and account for premium reductions (newer commercial buildings, and even some residential properties, are constructed with fire sprinklers and alarms that will reduce your insurance premiums, as will monitored intrusion alarms).

Some insurance companies have a co-insurance clause that requires rental property owners to carry a minimum amount of coverage. If you carry less than the minimum amount of coverage, the insurance company will impose a co-insurance penalty that reduces the payment on the loss by the same percentage of the insurance shortfall. For example, if you carry only $300,000 in coverage when you should have $600,000, you're carrying only 50 per cent of the minimum required insured value. If the building suffers a loss (of, say, $100,000), the insurance company might pay only 50 per cent of the loss (or $50,000).

WARNING

Some rental property owners first become investors by renting out their former personal residences when they buy new homes. They may not realise they should immediately contact their insurance agent and have their homeowner's policy changed for a more specific landlord's policy, which contains special coverage riders that aren't in the typical homeowner's policy. Obtaining proper landlord's coverage for your rental property is vital, or you could face the possibility of having your claim denied.

Some first-time investors of attached dwellings such as apartments, units and townhouses sometimes also fail to have their own contents insurance for their properties. They wrongly believe that the insurance provided by their body corporate or owner corporation is all that they need. While that insurance does cover the actual building and the majority of fittings and fixtures within each dwelling, additional contents insurance is required for such things as floor coverings, light fittings, curtains, air conditioning and public liability for inside the units.

Excess liability (umbrella) coverage

Excess liability (umbrella) coverage can be a cost-effective way to dramatically increase your liability protection and is designed to supplement your main or basic policies. An umbrella policy provides both additional and broader coverage beyond the limits of the basic commercial general liability insurance and other liability coverage, and this coverage is available only after the primary policy limits have been exhausted. Your primary policy may have liability limits of $1 million or $5 million, but an umbrella policy can provide additional $1 million increments. Umbrella coverage is designed to cover you for what might seem extremely rare circumstances. For example, if an accident on your property caused someone to lose his ability to work for the rest of his life, the claim may well be much higher than the standard cover allows. Paying an additional premium for umbrella coverage should stretch the policy to cover the full claim.

MOULD: THE HEIR-APPARENT TO ASBESTOS

Increasing legal actions suggests that moulds and fungus, as a long-term health issue for those exposed to potentially dangerous air particles, has the potential to become a significant legal issue in Australia (although mould and fungus are unlikely to be as big an issue as asbestos). You may wish to specifically enquire as to the exact protection included in your policy for mould.

The best way to avoid claims of property damage or personal injury from mould is to properly maintain your property and rent out the residential property or suite only when it's in good condition, and make sure you've got that agreed in writing. The challenge with most mould claims is that water intrusion and the subsequent concerns about mould typically occur within the tenant's space in areas where the owner has no access or control. Or the tenant can even be the cause of the source of moisture through negligence, poor ventilation or inadequate cleaning. The rental property owner must rely on the tenant to minimise the likelihood of mould, as well as to report any concerns immediately.

Additional insurance options

A variety of other insurance covers also make sense for most rental property owners, usually via landlord insurance policies:

TIP

>> **Loss-of-rent cover:** This insurance provides income if your property is severely damaged by fire or another calamity and allows you to continue making your mortgage and other payments.

>> **Workers' compensation insurance:** This cover pays employees (or contractors, potentially) and their medical expenses if they're injured or become ill as a result of their job. Workers' compensation laws differ from state to state; be sure to fully comply with them. This insurance coverage is often provided through government agencies, with private insurance companies offering backup cover. State and territory governments require businesses to have workers' compensation insurance for their employees. However, it's worth asking your insurance broker if taking out this cover is advisable. Don't take chances; if you're not properly covered, this insurance can often be added to your insurance policy for little cost.

>> **Flood, storm and earthquake insurance:** These are examples of coverage available for a separate cost. This coverage can be critical in the event of a natural disaster.

Determining the right excess

The excess is the amount of money that you must pay out-of-pocket before your insurance coverage kicks in, and is a form of self-insurance (covering the potential loss yourself). Typically, excesses for small rental property owners can be about $1,000 or more for each incident. That is, if you get flood damage in May and then a theft in June, you have to pay two excesses. The higher the excess, the lower your premium. As your financial ability to self-insure grows, evaluate the possibility of having a higher excess and using your savings to purchase other important coverage.

Selecting potential insurers

The coverage you can get as a rental property owner varies among insurers. As with any competitive product or service, conduct your research via an insurance comparison website, or speak with an insurance broker or two, to ensure that you receive the insurance cover you need at the best value. Keep in mind that the lowest premium is often not the best policy or value for your specific needs.

TIP

Be sure to select a qualified insurance broker or agent who understands your unique needs. The insurance professional or broker can then provide you with information on the kinds of coverage worth considering.

In addition to the price of a policy and the insurer's reputation and track record for paying claims, an insurer's financial health is an important consideration when you choose a company. Insurers can go belly up (as HIH did soon after the turn of the century in what was then Australia's biggest corporate collapse, where losses were estimated at around $5.3 billion). Having a cheap premium is pointless if the insurer won't be around to pay any claims.

TIP

After you've made your decision of which policies and insurers you want to do business with, be sure that the premium is paid and insist on written evidence that the insurance company has provided coverage.

Talking with tenants about contents insurance

Contents insurance is secured and paid for by your tenants and covers losses to the tenant's personal or business property as a result of fire, theft, water damage or other loss. As a rental property owner, you benefit from contents insurance because it covers any claims in the event that the tenant starts a fire or flood.

WARNING

Most commercial tenants have this coverage, but residential tenants often think they don't need contents insurance because they have few valuables, or they are covered under their landlord's insurance policies, when they are not. Contents insurance covers much more than just their personal possessions, because protection against liability claims made by injured guests or visitors is also often covered. The insurance also offers supplemental living expenses if the rental unit becomes uninhabitable due to fire or smoke damage. And it protects the tenant in the event that they cause damage to another's property. You can suggest that your tenants carry contents insurance but, because many renters choose not to, you'd have trouble keeping your properties occupied if you insisted that your tenants carry contents insurance.

Dealing with claims

Record all the facts as soon as an incident occurs on your rental property, particularly if it involves injury. Your property manager will be the first point of call for any incidents and should have set policies and procedures in the event of an incident at your rental property. Be sure to contact your insurance company or agent as soon as you have all the relevant information.

TIP

Because one of the primary issues in contention is often the property condition at the time of the incident, photos attached to the entry condition report will be invaluable at this time. Your property manager will have these on file.

Insuring Your Biggest Asset: You

Under-insurance in Australia is an enormous issue across the sphere of possible disasters, and nowhere is this shortcoming more obvious than in personal risk insurance. Incredibly, people think more about insuring their homes and their cars than their lives, health and incomes.

The four types of personal risk insurance (life/death, total and permanent disability, trauma and income protection) shouldn't be an afterthought for property investors. They're as important to making sure the endgame is achieved if something happens to you as any coverage you can put on your bricks and mortar investment.

What happens if you die five years into your property-investment program, leaving your spouse to look after the family and the multiple mortgages you've secured buying a few properties? If the aim of building your property portfolio was to secure your family's financial future, your untimely and unforeseen death may leave your spouse in a deep financial hole. Your spouse will not only be dealing with grief over having lost you, but may well also have to sell the very assets that were going to provide financial security in a decade or so.

How about if you were the sole breadwinner and you suffered a debilitating illness that stopped you from working for a year? Without income protection, the first thing to go could be your investment property.

Personal risk insurance can help to ensure that, if something goes wrong that has nothing to do with the investment itself, the bigger plan — building your family a secure financial future — isn't put in jeopardy.

Life (death) insurance

Life insurance pays out an agreed sum in the event of the insured's death. Arguably, everyone with dependants (a spouse or children) should consider life insurance to make sure no financial mess is left when you die, including that your funeral and final debts can be paid off.

If you're married, have a few young children and are the sole breadwinner, how is your partner going to bring your children up if you die? Sure, your spouse will probably get by, but often for a reasonable (and well worth it) cost, you can insure your life for many hundred thousand dollars — enough to pay off the mortgage and have some left over to invest to help put the children through school. Your family is already dealing with the grief of having lost you. Why turn that emotional grief into a financial nightmare?

The argument for life insurance is even more compelling for property investors. The reason for beginning a property-investment strategy is usually to create significant wealth for your family in 10 to 20 years' time. This strategy involves a long-term plan that necessitates taking on risk and a significant amount of debt.

Even if you buy only one investment property, you could have $500,000 to $700,000 of debt. If you're also paying off your own home, your total debt could be double that. What would happen if, in the first couple of years of your property-investment plan, you had bought three properties? And you've got children and a partner who's been out of the workforce for a few years to look after them? Having, for example, a $2 million life insurance policy would (in the event of your death) allow your spouse to potentially pay off the mortgages on the home and the investment properties, which would leave the rent from the properties as income to bring up the children.

So how much cover should you have? Every person's situation is different. The amount of cover you should consider depends on your personal situation. How much can you afford? How many assets do you currently have? How old are you? How many dependants do you have? How long until they're no longer financial dependants?

Two basic concepts are used by financial advisers (who we recommend you talk to in order to take out a complete personal risk insurance package) when thinking about life insurance. Bruce, a licensed financial adviser with significant experience in insurance, recommends the following as a guide to determining how much insurance you should consider taking:

>> **Ten to thirteen times earnings:** If you earn $80,000 a year, cover of $800,000 to $1,050,000 would cover most people's debts and leave a sum that could be invested to provide a future income for the family.

>> **Covering your debts:** Whatever your debts are, cover them. If you have $1.5 million worth of debts over your home and investment properties, take out enough cover to pay that debt out. If your home is paid out, you'll no longer have a mortgage. And if the investment property debt is paid out, your family will have the rental income coming in to help them cover their living expenses.

TIP

For most Australians, straight life insurance cover can be taken within their super funds, and we recommend doing this. You don't have to pay up-front for the insurance, as it's essentially paid for out of the Superannuation Guarantee contributions that most businesses must pay their employees. And the premiums are paid for with money that has had only a maximum of 15 per cent tax taken out. Life insurance premiums inside a super fund are also a tax deduction for the fund, while life insurance taken out in personal names doesn't qualify for a tax deduction.

REMEMBER

If you die and the life insurance is inside your super fund, the money is paid to your super fund. You need to have told your super fund who you want the proceeds of the fund to be paid to, preferably through a binding nomination, if your super fund offers that option. If the nomination is binding, the fund's trustees must pay it to your nominated beneficiary. If the nomination is non-binding, the trustees take your wishes into consideration, but they ultimately have the power to decide who the proceeds are paid to. (Trustees have been known to take the claims of others, such as estranged partners or children, into account when determining who to pay the funds to.)

Life insurance premiums are based on age, occupation, lifestyle choices and address (some states have lower life expectancies than others). The older the insured person is, the higher the premium, because the insured person has a statistically higher chance of dying. The same applies to factors such as occupation, hobbies and the state you live in. Also, pre-existing medical conditions that essentially lower your life expectancy can also have the impact of increasing the premium you must pay.

Those in their 20s and 30s can usually buy insurance extremely cheaply. Each year, as you age, the premiums become more expensive (or, with some policies, the premium stays the same, but the level of coverage drops). By the time most people turn 55 or 60, their assets and liabilities balance sheet has evolved to the point where they may no longer really need life insurance, or it has become too expensive. By this stage of their life, they may have grown their assets to a level they're comfortable with or have reduced their debts to manageable levels. (If they haven't reached a net wealth position with which they're comfortable, their other choices may include continuing to pay the higher premiums or reducing their level of life insurance cover.)

Total and permanent disability insurance

Total and permanent disability (TPD) insurance covers major accidents and ill-nesses through the payment of a lump sum (similar to life insurance). A TPD event can be an accident that causes the loss of limbs or eyesight, a combination of these, or an illness that permanently prevents you from working (usually paid after incapacity for a period longer than six months).

TPD insurance is usually bought as a rider to life insurance. If you were to buy, say, $1 million of life insurance, you may insure yourself for the same amount of TPD insurance, roughly doubling the cost of life insurance. The price of premiums for these do vary widely depending on your age and lifestyle, as well as other factors.

The lump sum payment is designed to help you make required lifestyle changes. If you've had a TPD injury or illness, you may want to have your home mortgage paid out because you'll no longer have your former income. If you're a property investor, you may also want all, or a portion, of your investment debt wiped out so that you can derive a positive income from your properties and not be forced to sell them.

TPD events covered under each insurer's list vary widely. Make sure you read the product disclosure statement (PDS) that covers the policy you're considering, to find out what TPD events are covered and what aren't. Financial advisers can be very useful here, because most have access to software programs that rate the policies of all the major life insurers.

TPD insurance, like life insurance, is a tax deduction when the policy owner is a super fund. The policy isn't a tax deduction when paid for by an individual. A TPD payout inside a super fund also relies on the trustees of the fund agreeing to pay out to the individual. This condition is a formality in most cases, but is a small risk of having the policy inside your super fund, compared with holding the policy in your own name. In most cases, if the TPD payout is going to be paid out of the super fund, the payment incurs tax, which you should take into consideration when determining your level of cover. Again, a financial adviser with insurance experience can be invaluable here.

Trauma insurance

Trauma insurance was devised only in the early 1980s by South African doctors, when it became apparent that modern medicine was allowing many people to survive traumatic illnesses that used to be a death sentence. The most common of these are heart attacks, cancers and strokes.

Although patients may survive, they can be left with monstrous medical bills for the treatment (or ongoing treatment for expensive medicines that aren't covered by the Pharmaceutical Benefits Scheme) and may need to make some adjustments to their home or lifestyle. Such a patient may be off work for several months (or longer) recuperating. The level of cover required again varies with every investor's circumstances. Most commonly, a trauma insurance package of $250,000 or $400,000 would cover the majority of your needs, but many investors may wish to have $1 million or more to cover substantial debts.

Trauma insurance (like TPD insurance, described in the previous section) is another product that requires proper reading of a product disclosure statement or advice from a financial adviser. Some policies are very, very basic, while others cover a wider range of illnesses.

Trauma insurance isn't tax-deductible, whether the policy is held by an individual or a super fund, making it a more expensive form of insurance.

Income-protection insurance

Take a second to think about this question: What is your biggest financial asset? If you just answered your home, your car or your share or managed-fund investment portfolio, in most cases you're going to be very wrong. For most people under the age of 50 (possibly even 55), the biggest asset you have is your ability to work. If you're 35 years old and earning $100,000 a year, then you're likely to earn $2.5 million in today's money (not including any cost-of-living or general pay increases you may receive) by the time you turn 60.

Income from wages and salaries, and how that funds your investment strategy, is fundamental to any wealth you create over your lifetime. Most people spend $1,000 a year to insure a $30,000 car (which consistently falls in value), but have never considered spending the same amount to insure their $100,000 or $150,000 incomes.

Income-protection insurance generally allows the insured to cover 75 per cent of their salary for defined periods — usually two or five years, or until age 60 or 65 — and can be paid monthly, half-yearly or yearly. If you're on a salary of $80,000 a year, you'd insure for a benefit of $5,000 a month ($80,000 × 75 per cent × 1/12). Income-protection insurance can only be taken out to cover income earned from 'personal exertion'. It can't be taken to cover rental income or dividends because these will continue to be paid regardless of your ability to work.

Income-protection insurance is also the most flexible of the personal risk insurance policies, but arguably the most important for property investors. The longer you're prepared to wait for the benefit to cut in (the waiting period), the smaller your premiums will be. Waiting periods are usually 14, 30, 60, 90 or 180 days, or one or two years. If you nominate that you're prepared to wait 90 days before your $5,000 monthly benefit cuts in, you'll have a significantly lower premium than if you chose a 14- or 30-day waiting period. When considering how long you can or should wait before receiving a benefit, take into account how much sick leave, holidays, long-service leave and other paid leave you can take from your current employer, as well as whether you're the sort of person who has ready access to cash, through savings or a share portfolio that could readily be sold down.

In the majority of cases, money earned from a regular job will be the main source of income until retirement, even for a property investor. Property investors often rely on the base income from their full-time employment to gain tax deductions that make the property a worthwhile investment to hold.

For example, if you're on an income of $100,000 and are no longer able to work, the loss of you income would be bad enough. But if you had two investment properties that were negatively geared to the tune of $20,000 a year (see Chapter 15 for an explanation of gearing strategies), the loss of income could be disastrous. The $20,000 is a cost you can wear when you have an income of $100,000 a year. If an accident or illness saw your income fall to zero (or to the level of a government disability pension), that $20,000 of annual losses would no longer be affordable. Unless you had significant and easily retrievable savings, both properties would probably have to be sold if you were going to be off work for many months or years.

If your $100,000 income was fully insured, you would begin to receive a monthly income payment of $6,250 ($100,000 × 75% × 1/12), or the equivalent of $75,000 a year at the end of your waiting period. While you'd still have lost a sizeable portion of your overall salary, you may be able to hold on to your two properties, or may need to sell only one, if the illness or injury was to keep you out of work for many years.

TIP

Income-protection insurance is arguably more important for the self-employed than it is for salaried employees. If you're self-employed and you can't work, you're unlikely to be able to afford to pay yourself sick pay, holiday leave or long-service leave for extended periods, which can be used by regular employees for shorter term illnesses.

REMEMBER

Income-protection insurance is generally a tax deduction when purchased inside a superannuation fund or when held personally. The tax deduction is at the marginal tax rate (of the person or the super fund). Because super funds get a maximum tax deduction of 15 per cent, paying for income-protection insurance in your own name, if your marginal tax rate is higher than your super fund account, is usually wiser.

WARNING

The quality of income-protection policies varies widely — inside and outside of superannuation funds. Seek professional advice from a licensed financial adviser on the suitability of the policy for your personal circumstances.

IN THIS CHAPTER

» **Mastering the tax advantages of real estate investing**

» **Handling interest**

» **Getting into gearing**

» **Assessing capital gains tax**

» **Transforming your home into an investment**

» **Looking into exit strategies**

Chapter **15**

Tax Considerations and Exit Strategies

R eal estate is a great investment that offers you the opportunity to leverage a small cash investment to own and control large holdings that can generate cash flow and appreciate significantly over time. But cash flow, leverage and appreciation don't operate on their own. Using real estate tax laws has always been an imperative for real estate investors to get the full financial benefits available.

TIP

Applying tax strategies properly allows rental property investors to potentially reduce income tax and manage capital gains tax. Success in real estate, like all investments, is determined by how much money you keep on an after-tax basis. Real estate offers the potential to minimise tax, so real estate investors need a thorough understanding of the best techniques to optimise their financial positions; however, don't consider tax minimisation to be a wealth creation tool — because it isn't. Rather, the ability to reduce tax via negative gearing is usually temporary, with more investors expecting to be neutral or positively geared within 5 to 10 years of investment property ownership.

REMEMBER

While we discuss tax advantages in this chapter, don't let tax considerations be the primary driver of your decisions. Purchasing real estate should first be a sound investment decision. Only when a deal makes investment sense (both at the time of purchase and after sale) should you consider the tax aspects. Also, real estate taxation is a constantly changing, complicated area. Although this chapter covers the key concepts, it isn't a substitute for professional tax advice. All real estate investors need a competent accountant (who knows real estate and preferably has additional training such as being a QPIA) on their investment team. Meet with your tax advisers regularly, rather than only before the end of the financial year.

Because the subject is so entwined in tax considerations, we also cover real estate sales in this chapter — also known as *exit strategies*. The tax implications of various exit strategies are important to understand so you can potentially minimise the tax consequences of selling real estate holdings.

Understanding the Tax Angles

The tax laws regarding investment real estate are far more complex than those regarding home ownership. For example, homeowners can't deduct their interest costs or the repairs and maintenance costs of their home from their income earned — but, as the owner of a rental property, you can deduct such costs. Also, the benefits of depreciation apply only to rental real estate and aren't available for the home you live in.

TIP

Tax laws change frequently, so check with your tax adviser before taking any action. Use a licensed tax agent to prepare your tax returns if you have investment property. In the sections that follow, we discuss some important rental real estate tax concepts that you should understand if you want to make the most of your property investments.

Property taxes

With property investment, investors need to know specifically about two types of income:

>> **Ordinary income:** This includes salaries, bonuses and commissions, rents and interest, and is taxed at up to 45 per cent. Net rent receipts (that is, after deductible expenses) are subject to tax as ordinary income.

>> **Capital gains:** These are generated when investments (such as real estate and shares) are sold for a profit. The income you realise upon the sale of your investment property is subject to tax as a capital gain. Although capital gains tax laws have changed considerably since their introduction in the mid-1980s (see 'Capital Gains Tax', later in this chapter), capital gains are classified in two ways at the time of writing:

  • **Short-term:** For property held for 12 months or less, capital gains are taxed at the same rate as ordinary income, at your marginal tax rate (MTR).

  • **Long-term:** For property held for longer than 12 months, only half of the gain is taxed, still at your MTR, meaning an effective maximum tax of 22.5 per cent (not including the Medicare Levy).

But you can't pay tax until you figure out exactly what part of your income will be taxed. Again, we recommend that you have a qualified accountant do your tax (refer to Chapter 4). But we do show you here how to perform your own cash-flow analysis. The cash flow from a property — positive or negative — is determined by deducting all operating expenses, mortgage interest, capital-improvement expenses, damages and depreciation from rental income and then against your own ordinary income (see 'Negative gearing', later in this chapter).

Calculating the cash flow of a property follows the format shown in Table 15-1. Here, we provide a quick summary, based on a single residential investment property rented at $600 a week for an owner whose ordinary taxable income is $100,000 a year. The same principles apply for blocks of flats, commercial properties and whole property portfolios. Of course, property managers will provide you with a statement at the end of each financial year that lists all rental income and expenses, including their fee.

If you wish to run the numbers yourself, here is a way to do so:

1. **Start with the actual rental income collected for the property.**

   Make sure you take account of vacancy periods.

2. **Add any other income not affected by occupancy to establish the gross income.**

   The income from the rental of a mobile phone tower on the roof is an example of this kind of income.

3. **Subtract the operating expenses (general repairs and maintenance) from the gross income to calculate the net income.**

4. **Subtract the interest paid on the mortgage from the net income to arrive at the before-tax cash flow.**

5. **Subtract the building capital allowance from the before-tax cash flow. Then subtract depreciation on the depreciable fixtures and fittings. The result is the taxable income or loss from the property.**

The building capital allowance is a non-cash accounting deduction that reduces your tax liability without requiring actual expenditure. Depreciable fixtures and fitting may include carpets, curtains, blinds, ovens and light fittings, depending on a number of factors including the year you purchased the investment property. Engaging a professional quantity surveyor is vital to determine any depreciation deductions for each investment property.

6. **Add your taxable income to (or subtract your loss from) your annual salary to determine the new income on which you'll be taxed at your ordinary marginal tax rate (MTR).**

For most pay-as-you-go (PAYG) employees, the difference in tax paid will be refunded through their tax return.

Note: References in this chapter to income tax rates, or marginal tax rates (MTR), include the 2 per cent Medicare levy that's payable in Australia on most incomes, when applicable. Although the levy is treated as a separate impost by the Australian Taxation Office (ATO), the vast majority of property investors have to pay this as a tax on their investment earnings (and, indeed, claim back as a tax deduction if negatively geared).

TABLE 15-1   ## Calculating Net Taxable Income

Actual rental income	**$31,200**
Plus other income	Nil
Gross income	**$31,200**
Minus operating expenses	($6,496)
Net income	**$24,707**
Minus annual mortgage interest	($25,000)
Before-tax cash flow	**–$293**
Minus building depreciation	($4,500)
Minus depreciable fixtures and fittings	($1,500)
Net tax loss from the property	**($6,293)**
Owner's ordinary income	$100,000
Net taxable income	$93,717

The property in the example shown in Table 15-1 is moderately negatively geared, which will lead to a reasonable impact on this investor's net tax position. Using the 2022–23 tax rates, the reduction of $6,293 in net taxable income for an investor earning $100,000 has the effect of reducing the income tax she's required to pay for the year by $2045, which is the loss ($6,293) multiplied by the investor's marginal tax rate (32.5 per cent, not including the Medicare Levy).

Depreciation as de facto income

Depreciation is the write-off of the cost of an asset over its estimated useful economic life, which allows you to claim a deduction for certain non-cash 'expenses' in regard to a rental property because the parts of the assets associated with the investment 'wear out' over time. The write-off allows you to claim a portion of the falling value of the asset against your other income.

Depreciation is an expense, but it doesn't actually take cash out of your bank account. Instead, you treat the depreciation amount as an expense when working out your total income from the property (and, essentially, your total income from all other sources), decreasing your taxable income and, therefore, the tax on the income from the property.

Essentially, three types of assets are 'depreciated' (for building costs and capital works it's technically termed an *allowance*) in relation to investment properties: building cost (construction cost), capital works, and fixtures and fittings. The rules differ slightly between residential properties and commercial properties, and we touch on those differences here.

TECHNICAL STUFF

The Australian Taxation Office sets out in its 'Rental Properties' guide, published most years, the current depreciation allowances for residential investment properties. The guide lists many depreciable items and you'll find most household items on the list. You can find this list by searching for 'rental properties' on the ATO's website (www.ato.gov.au).

REMEMBER

Land is not a depreciable asset. The reasoning is that, even if a house is demolished or destroyed (or blown over by the wolf chasing the three little pigs), the value of the land itself won't be affected. This principle leads to an important axiom to keep in mind throughout your property investing career: land appreciates; buildings depreciate.

The tax basis for depreciation is that, from the time an item is bought, that item loses its value through wear and tear. Depreciation takes into account the falling value of an asset by allowing most investors to slowly reclaim a portion of the costs associated with the capital that will eventually be needed to replace the item. Some items lose value faster than others. Although an actual residential building is deemed to have a lifespan of 40 years (see 'Building cost depreciation', following) for the purposes of the capital works allowance, carpets are written down over 10 years, ceiling fans over 5 years and electric hot water systems over 12 years. Changes to legislation in relation to depreciation happen quite regularly, which is why working with experts or researching the current capital works allowances via the ATO is important.

Building cost depreciation

Over time, buildings suffer from wear and tear. Although the oldest buildings in any city often rank as the most beautiful, keeping them that way involves considerable maintenance costs. If a house doesn't receive proper maintenance, it will slowly fall into disrepair. Depreciation allows a property owner to claim back on tax a portion of the cost of the item. (Getting back a portion of its replacement cost is another way of looking at it.)

Two important dates impinge on building cost depreciation when it comes to residential real estate. Where construction of a building commenced before 18 July 1985, no claim for depreciation is allowed for the cost of the bricks and mortar. The other important date is 15 September 1987, after which the original construction cost of the building can be depreciated at 2.5 per cent a year for the first 40 years of the building's life (after which time, for tax purposes, the building is essentially considered worthless). However, depreciation can still be available for costs associated with buildings that are older than this date — for example, due to structural or cosmetic renovations that have taken place.

TECHNICAL STUFF

Between those two dates — about two years and two months — is a period when properties could be depreciated at a higher rate. If construction commenced on a property between 18 July 1985 and 15 September 1987, that property was depreciated at 4 per cent a year over 25 years. Therefore, the depreciation on those properties ran out in about 2013 — allowing for about a year for completion of the building works if construction commenced just before or on 15 September 1987.

WARNING

Investors can use the construction-cost depreciation to defer and reduce, but not eliminate, tax. Annual depreciation for properties acquired, or structural improvements made, after 13 May 1997, actually reduces the *cost basis* (calculated as the original cost of the property plus certain other purchase costs and capital improvements) of the rental property. This deduction is partially *recaptured* (added to your taxable profit) and taxed upon sale. However, it's still likely to be a tax saving, because you get the depreciation at your current marginal tax rate (up to 45 per cent) but, when you sell and the tax is 'recaptured', you pay at CGT rates, paying tax only on half your gain (meaning an effective maximum tax rate of 22.5 per cent, not including the Medicare Levy). Depreciation lowers your income tax in the current year by essentially providing a government interest-free loan until the property is sold. Of course, this can improve your cash flow throughout the investment property ownership period — but always remember that depreciation is not 'free money'.

TIP

Because depreciation is allowed only for the value of the buildings and other improvements, the amount of your depreciation deduction depends on the highest portion of the overall property value being attributable to the buildings. Therefore, it's advantageous to allocate the highest fair market value of your property value to the improvements to increase your potential deductions. But don't overstate the value. Getting a professional quantity surveyor to do the estimates is always advisable (refer to Chapter 4 for information on valuers and other investment team members). The Tax Office will be suspicious (and may 'red flag' you for an audit) if they consider construction-cost depreciation numbers to be too high. The ATO recognises professionally prepared depreciation schedules as just that — undertaken by professionals.

Building-depreciation deductions for both the year of acquisition and the year of sale are for the actual number of days held. That is, if the property was bought on 10 May, depreciation will be for the rest of May and June, or 52 days. If sold on 10 May, it will be for the 314 days of the year already passed. Therefore, if the annual deduction is $2,000, the buyer would get 52/365 of the $2,000 deduction, or $284.93.

TIP

Investors are strongly advised to pay to get an expert to compile a 'depreciation schedule' (many accounting firms or quantity surveyors will visit the property and create a cost-estimate schedule for around $1000 to $1500 for a residential property). A property-depreciation schedule contains estimates of the cost of the building, plus other depreciable items, in a form that allows your accountant to account for it quite simply.

Capital works

Capital works are those major construction items that may or may not form part of the house itself, but for which the ATO will allow a deduction only at the same rate as for bricks and mortar. These works include things such as the driveway, a built-in barbeque, shutters, skylights, water tanks and awnings. These items must be depreciated over 40 years at 2.5 per cent a year.

REMEMBER

Commercial property owners typically modify vacant spaces to get potential tenants to sign a lease. The ATO requires that the cost of those improvements be depreciated over 40 years, even if the lease and the actual useful life of the improvements are much shorter. If the tenant moves out before 40 years are up (which most will), the good news is that you can depreciate the full remaining portion of the improvements that are torn out as a result of the tenant vacating.

Fixtures and fittings

A house without fittings is barely a house at all. Finding tenants for a residential investment property without floor coverings (or polished boards), light fittings, a bath or shower and a stove would be difficult. These items can also be depreciated, depending on when you purchased the property.

In general terms, the ATO's allowances for depreciation of these items are roughly in line with a reasonable lifespan for the item itself. Carpets, for example, can be depreciated over ten years — 10 per cent of the cost of the carpet can be depreciated each year.

The full list of depreciable items and their rates is also available from the Australian Taxation Office website (go to www.ato.gov.au and search for 'rental properties').

Low-value pool

Assets bought for an investment property at relatively low cost can be allocated to the 'low-value pool', for which special depreciation rates apply. The items must be less than $1,000 in value (items up to $300 can be fully claimed as an expense in the current year). Any items placed in the low-value pool must remain there.

TECHNICAL STUFF

Items already in the low-value pool from previous years at the start of a year are depreciated at 37.5 per cent a year at a diminishing rate. Therefore, if five items valued at $2,000 were included for the year, the depreciation of those items for that year would be $750 ($2,000 × 37.5%). Those items would then start the following year valued at $1,250 ($2,000 − $750).

Items that are added to the pool for the first time during the year are depreciated at 18.75 per cent. If three items worth a total of $1,000 were added to the low-value pool during the year, a depreciation deduction of $187.50 ($1,000 × 18.75%) would be allowed. These items would start the following year valued at $812.50.

Combining these examples shows that an existing pool worth $2,000, with $1,000 worth of low-cost goods added during the year, would have a first-year deduction of $937.50 ($750 + $187.50). The entire pool would start the following year valued at $2,062.50 ($1,250 + $812.50).

REMEMBER

What sort of items may go into a low-cost pool? Examples include television sets, portable gas heaters and small items of furniture. Each item must be worth less than $1,000.

Recollection after sale

Although depreciation may feel like free money being handed back from the Tax Office, be sure to note these few important points.

When it comes to fixtures and fittings and the low-value pool, you're dealing with items that will need replacement at some stage. Carpets and electrical appliances don't last forever. The money you claim back via depreciation is an acceptance of the need to update or replace these items. You can look at the scenario in one of two ways — you're either getting back a portion of what you've already paid for the goods, or you're receiving a partial pre-payment to help with the cost of replacing the item later.

However, when it comes to building and capital works, if the asset was acquired or the cost incurred after 13 May 1997, a partial recollection of what you've claimed as depreciation will be applied if you ever sell the asset. This recollection occurs through a reduction in the 'cost base' of the property.

TECHNICAL STUFF

Here's an example of how the cost base of the property may be reduced: If you bought a property ten years ago for $400,000 and the cost of the building was $200,000, you may have claimed $50,000 in depreciation over that 10 years ($200,000 × 2.5% × 10 years). You've now sold the property for $600,000 — a $200,000 profit. However, as depreciation has been claimed on the building, the property now has a reduced cost base of $150,000, meaning that the profit, as far as capital gains tax is concerned, is $250,000. You may ask, 'Isn't this just a case of paying back the tax you claimed earlier?' The answer is, 'No, not necessarily.' First, the value of that tax deduction of $50,000 over the years was claimed at your MTR against your personal income. But, when paying CGT on the extra $50,000, you pay it only on half the gain, or $25,000. That would increase the CGT you have to pay by between $8,125 (at 32.5 per cent MTR) and $11,250 (at 45 per cent MTR), which would still be a reduction on the tax you claimed as a deduction earlier.

REMEMBER

If you never sell, you'll never have to repay that portion of the tax. If you sell the property while in retirement, the CGT payable will likely be reduced due to your lower annual income.

The Biggest Expense of All — Interest

Of all the costs associated with real estate investment, the biggest one for the majority is going to be the cost of servicing the mortgage. Unless you bought with cash or have owned the property long enough to have paid the mortgage off, you'll have an interest expense. And, in the first few years of holding a property, that cost is likely to be significant.

The ATO allows deductions for the interest expense associated with holding an income-producing asset. If you have an interest-only loan on your property, the full cost of servicing your loan is likely to be a tax deduction. The repayment of capital, however, is not a tax deduction. If you have a principal and interest loan, you can claim only the interest portion of the repayments.

No restrictions exist at the time of writing on how much interest you can claim against your income (as long as the rent is considered to be on a commercial, or market, basis), if the expense relates directly to an income-producing investment.

Gearing Strategies and Tax

Australians normally associate the term 'gearing' with its buddy, 'negative'. Negative gearing is a popular tax strategy in this country — and indeed in many places around the world — but, for many, the term has connotations of tax avoidance (which it most certainly isn't). With investment, gearing is another term for borrowing. Investment in property usually requires some borrowings, at least in the early years of ownership. Three types of gearing strategy exist — negative, positive and neutral. Different investors will feel comfortable with different types.

Negative gearing

When the costs of holding an asset exceed the income the asset earns, an asset is said to be *negatively geared*. When a person has holding costs higher than the income being generated, the investor is losing money on a cash basis.

For example, say an investor paid $625,000 for a property two years ago and rented it out at $500 a week ($26,000 a year on full tenancy). She took a loan of $500,000 for the purchase and, with an interest rate of 4.3 per cent, pays nearly $21,500 a year in interest. Further costs of nearly $8,000 a year are incurred (for council rates, insurance, agent's fees, maintenance costs and so on). The total annual cost of holding the property is approximately $29,500, but the income from the property is $26,000. This investment is negatively geared to the tune of $3,500.

Why would this investor hold a property that's losing her money on an ongoing annual basis? Several, potentially intertwining, reasons can make sense. One reason is that she can claim the losses as a tax deduction against her other income, which reduces the cost by her marginal tax rate (that is, up to 45 per cent plus the Medicare Levy). A second reason is that, over time, the rent will rise, hopefully enough to make up for the other costs and eventually even create a positive income.

The third reason is the most important. And that is that the property should increase in value by more than the ongoing cash losses of the property over time. If the property is costing a net (after tax) total of $3,500 a year to hold over a four-year period (a total of $14,000) but increases in value by $120,000 over that four-year period, then the investor is well ahead.

REMEMBER

While it is true that those with higher incomes get the most benefit, negative gearing isn't a tool for the wealthy, because the vast majority of investors own just one property (71 per cent) or two (90 per cent). That is, about 90 per cent of investors own only one or two investment properties. Negative gearing is always a hot political topic in Australia. But an individual's opportunity to use negative gearing as a tax strategy is, at the time of writing, maintained.

Positive gearing

The opposite of negative gearing — to state the bleeding obvious — is *positive gearing*, when the income (rent) from a property exceeds the costs associated with holding it. If an investor owns a property commanding rent of $500 a week ($26,000 a year) and the overall costs are only $15,000, then the investor is making $11,000 a year as income from the property.

Positively geared properties can result from a number of circumstances:

> **The income from the property is high.** Higher rents can occur over time or because the property has been made more attractive to tenants.

> **The holding costs on the property are low.** An investor who has held a property for many years may have paid down the loan to the point where interest repayments are quite low.

> **Interest rates have fallen.** A decrease in mortgage rates can occur when the Reserve Bank cuts interest rates aggressively.

The aim of most property investors is to eventually get a 'passive' income stream from their investment properties. They may not mind having big tax deductions from negatively geared property while they're working and earning a good income. But most investors plan for the rent from the property to become an income stream in retirement.

Neutral gearing

In Australia, a property that is exactly neutrally geared is unlikely to exist often — if one did exist, it would be either a fluke or the result of highly engineered accounting. But, in a broad sense, any property where the income is roughly equal to the holding costs can be considered *neutrally geared*. In the case of residential investment property, that would probably be when the after-tax cost of holding the property is within about $2,000 of costing nothing.

Little or no tax is paid on neutrally geared properties. The aim, of course, is for neutrally geared properties to turn into positively geared properties within a few years, usually as a result of rising rents.

Capital Gains Tax

Capital gains tax (CGT) has been in existence in Australia only since 1985. CGT is the tax paid when investments are disposed of for a profit. The most important phrase to read there is 'disposed of'. Many real estate investors never, ever pay CGT because they never sell their properties — although they are generally sold at some point in the future by one of their beneficiaries. Although CGT is not payable on everything — the family home has a general exemption from CGT — it is payable on investment property.

CGT has undergone some major changes since its introduction. The most significant overhaul was in 1999, when the federal government removed cost-base indexation of CGT assets and also introduced the 50 per cent capital gains discount for assets held for longer than 12 months.

Pre-CGT assets

Assets bought prior to 11.45 am on 19 September 1985 are exempt from capital gains tax. No tax will be paid on the profit regardless of when the asset is sold or what the gain is. Most pre-CGT assets would now be earning considerable income, so, although they'll never be taxed on their capital gains, they'll probably incur an increasing amount of tax on the income the investment is spinning off.

Post-CGT assets

Any investment bought after 11.45 am on 19 September 1985 is a CGT asset. And any investment property bought now will be a CGT asset. But the rules have been tinkered with a few times since their introduction, creating several classes of CGT assets in regards to investment property.

Properties bought between 19 September 1985 and 21 September 1999

Investors who bought their properties during this period have two options for working out their capital gain. The first option is indexation, which is becoming increasingly unattractive because indexation was frozen on 30 September 1999. Under the indexation method, an asset's cost base was increased by inflation from the time the asset was bought to the time it was sold.

The second option for working out the capital gain is to simply reduce the profit by 50 per cent, add that to your taxable income and then pay the MTR on that amount. Take the sale price and subtract the cost base. If you ignore depreciation and purchase and sale costs, a property with a cost base of $150,000 that was sold for $400,000 will have a taxable capital gain of $125,000 (half of $250,000).

The ATO allows investors who bought assets in this period to choose either indexation or the 50 per cent profit-reduction method. However, the indexation method would rarely be the best choice for investors nowadays.

Properties bought on or after 21 September 1999

Properties bought after 21 September 1999 that are held for longer than 12 months qualify for a 50 per cent reduction in the profit on which CGT is paid. If an asset is not held for 12 months, the profit is simply considered income and marginal tax rates apply on the full amount of the gain. With these assets, the profit is determined to be the sale price less the cost base of the asset. The cost base can be affected by the depreciation (refer to 'Depreciation as de facto income', earlier in this chapter).

TECHNICAL STUFF

An asset bought for $250,000 in 2002 and sold for $500,000 in 2012 had a profit of $250,000. If the investor applied $20,000 of depreciation because the asset was built in 1998 (refer to 'Building cost depreciation', earlier this chapter), then the reduced cost base would be $230,000. The investor's gain would be $270,000. As the asset was held for longer than 12 months, tax would be paid on $135,000 (half of the $270,000 gain).

The home exemption

One of the main exemptions for CGT is your own home — which is one of the reasons your home is not an investment property (and why we separate them as assets in this book).

As long as the home is owned by an individual and is that individual's main residence for the period of ownership, a general exemption from CGT applies. Even if the home was bought for $10,000 and is now sold for $2 million, the whole profit will be non-taxable if the ATO accepts that the property was the principal place of residence.

A few exceptions to the home exemption exist. First, if a house passes through an estate to an individual (say, a parent's family home passing to a child), the individual has two years from the deceased's date of death to sell the property CGT-free. If the property is not sold within two years of death, the recipient will get a new cost base of the asset's value at the time of the deceased's death. A profit made above that cost base will incur CGT. (However, if the beneficiary were to make the property the principal place of residence, the home could continue to be a CGT-free asset.)

A portion of the profit from the sale of a home could be taxed in some circumstances. These circumstances include if the individual has ever rented the house out during the period of ownership (see the next section) or if deductions for the cost of the home have been claimed (for example, if the owner claimed expenses associated with running a business from the premises).

Turning Your Home into an Investment Property

You've lived in your home for five or ten years, but the time has come to move to something bigger or just out of the city and into a place with a yard for the kids. You don't want to give up your home and you think it would be the perfect rental — after all, you've turned the place into something special. Turning your home into an investment property is possible, but requires some extra consideration from a tax perspective to ensure you avoid the pitfalls.

Tax-deductibility

When a property switches from being a home to an investment property, a whole raft of items that weren't tax-deductible or depreciable now may be.

Recouping for all those makeovers

If you spent $20,000 doing up your kitchen, another $30,000 fixing the bathroom and $15,000 putting bookcases, cupboards and an office in last year, that expenditure may well now become a tax deduction or form part of a depreciation allowance — but expert advice is required here.

TIP

Keep records of everything you do to your home while you're living there, if you ever intend to turn it into a rental. Those receipts could be very valuable one day. If you haven't kept records, you can get a similar outcome by paying an expert to complete a full depreciation schedule.

However, from 1 July 2017, there are new rules for deductions for decline in value of certain second-hand depreciating assets in your residential rental property.

According to the ATO, if you use these assets to produce rental income from your residential rental property, you cannot claim a deduction for their decline in value unless you are using the property in carrying on a business (including a business of letting rental properties), or you are an excluded entity.

Second-hand depreciating assets are depreciating assets previously installed ready for use or used:

>> by another entity (except as trading stock)

>> in your private residence

>> for a non-taxable purpose, unless that use was occasional (for example, staying at the property for one evening while carrying out maintenance activities would be considered an occasional use).

This change generally applies to the depreciating assets that you:

>> entered into a contract to acquire, or otherwise acquired, at or after 7.30 pm on 9 May 2017, or

>> used or had installed ready for use for any private purpose in 2016–17 or earlier income years, for which you were not entitled to a deduction for a decline in value in 2016–17 (for example, depreciating assets in a property that was your home in 2016–17 that you turned into your residential rental property in 2017–18).

Changing the terms of your home loan

Renegotiating the terms of your home loan usually makes sense. For a start, if you take out a loan for your new home, you'll certainly be better off turning your old home loan into interest-only and using any excess cash to pay down the non-deductible debt on your new home loan.

WARNING

Be very careful when renegotiating the terms of your home loan if you're going to turn it into an investment property. The ATO won't allow you to pull large sums of equity out of your home to maximise the tax deductions when you convert it to a rental (potentially to reduce the loan on your new home). If you've repaid large slabs of your home loan early, the loan, for tax-deductibility purposes, will be the lowest point that the loan reached. If you have a home worth $900,000 with a loan of $550,000, the ATO won't let you withdraw $200,000 of the equity to maximise the borrowings on your old home and minimise the loan on your new home.

TIP

Plan ahead if you want to turn your home into an investment property within the next year or two. A few legal tax moves may be available to increase the tax-deductibility of your current home when you move out and decrease the home loan on the house you're intending to move into. First, stop paying any extra capital off your current home loan (and don't put spare cash into the redraw account — refer to Chapter 7 for details on banking products). If you have extra money you'd like to have working against your loan, put it into an offset account. You could even consider going interest-only on your home loan, if your bank will allow you to, and putting the principal you'd then save into an offset account.

From the ATO's perspective, redraw and offset accounts are specifically different. Money placed into a redraw account is considered early repayment of capital. If you try to withdraw it, you may not regain the tax-deductibility on the withdrawn sum. However, savings sitting in an offset account is not repayment of capital and can be taken with you to help pay down the non-deductible debt on the new home.

WARNING

Do you really want to turn your home into a rental property? If you've spent five to ten years doing your place up, you may well have spent a fortune getting everything right. Tenants, even the really good ones, tend not to treat a rental residence as they would their own home. Would finding damage to the house from careless tenants cause you heartache?

Home CGT liabilities

The first major impact of turning your home into an investment property is that it will lose its blanket CGT-exempt status. You won't have to pay CGT on all gains the property has made, but, effectively, the amount of CGT you'll pay when the property is sold in the future will be proportional to the amount of time the house spent as a primary residence, versus the time spent as an investment property.

That is, if you held a property for ten years and had it rented out for three of those years, you may pay a proportionate amount of CGT — in this case, 30 per cent of the gain would be considered taxable. (The taxable portion is actually worked out through the number of days the property was held.) If the property made a $200,000 profit over that ten-year period, $140,000 may be exempt and $60,000 may be considered a taxable capital gain.

The six-year rule

According to the Tax Office, a property stops being your main residence when you stop living in it. However, for CGT purposes, you can continue treating a property as your main residence in the following situations:

>> **For up to 6 years** if it's used to produce income, such as rent (sometimes called the *6-year rule*)

>> **Indefinitely** if it is not used to produce income

During the time that you treat the property as your main residence after you stop living in it:

>> It continues to be exempt from CGT (the same as if you were still living in it, even if you start renting it out after you leave).

>> You can't treat any other property as your main residence (except for up to six months if you are moving house).

The six-year rule may apply, for example, if you move interstate and rent a property there, while renting out the home you own.

Foreign and temporary residents

Foreign and temporary residents are subject to CGT only on taxable Australian property, such as real estate in Australia and assets used to carry on a business in Australia, according to the Tax Office.

The 50 per cent CGT discount is generally not available to foreign and temporary residents for assets acquired after 8 May 2012. Foreign residents are not entitled to the main residence exemption, unless they satisfy the requirements of the life events test.

If you become an Australian resident, or stop being one, the assets on which you pay CGT in Australia will change. Assets you acquired before CGT started on 20 September 1985 are not subject to CGT.

REMEMBER

Seeking advice from a qualified tax accountant is vital when checking how your residency status may impact your current and future property taxes.

Holiday homes

Wouldn't it be lovely to have a second home by the beach, or in the mountains, that was yours to use when you wanted to, but that was also a tax deduction? The Tax Office regularly raises concern over the tax-deductibility of holiday homes, making it a potential trap for the novice property investor. Refer to Chapter 2 for a general discussion of holiday homes and Chapter 10 for more detail.

The important thing to remember when it comes to claiming tax deductions for what is essentially a holiday home is 'proportionality' — you can claim expenses for the house only for the proportion of the year for which it's honestly available for rent. If you use the home personally for half the year, then you're likely to be able to claim only half of some of the expenses. However, traps exist here also. If you use the home for the half of the year that's peak season, the ATO may not let you claim 50 per cent of the deductions — they may only let you claim a lesser portion.

WARNING

A trap for any wannabe tax dodgers is weekend use of a holiday home. You can't use the house on weekends, have it available for rent during the week and claim 5/7 of the expenses (because it was available for five out of seven days each week). The Tax Office is awake to the fact that the peak renting time for holiday homes is weekends and entire weeks rather than weekdays.

Exit Strategies

A successful investment strategy doesn't simply involve buying and operating properties. The exit strategy has a significant impact on overall success. What good is a real estate wealth-building plan if you put little or no thought into the endgame? Begin your exit strategy planning before you buy the asset. You can always change or modify your plans, but proper planning prior to acquisition is essential to the success of your exit strategy.

TIP

When you're looking to buy rental real estate with upside potential, seek properties that have deferred maintenance and cosmetic problems that allow you to buy at a good price. When you go to sell your property, you want to get full value; so, before you begin to show your available property, scrutinise the kerbside appeal and physical condition for items that need attention. Don't rely on your own eye; ask a trained professional real estate agent or property manager who isn't familiar with the property to give you some feedback. Even a trusted friend could provide the 'fresh set of eyes' needed to see little problems that could reduce a buyer's offer price.

When the time comes to sell the property, you have several options, but not all of them will have the same tax consequences.

Outright sale

One exit strategy is to simply sell the property and report the sale to the ATO. With the capital gains tax rates, this strategy may work for taxpayers nearing the end of their prime real estate investing years who are looking to slow down and simplify their lives.

In an outright or all-cash sale, you simply sell the property and determine whether you have a taxable gain or loss when compiling your tax return. If you have a gain, CGT is due and, if the property has been held for at least 12 months, half of the capital gain is waived, making an effective maximum of 23.5 per cent apply.

In Australia, capital gains tax is due when 'a CGT event occurs'. For most sales, a CGT event usually occurs at the time a contract for sale is signed. However, some exemptions may apply, and property sellers are recommended to see their accountant prior to signing any contract to sell.

TIP

Although the sale of a property can make sense, you may consider refinancing an investment property with substantial equity as an alternative way to free up cash for other real estate acquisitions or other investments.

Calculating gain or loss and tax liability on sale

Preparing and retaining accurate records, from the initial purchase of your rental property and throughout your ownership, is extremely important because you must report a capital gain or loss involving real estate investment property to the ATO. These days, it is simple to retain records for your investment property and portfolio in special folders on your computer, plus professional property managers will provide you with annual financial reports for each of your properties.

Several factors go into the required calculation to determine whether the sale produces a gain or a loss:

>> The sale price is a major factor.

>> Any capital improvements made to the property should be included.

>> Accumulated building depreciation claimed during the holding period increases your taxes when it's partially recaptured.

The following series of five steps outlines the calculation of net sales on proceeds, total gain or loss on sale, the adjusted cost basis (taking into account capital improvements and building depreciation), reportable capital gain (after deducting previous unused losses) and, finally, the total tax liability from capital gains tax.

Step 1: Determine the net sales proceeds

The net sales proceeds are the gross sales price minus the selling expenses (see Table 15-2). The selling expenses are those costs incurred to consummate the sale, such as agent commissions, legal and accounting fees, settlement fees, title insurance and other closing costs.

TABLE 15-2

Calculating Net Sales Proceeds

Gross sales price	$900,000
Minus selling expenses	(40,000)
Net sales proceeds	$860,000

Step 2: Determine the adjusted-cost basis for the property

When the property is acquired, the cost basis is simply the original cost of the property (the purchase price) plus stamp duty, transfer costs and valuation costs.

If the owner didn't purchase the property, as in the case of property received as an inheritance or gift that was purchased before CGT came into existence, the basis is usually the fair market value at the time of transfer.

However, the basis isn't static and changes during the ownership period. To adjust the original basis, three factors are taken into account (see Table 15-3 for the sample calculations):

>> **Capital improvements:** During the holding period, owners often make some capital improvements or additions to the property. *Capital improvements* are defined as money spent on capital works to improve the existing property or construct a new building or additions. The adjusted basis is increased by capital improvements, because capital works are normally written down as building depreciation. (The cost of capital improvements is added to the original acquisition cost to determine the adjusted basis.)

Routine and normal repairs required to keep the property in good working order over its useful life are deductible expenses during the tax year in which they're incurred. They're not capital improvements for the purpose of the adjusted-basis calculation. For example, replacing a few tiles or even reroofing a portion of the building is a repair, but completely replacing the roof is a capital improvement. A newly constructed addition that increases the rentable square metreage of the rental property is a capital improvement. The capital improvement includes all costs incurred, such as contractor payments, architect fees, building permits, construction materials and labour costs.

>> **Recovering building and capital works depreciation:** At the same time, building depreciation claimed each tax year is accumulated and reduces the adjusted basis of the property (if it was acquired, or the cost was incurred, after 13 May 1997).

TABLE 15-3

Calculating Adjusted-Cost Basis

Original acquisition cost or basis	**$520,000**
Plus capital improvements	40,000
Minus accumulated building depreciation*	(50,000)
Adjusted basis	**$510,000**

*If acquired after 13 May 1997.

Step 3: Determine the total gain or loss on the sale

The total gain or loss is determined by taking the net sales price and subtracting the adjusted basis (see Table 15-4).

TABLE 15-4

Calculating Total Gain or Loss on Sale

Net sales proceeds (from Table 15-2)	**$860,000**
Minus adjusted-cost basis (from Table 15-3)	(510,000)
Total gain (or loss) on sale	**$350,000**

Step 4: Adjust the total gain by previous years' capital losses

If you have unused capital losses (from, say, a previous rental property sale or shares sold at a loss) from previous tax years, deduct them from the net sales proceeds (see Table 15-5). The previous years' unused capital losses are those losses that you couldn't use in prior tax years because you didn't have offsetting gains.

TABLE 15-5

Calculating Reportable Capital Gains

Total gains on sale (from Table 15-4)	**$350,000**
Minus unused capital losses	(25,000)
Reportable capital gain	**$325,000**

Step 5: Determine total tax liability

The reportable capital gain is considered assessable income unless the property was held for more than 12 months. Most real estate investors hold property for more than 12 months and qualify to have the capital gain reduced by 50 per cent. (Also, if the property has been held for less than 12 months, all cost recovery that has been taken will be recaptured as ordinary income.)

Half of the capital gain, or appreciation gain, is taxed at the taxpayer's MTR (if the property was held for more than 12 months). The following example in Table 15-6 assumes the maximum MTR, including Medicare Levy (47 per cent) is being paid, resulting in a tax liability of $102,225. If you've already retired when the sale of your property (or CGT event) occurs, your MTR is likely to be lower.

TABLE 15-6

Calculating Total Tax Liability

Reportable capital gain (from Table 15-5)	**$325,000**
Times CGT discount rate	50%
Capital gain (added to ordinary income)	**$162,500**
Times marginal tax rate	47%
Total tax liability	**$102,225**

REMEMBER

The taxation of real estate is complicated and constantly changing, so we've just covered the tip of the proverbial iceberg here. Proper tax advice from accounting professionals is a must.

Gifts and bequests

Gifting a property during your lifetime is usually not a great idea, except in rare circumstances, because it will set off tax implications for the person making the gift. In most cases, a capital gains tax event occurs for the original owner at the time of transfer, meaning CGT needs to be paid for the year of transfer. For instance, if a property had originally been bought for $100,000 and was now worth $500,000, the original owner might have a capital gain of $400,000 on which tax would be paid (if a post-1985 asset), and the new owner would have a new cost basis of $500,000.

An investment property bequeathed at death carries the same tax cost basis from the original owner to the new owner. For example, if the cost basis of the property is $100,000, even though the fair market value at the time of the gift is $500,000, the recipient's tax basis remains $100,000. If the recipient were to immediately sell the property, she would have a taxable gain of $400,000.

However, for the deceased's principal place of residence (home), death provides a tax-free transfer (unless the home was used for income-producing purposes, such as having it rented out, immediately before the death). That is, if the home was bought 20 years ago for $100,000 and is worth $500,000 on the day the deceased died, then the recipient gets a new cost base of $500,000. Further, the recipient has two years from the date of death to sell the house for the proceeds to remain CGT-free.

So, if you want to make your real estate wealth-creation strategy span multiple generations, consider taking advantage of these tax benefits!

Chapter **16**

Building a Portfolio

'The journey of 10,000 miles starts with a single step'. This old proverb can be easily adapted to explain the most important concept in the world of investment. That is, if you have a certain dream or ambition — to be that successful businessperson, self-made investment millionaire or property tycoon — you don't just magically become that person. You have to make a start or *take that first step*.

Property portfolios don't just appear (unless your property-portfolio-owning parents died and left you the lot). The most successful real estate investors inevitably start with a single property. How they move from there to being the owners of a 'multimillion-dollar portfolio' is a well-worn path that has been followed by millions of people around the world. Investing in property isn't a step-by-step process that guarantees success, but offers enough common principles for those with commitment to follow.

Property investment isn't necessarily easy. And it requires years of patience and probably a bit of luck. Property prices can go through long periods of stagnation or even falling real prices (that is, after taking into account inflation), which removes the easiest way to having your properties create wealth — capital growth. During some cycles, rents can also refuse to nudge higher, which can dull returns and deny the cash funding for subsequent property purchases. Both of these regular cycles can knock the commitment out of people who are initially enthusiastic about building a portfolio before they've really tasted success.

Getting your mind around building a portfolio largely comes down to understanding a few basic principles — the laws of investment that are the building blocks upon which real property wealth is created. Once grasped, it will be an easier stretch to accept some of the realities of managing a property portfolio — being a landlord to many, diversifying your property holdings, maximising your tax position and owing a bank, potentially, a few million dollars — all of which we discuss in this chapter.

Using Property's Power Tools

The power of compounding returns and the power of leverage are the real secrets behind building a profitable real estate portfolio. They allow even those with relatively modest incomes to control multimillion-dollar portfolios. Along with knowing the basics of the property market itself, a deep understanding of how these two forces can be harnessed to build a portfolio is an imperative.

Compounding returns

School maths classes taught you about the 'power of compounding interest'. If you put $100 into a bank account earning 10 per cent interest, at the end of a year, your $100 will be worth $110. That is, it will have grown by $10. If you leave that $110 in for another year at 10 per cent interest, it will be worth $121. In the second year it will have grown by $11, or $1 more than its growth in the first year. In the third year, it will grow by $12.10; in the fifth year, by $14.64; in the tenth year, by $23.58.

Property investment can be an incredibly powerful investment tool because of the power of compounding. A $600,000 property that rises by a consistent 5 per cent each year will be worth about $631,000 at the end of the first year, $661,000 at the end of the second year, $770,000 at the end of year five and $988,000 at the end of the tenth year.

REMEMBER

No property increases in price that uniformly. In some years, prices may rise 20 or 25 per cent, while in others they may stay stable. Worse — and don't let seminar-based property spruikers fool you — prices can go backwards in real and in actual terms. But the theory of compounding is an important one for property investors, because it's the basis for the development of all portfolios.

Powering with leverage

Aside from the power of compounding, an even more important concept behind property wealth is the power of leverage. Leverage, also known as gearing, is probably the pivotal reason that property is a favoured investment form for many of the world's most financially successful people.

In investment terms, leverage is simply another name for borrowing money to invest. Leveraging is about using OPM (other people's money) to buy property. Like all loans, you're renting OPM, the price of which is called 'interest'.

The fact is that few people buy property with their own cash (and many people invest in property using almost entirely OPM). Most people buy their first property by saving up a deposit, and then borrowing the remaining necessary funds from a bank or other lender to purchase the property.

REMEMBER

Almost all property is bought with some size of loan attached. Often, especially for property investors with substantial equity in other properties, almost the entire purchase price of the property is borrowed (refer to Chapter 5 for information on how much to borrow).

WARNING

Borrowing for property investment means you're taking higher risks. The concept of leverage applies to both rising and falling property values. If you're leveraged and prices fall, your financial position deteriorates faster than someone who doesn't have as much debt. Although investment debt is a proven wealth accumulator over long periods, you need to make sure you understand the risks on both the upside and the downside before borrowing large sums to invest.

Combining compound returns and leverage

The real attraction of property to those who've built, or are building, their own property portfolio, is what happens when the two powerful forces of compound returns and leverage are put together over an extended period.

TECHNICAL
STUFF

A $600,000 property that increases by 5 per cent in a year will be worth $630,000 at the end of that year. But what happens if the buyer who paid the $600,000 for the property in the first place put down only 10 per cent of the purchase price ($60,000) as his own money and borrowed the rest ($540,000)? At the end of a year, if the property has grown by 5 per cent, he will now have equity in the property of $90,000 ($630,000 less the $540,000 loan). The initial $60,000 equity in the property has grown by 50 per cent in a year, to be worth $90,000. After two years, his ownership will have grown to $122,000 and at the end of year ten (assuming no loan principal has been paid off), his equity will have grown to approximately $448,000. Not a bad return on the initial $60,000 investment in ten years.

And what happens to an investor who owns a $2 million portfolio when a 5 per cent rise in values occurs in a year? The portfolio rises in value by $100,000. However, if the investor had equity of $500,000 on the $2 million portfolio (and, therefore, had debt of around $1.5 million) and the portfolio rose by 5 per cent, the investor's $500,000 in equity grows to $600,000, or by 20 per cent.

Buying Your Second Investment Property

Putting the theory into action to build a property portfolio isn't as hard as it may sound. For a start, the good news is that by the time you're in a position to buy your second investment property, you've obviously already learned enough to buy your first — therefore, you don't need to relearn the basics of investment. Additionally, and somewhat inevitably, you'll have made a few mistakes along the way. And we're sure you'll have learned from those, too.

REMEMBER

Typically, buying your second investment property will occur after you've developed some equity in your home and your first investment property. (We don't include your home as an investment property for reasons explained in Chapter 2, but for many the second investment property will be the third property they buy.) For those without a home, the theory of moving from your first investment property to your second is the same as it is for those with a home. The purchase is usually made possible by using the equity already built from previous purchases to help cover the next purchase.

While the value of properties grows, the usual occurrence is that the debt either stays the same or perhaps even falls slowly (if you're paying principal and interest on one or more of your loans). Rising property values give you growing equity — and it's equity that will both bring you wealth from your property and give the bank the security it needs to be confident to lend you more money.

TECHNICAL STUFF

Here's a typical example of increasing equity: A couple bought their home ten years ago and, after spending six years paying down some of their home loan, they bought an investment property. The initial cost of their home was $550,000, which has now grown in value to $850,000 (after some renovations helped improve the property's value). They did their best to pay down the debt on their home in the first few years, but they still retain a debt of $300,000. The investment property they bought four years ago for $680,000 is now worth $840,000. Because they took out an interest-only loan on the investment property, the loan is still $544,000. They're considering buying another investment property valued at $660,000.

Current position:

Home value: $850,000

Home loan: $300,000

Investment property value: $840,000

Investment property loan: $544,000

Total loan-to-value ratio (LVR): 49.9 per cent

Second investment loan request:

Investment property value: $660,000

Investment property loan: $660,000 (using equity from their existing portfolio for deposit effectively means this loan is a 100 per cent loan)

LVR of second investment property: 100 per cent

Combined position (home and two investment properties):

Value of joint properties: $2,350,000

Value of joint loans: $1,504,000

LVR of all properties: 64 per cent

The investor couple now have two purely investment properties worth $1.5 million. However, including their home, they now have property assets worth $2.35 million (although the home is not an investment property, the equity it holds can be used to help fund property investments).

In most cases, assuming the couple have a reasonable income, a lender would usually be comfortable lending them the extra funds for their second investment property, assuming their financial circumstances haven't changed significantly since they bought their first investment property.

Now the couple have an investment debt of $1.504 million — more than the value of their own home. Of that, they get to claim against their tax the interest paid on the investment property loans, depending on a few variables.

REMEMBER

Over time, rents themselves also rise. Apart from paying down the debt on your investment property (which many investors rightly choose not to do if they still have non-investment debt in their names, such as a home mortgage), rising rents should also help you turn negatively geared property into positively geared property, or help you pay down non-deductible personal debt.

Buying the Third, Fourth, Fifth and Beyond

Buying your second investment property is usually much less nerve-wracking than buying your first because you've had some experience. By the time you're in a position to buy your third investment property, the basic theory should be deeply ingrained and you'll have refined your own processes, including location search criteria (see 'Diversifying Your Portfolio', later in this chapter), property style and desired house traits. With that in mind, we take a look at buying that third property and then buying, say, a sixth property.

Property three

For the purposes of this example, we again assume that the investors' first property purchase was a home. Since then, they've bought two investment properties. We continue with the example couple from earlier in this chapter, but we're now three years later. By this time, their entire property-holding portfolio has increased by 5 per cent per annum.

REMEMBER

As the general price of properties rise, so does the value of the average property investment.

Current position:

Home value: $984,000

Investment properties value: $1.736 million

Value of all properties: $2.720 million

Home loan: $300,000

Investment property loans: $1.204 million

Total loans: $1.504 million

Total LVR: 55.3 per cent

Third investment loan request:

Investment property value: $700,000

Investment property loan: $700,000 (using equity from their existing portfolio for deposit)

LVR of new investment property: 100 per cent

Combined position (home and three investment properties):

Value of all properties: $3.420 million

Value of all loans: $2.204 million

Total LVR: 64.4 per cent

The couple now have properties that, combined, are worth $3.420 million, with debts of about $2.204 million. Some people simply can't get their heads around this — the thought of owing a bank nearly $2.2 million wouldn't allow them to sleep properly at night. For them, property investment may be too difficult a step to take. But property investment and significant debt go hand in hand. And what usually occurs is that those who begin property investment learn to understand the nature of investment debt (see 'Understanding Good Debt versus Bad Debt', later in this chapter) and become comfortable with more and more debt over time.

But, if you want to see some serious (good) debt, read on.

Property six

For the investors' sixth property, we've continued to assume growth of 5 per cent a year and that our investor couple have (after their second investment property, bought in year 10) bought an investment property every three years. To give the timeline some perspective, 22 years have passed since they bought their home, 16 years since they bought their first investment property and 9 years since they bought investment property number three. They bought their fourth investment property 6 years ago and their fifth investment property 3 years ago.

If we assume that the couple bought their home when they were 30, they're now 52 years old. (They're probably near the height of their careers and have probably had a couple of children.) They've nearly paid off their home and have five invest-ment properties.

Current position:

Combined property values: $5.849 million

Combined property loans: $2.204 million

Total LVR: 37 per cent

Sixth investment loan request:

Investment property value: $700,000

Investment property loan: $700,000

Total LVR of sixth investment property: 100 per cent

Combined position (home and six investment properties):

Combined property values: $6.549 million

Combined property loans: $2.904 million

Total LVR: 44 per cent

The investors now have a portfolio worth more than $6.5 million. If they stop right there, their property portfolio will be worth approximately more than $12.5 million by the time they turn 60, or $16 million by the time they're 65. That should be enough to retire on!

In these examples, we have assumed no repayment of debt, although rising rents and positive gearing would probably have allowed this to happen.

Even though this example is looking at a scenario that's years from now, the couple now has a clearly large debt by anyone's standards. Many will dismiss this concept as not being possible for them: 'There's no way a bank will lend me that much money!'

If you're thinking that, what you might be forgetting is that the investors don't just have their normal wages to help them meet the mortgage repayments. They also have tenants helping by paying rent (see 'Getting comfortable with big debt', later in this chapter) and the Tax Office will be helping with tax deductions and allowances for depreciation (refer to Chapter 15 for more on tax considerations).

Growing Equity

Property investors tend to continue to hold on to their properties, meaning most wealth made from property continues to sit inside the property asset class, essentially for two reasons. The first is that property entry and exit fees are usually large (up to 6 per cent for entry and about 3 per cent to exit). The second reason is tax — the moment you sell a property (or, more accurately, when the beneficial ownership changes), capital gains tax (CGT) becomes payable and, therefore, a portion of your gains are handed back to the government.

To avoid the high entry and exit fees and capital gains tax, property investors don't buy and sell properties like some investors turn over their shares. If you have to make up to 6 per cent in entry costs and 3 per cent in exit costs, your property has to make at least 9 per cent before you make a cent of profit, plus the time cost of holding the investment. This fact is one of the reasons that property is considered a long-term investment, particularly in Australia. (As a comparison,

New Zealand has no stamp duty or capital gains tax. And, in the US, you can escape CGT by reinvesting the proceeds of your investment within a year.)

If you have a portfolio of properties, like the six-strong portfolio modelled earlier in this chapter, you could manage your holdings so that, when the time comes to sell, you have some choice over how much tax you pay (refer to Chapter 11 for more information on how to hold title).

Getting comfortable with big debt

If you're aiming to become a property mogul, you'd best get used to the idea of owing banks large sums of money. Direct property is an expensive asset class to buy into and it almost inevitably requires putting up some of your own equity and borrowing the rest from a lender.

If you own six properties, as in the example earlier in this chapter (refer to 'Property six') and you've made the most of tax laws to do so, you'll have large debt — nearly $3 million in the example we looked at. That's a difficult thing for many people to understand. Some experts believe in paying down the debt on a property as fast as possible to ensure that the investment becomes positively geared. They also argue that the size of the portfolio doesn't change that position. But, particularly in the early years of buying a property, paying down the debt often doesn't make sense (see 'Understanding Good Debt versus Bad Debt', later in this chapter).

Servicing a 'menagerie of mortgages'

Along with that property portfolio comes the menagerie of mortgages — an array of loans that will often be wildly different in size (and occasionally lenders), even if the beast is always the same (it's still the same old money).

How do you service six properties with millions of dollars of debt (refer to the example in 'Property six', earlier this chapter)? We wouldn't dare say 'easy'. But you don't have to come up with $150,000 a year (that's about 5 per cent, our preferred average rate for considering medium-term interest rates, of $3 million) yourself.

First, you have tenants paying rent. In many cases, over the time you've taken to build the portfolio, the first few properties bought will have seen rent increases and they may now be individually positively geared. Second, depending on the type of property you've bought, you may have a fair amount of depreciation on the capital cost of the houses, providing significant tax deductions (refer to Chapter 15). Depreciation is a de facto form of income for a property investor, by way of a tax return for the depreciation in value of the bricks and mortar.

NEGATIVE GEARING IS (LIKELY) HERE TO STAY

Every decade or so — usually when property prices are hitting new peaks and a chorus of concern is raised about whether young people will ever be able to buy their own property — comes the inevitable call for the abolition of negative-gearing tax breaks. The urgings usually come from individual federal politicians (who aren't speaking on behalf of their party) and state politicians (who have no power over federal tax law), perhaps a few welfare groups, who are keen to be seen to be doing or saying something about the plight of first-home buyers.

The theory is that, if you remove the tax incentives for negative gearing, investors won't be as keen to invest in property. Many would sell out of their negatively geared investments, putting downward pressure on prices, allowing younger people to buy in — a logical argument.

The problem, not usually thought through by those proposing the abolition of tax breaks, is the flow-on effect of investors either selling property en masse, or refusing to invest in property.

What happens if investors aren't interested in property? Two things. First, lower demand means the price of property will fall (as is intended). And, although that may allow first-home buyers to enter the market, it will also dramatically cut the wealth of those who've already bought their own houses. Those people who've already bought their homes are voters too. And they're not going to be too happy with falling house prices.

Second (this point is what's usually forgotten), if investors aren't buying property to rent out, those who wish to rent have fewer places to live. If there's less supply of rental housing, those who still can't afford to buy, or don't want to buy, will have to pay higher rents.

This 'theory' went into practice in Australia in the mid-1980s, when the then Labor government removed negative-gearing provisions. What followed was falling house prices and aggressive rent increases. Within two years, negative-gearing tax breaks were reintroduced. (Arguably, if the law had stayed, the market would have eventually settled itself into some sort of equilibrium. But the backlash was so strong — by investors and tenants — that immediate action was taken.)

Negative gearing isn't necessarily permanently entrenched — but it will be a brave government that tries to remove it again.

If rent and depreciation don't cover your costs, you have a third prong. The Tax Office gives you a portion of your losses back each year because of existing tax rules on negative gearing.

This combination of 'incomes' — rent, depreciation and negative-gearing tax returns — could possibly give an investor with a $3 million loan portfolio a neutrally or even positively geared investment portfolio.

Keeping an eye on leverage

The sorts of debts that are racked up in property portfolios are significant and should be constantly monitored. Your lender, or lenders, will monitor your debt level themselves anyway and won't lend you money if they perceive a big enough risk that you might 'fall over'. But, the more property investors get used to debt, the more debt they tend to be happy to take on. Getting used to the debt that comes with the first investment property is significantly harder than signing up for the debt that takes you from $2.2 million to $2.9 million.

What is more important is the level of leverage in your portfolio. Banks essentially issue their own warning when an investor's overall level of debt exceeds 80 per cent on assets by insisting on lenders' mortgage insurance (refer to Chapter 7) being paid. Say the value of your properties is $2 million. Some banks will let you borrow up to $1.6 million (80 per cent) without charging lenders' mortgage insurance (but this will depend on a number of other factors, including your personal income and rent-related income).

TIP

Be sure to keep your own eye on your debt levels and what you're comfortable with. Keep a constant eye on what property prices are in your area to give you a good idea of what your property's worth. Also be aware of the debt you're carrying. Divide the debt by the total property value and multiply that by 100 to find your personal loan-to-value ratio (LVR). For example:

$$\text{Leverage (LVR)} = \frac{\$1.3 \text{ million}}{\$1.7 \text{ million}} \times 100 = 76.5\%$$

WARNING

Although occasionally going over 80 per cent LVR (and so incurring lenders' mortgage insurance) may be okay in the early stages of your property portfolio development, going over every time you invest in another property would be highly inadvisable. Indeed, this is generally no longer possible due to increased regulation on lenders and some fringe lending opportunities. Lenders' mortgage insurance is expensive in most instances but can make the difference between purchasing a property or not at all, so can be useful for first-time investors.

Understanding Good Debt versus Bad Debt

The concepts of 'good debt' and 'bad debt' need to be discussed here because of their importance to paying down debt when an investor has a lot of it. Bad debt is debt that you can't claim a tax deduction for. It's essentially for consumer goods and includes debt on credit cards, cars, holidays, home renovations and your own home. Good debt is debt that you can claim a tax deduction for, which is predominantly investment debt.

Why is there a difference? The cost of servicing $100 of interest on bad debt is $100. The cost of servicing $100 of interest on a good debt can be as little as $55, if you're on the top marginal tax rate, because of the tax-deductibility of investment debt. (Refer to Chapter 15 for more on tax considerations.)

TIP

What does the concept of good debt versus bad debt mean for investors? It means that, if investors have a mix of good and bad debt in their lives, any spare money they have for debt reduction should be used to pay down the bad debt. Investors, particularly in their early years, often still owe money on their own home. That's the debt they should concentrate on reducing with spare capital. Because of the tax-deductibility of investment debt, no point exists in paying down investment debt while you still have bad debt — including for your own home — on your books.

Diversifying Your Portfolio

The concept of diversification is simple: If you have all your eggs in one basket and the person holding the basket lets go or stumbles, all of your eggs are going to smash. If you have several people holding your eggs in several baskets and one of these people drops a basket, you've still got a lot of other people (hopefully) safely holding your other eggs. (Refer to Chapter 2 for a discussion of diversification.)

Too many Australians break this important rule when it comes to property investment. The temptation to buy an investment property 'just around the corner' from home really should be overcome. If property in your home suburb went through an extended down period, that would be bad enough. But, if your only other major asset was an investment property in that same suburb, you'd be hit twice.

TIP

Diversification doesn't necessarily mean buying on the opposite side of the city to which you live (if you live in a state capital). But it does mean buying somewhere significantly far enough from your home that the direct financial impact of, say, a local major employer going bust would not directly impact on both properties.

If, however, you bought an investment property 20 kilometres away from where you lived (and from the employer that went bust), it's unlikely that very many people employed by that company will be living in that part of town. And although it's possible that the reverse could occur — in trying to diversify, you may end up choosing to buy a property in an area where another major employer falls over — the theory is the same. Having a slightly higher risk of losing one egg is better than having a smaller risk of losing all of your eggs.

Across a city or state

Diversification is easily achievable across large cities. If you live in the northern or eastern suburbs of a major state capital, you could investigate suburbs to the south or west that you think are undervalued, and try to find a property that fits your criteria to buy there.

Only five Australian cities have one-million-plus populations. In cities of that size, even if the largest private employer in town collapsed, there's enough industry to keep the impact to less than about 1 per cent of the population. With virtually all other towns in Australia having fewer than 500,000 people, at least one employer would represent 2 or 3 per cent and as much as 5 or 6 per cent of the entire local workforce.

If you live outside a major capital city, consider buying in your state capital to give you the diversification benefits of a big city, particularly as it relates to employment opportunities.

Across Australia

Buying interstate can be advantageous. Australia is a large country with a small population. And it's very rare indeed that the pistons that fire the various economies of this country are firing at the same speed at the same time.

Indeed, the term 'two-speed economy' was coined in Australia in 2006 to explain how the 'resource-rich' states of Western Australia and Queensland were experiencing superior economic growth to the non-resource-rich states of New South Wales, Victoria and Tasmania. This was particularly true of property prices. Property prices in Melbourne, Sydney and Brisbane went for a canter between about 1996 and 2003–04. During that time, little out of the ordinary happened with Perth and Adelaide property prices. But during 2005 and 2006, Melbourne and Sydney property prices either tumbled or stagnated, while Perth (and more broadly Western Australian) property prices took off like a rocket, as money poured into the state as a result of the resources boom. Outside of their state capitals, Queensland and South Australian real estate prices showed similar strength on the back of resources.

It is generally accepted that property markets are doing different things at the same time for a variety of factors, including the strength or weakness of the local economy, jobs growth, migration patterns, as well as affordability considerations. The rise in interstate investors over recent years has been predominantly due to investors taking advantage of differing market cycles around the nation.

You can find plenty of opportunities interstate and there may be benefits in regards to land tax (refer to Chapter 9). But you need to spend even more time than normal making sure that all the right research is done, because you won't have a good idea about the suburbs or towns there to start with. When considering buying interstate, or anywhere where you are not familiar, working with experts, such as buyers' agents and QPIAs, is advisable. Look for experts who not only research different markets across the country but also have had success in purchasing there for their clients.

Building an income stream

You make your money from real estate in two ways — through capital gains from the value of the property rising or through having properties that provide a passive income. Of course, you can make your money from a combination of both.

Like actual property prices, rents can stay dormant for long periods. During these times, rents can rise less than inflation for several years, meaning your income is effectively going backwards in the same way that it can go backwards sitting in a low-interest bank account. But, over longer periods, rents would have to rise or there'd be no incentive to buy (either as a home or for investment).

Assuming that the six-strong property portfolio outlined earlier in this chapter had a 4 per cent yield from rent (which is about average for yields generally), that portfolio would be producing an income of approximately $660,000 a year by the time the couple were age 65. And, if the rents from those properties rise by 4 to 5 per cent a year, that's a very healthy income indeed.

The Part of Tens

Discover ten proven ways to enhance the value of a property.

Keep in mind our ten favourite real estate wealth-building strategies.

Chapter **17**

Ten Ways to Increase a Property's Return

As we cover through this book, you receive a return on your real estate investments essentially from four basic factors — positive cash flow, equity build-up from paying down your loan, tax benefits and property appreciation. A great aspect of real estate is that you can buy properties according to your particular financial and personal needs. Different properties are geared towards achieving more of one of these types of return than another. For example, investors with significant income from other sources may be able to take the longer term focus that negatively geared properties offer, taking in the tax benefits, and not worry as much about positive cash flow. Investors nearing retirement will prefer properties that create a positive income from day one. And all investors look forward to appreciation (though properties that are negatively geared from day one usually appreciate faster than those that are positively geared from day one).

Successful real estate investors continually ask themselves: How can I improve the returns on my real estate investment in each category? In this chapter, we highlight ten of the best ways you can enhance your return on investment with rental properties.

Raising Rents

Although rental properties may have other sources of income, the largest source is inevitably rent. So real estate investors wisely begin with an understanding that rent increases lead to greater cash flow.

However, setting the weekly or monthly rents and maintaining them at optimum market levels is one of the most common challenges faced by property owners. Many rental property owners are reluctant to raise rents, out of fear they'll lose good tenants. This is a valid concern but shouldn't prevent you from getting rents to market level and maintaining them there — one of the fastest and simplest ways to improve your cash flow. Of course, you should always look for cost-effective ways to improve the property and make sure that your rents are competitive and fair.

TIP

We recommend raising the rental rate modestly each year rather than waiting for two or three years and then hitting your tenants with a major increase all at once. Tenants are less likely to move as they understand that the costs of operation rise slightly each year.

If your rents are already at market levels, look to make upgrades to the property to justify higher rents. Maybe the addition of a dishwasher, air conditioning unit, remote control for the garage, an exhaust-vent unit above the stove or the addition of a deck or awning will be an improvement that justifies higher rent. Any improvements that enhance the quality of living or bring the property to a level similar to higher priced properties in the area can justify an increase to the rent being charged, and will probably be a deductible expense, or an item that can be depreciated or claimed as a building cost write-off.

Reducing Turnover

The single most important factor in determining the expenses of most rental properties is turnover of tenants. In both residential and commercial properties, turnover is simply bad for the bottom line. A tenant moving out almost certainly means a loss in rental income (on average, up to three weeks for a residential property, longer for commercial properties), plus you may be hit with some expenses (cleaning, maintenance, repairs and capital improvements) to make the place attractive to show the next prospective tenant. Signing long-term leases with quality tenants, continually maintaining the property in top condition and being responsive to tenant concerns can help reduce turnover, which directly improves the property's profitability.

Another effective tool to reduce the loss of rent when a tenant vacates is to get the premises advertised as being 'available soon' or 'available from 27 August', for example. As most tenants now first see their new home online (and can elect to receive automatic updates by email), you can almost have your place re-let the first day it's vacant, dramatically cutting your income losses. If you want to show prospective tenants through your property before the current tenant has vacated, make sure you seek permission and give the requisite notice. Also, as soon as you receive a tenant's notice to vacate, immediately seek permission to enter and determine what you need to do to make the property ready for the next tenant.

Subdividing and Developing

Properties on large blocks of land can be perfect candidates for development through subdividing the block and building a second income-producing dwelling. Houses built in the 1950s, 1960s and 1970s in major metropolitan cities in that 'middle ring' out from the CBD were often built on enormous blocks of land (the old quarter-acre block, or bigger). Often, the house was built nearer the front of the land (deliberately to leave a big backyard). In those circumstances, you may have the scope to build a second income-producing house or unit on the back half of the block, with an easement up the side for access, often called a *battleaxe block* because of the shape of the new lot created.

Councils and state governments usually encourage this type of development, because it helps to slow a city's urban sprawl, creates more efficient use of scarce land and adds critical mass for use of local facilities (particularly public transport, schools, hospitals, parks and other council and government-run services). The first port of call for anyone considering any sort of subdivision should be the local council, where you can find out how their process works and what development obstacles you may encounter.

WARNING

Property development is a different game to property investment and requires a different set of skills. Although investing in real estate is accepted as being at the low end of the risk-and-reward scale, property development is another step up the risk chain. You're betting not only on property, but also on your skills as a project manager, as you try to tie together your planning, organising and negotiating skills for the development of a house. Obviously, the increase in risk comes with the potential increase in reward also.

Keeping Your Bank on Its Toes

Banks need regular reminding that they shouldn't be taking your business for granted. They occasionally need to make you feel special in order to keep you as a satisfied customer. The problem is that banks, like all service providers, don't pay attention to customers who seem to be satisfied (or don't complain), even if they're getting a raw deal. Many customers don't know that they're getting a raw deal. The thinking is that, if the customer isn't whingeing, then they probably aren't unhappy. Those who are in regular contact with their service providers will get a better ongoing deal — 'It's the squeaky wheel that gets the oil'.

You don't have to be on the phone complaining to your bank manager or mortgage broker every month. But, even if everything is going fine and you're not in touch to complain, you should get on the phone to your personal representatives a couple of times a year to find out if they could, or should, be doing more for you.

Every two years, you should effectively put your banking business out to tender again. Find out exactly what's in your current deal and then go and talk to a mortgage broker to find out how your current deal stacks up against the competition. If it doesn't stack up, you've got two choices. The first is to take the new deal. The second is to go back to your bank and ask them to match it.

TIP

Don't let interest rates become the be-all and end-all of your decision to switch lenders. Interest rates are obviously important for real estate investors, but you should also take into consideration the other services your lender provides. Some of the other services (fee-free loans, zero application fees, free credit cards, discounted insurance and so on) may be worth keeping.

TIP

Although you can gain significant interest rate discounts by having all your business with the one lender, having two or more banks with parts of your business isn't necessarily wrong. You can play them off against each other as you look to build your portfolio by asking them to provide their best deal when you look to take out a new loan.

WARNING

Before signing up for new financing at another lender, always check to make sure that getting out of your current loan isn't going to cost you an arm and a leg in pre-payment penalties. Most loan products nowadays will let you out if you've been with them for a certain period. If exit fees apply, find out exactly how much they'll be — you may find switching lenders is still worthwhile, because the lower interest rate at the new lender will pay off the fees and charges within a few months or a year.

Maintaining and Renovating

The kerbside appeal or first impression that your property gives is critical to your overall success. Far and away the easiest way to increase cash flow and increase value is to simply clean up and address the deferred maintenance found in most properties. One of the fundamental rules of real estate is simple supply and demand. If your property really stands out and looks much better than comparable properties, you generate high demand; your rental will stay full at top market rents. That's what cash flow is all about.

Besides attending to the deferred maintenance, another great way to increase cash flow (and value) is to renovate the property. The key here is to spend money only on items that enhance the property and provide a quick payback.

TIP

For residential rentals, the best return on investment inside the property is in updating the bathrooms and kitchens. Off-street parking and security measures (such as key-operated locks on ground-floor doors and windows) can also be a positive enhancement in areas where crime is a concern.

One of the most cost-effective ways to increase the aesthetics and kerbside appeal of any type of property is through landscaping improvements. Often you can simply replace dead plants. If you want to do more, have a landscape gardener make suggestions. Whenever you consider these things, be sure to look into the installation of smart ways to conserve water.

Cutting Back on Operating Expenses

One of the first steps to take after you purchase a rental property is to evaluate current operating expenses, with a view to finding room for improvement, particularly without negatively impacting your tenants.

For larger properties, ask the local utility companies for tips to reduce usage. New technology is making the use of solar energy more attractive, and governments can have incentives for items such as rainwater tanks that can be used for gardening, rather than using town water. Many state governments and councils in Australia have passed laws making it possible (in some states compulsory for new properties) to install individual meters for each dwelling on a property. The rapidly increasing cost of water and sewerage services in many areas of the country may make the installation of individual meters cost-effective for your properties. Large water users who suddenly have to pay for their own consumption often soon learn to conserve a little better.

THE DANGERS OF CUTTING CORNERS

Although carefully screening your expenses can have a significant positive impact on your cash flow, don't go overboard and cut expenses too much. Always use licensed professionals where required and secure proper building permits. Being stingy with spending on your property is pointless — landlords who don't quickly attend to problems and make reasonable improvements to a property are the ones who have higher turnover. Tenant turnover is expensive (refer to 'Reducing Turnover' earlier in this chapter) because of lost rent and more regular updating being required.

For larger residential and commercial properties, ask each of the current contractors and service providers to present a proposal or bid for ongoing or new work required. Get some other local companies to provide quotes for the work and ultimately give your business to those firms that offer the best value. As your real estate portfolio grows, you'll find that contractors and service providers offer discounts based on volume.

Taking Advantage of Tax Benefits

The tax benefits received from real estate vary from investor to investor, but most rental property owners find tax benefits to be a boost to their return.

Even novice real estate buyers can take advantage of the generous tax savings with the capital gains exclusion for their principal residence. This exclusion allows vendors to avoid capital gains tax (CGT) on the profit from selling their homes. You can do up your home and sell it for a profit as many times as you like over a lifetime (as long as the ATO accepts that it was your principal place of residence — refer to Chapter 15). For investors willing to live in the property during renovation, serial home selling can produce significant tax-free profits (refer to Chapter 2 for this option).

Real estate investors, however, can't escape paying capital gains tax. If an investment property changes beneficial owners, CGT is payable. The good news is that the amount of your capital gain is halved for taxation if you've owned the asset for longer than 12 months.

As covered in Chapter 15, depreciation allows the owner to take a non-cash deduction that reduces the investor's taxable income or increases the negative gearing. Land isn't depreciable, so the amount of depreciation is determined by the value of the buildings (built after September 1985) or the value of improvements and contents, as the Tax Office allows most of those items to be written down. Always get a professional (perhaps your accountant could recommend a professional to you) to do a proper depreciation schedule of the property for you. Depreciation deductions are a non-cash item, so they often result in a taxable loss, even if the actual cash flow for the property is positive.

Being Prepared to Move On

When most people think about real estate, they correctly determine that capital appreciation is how the real money is made. Over time, property has proven to be an asset class that increases in value. Even an average annual rate of appreciation of 5 per cent dramatically increases your net worth over time. For an investor with $2 million of property assets, an increase of 5 per cent for a year is $100,000, which is certainly nothing to sneeze at.

However, appreciation can be heavily influenced by outside forces, such as the condition of the suburb, the local community and the local economy. That's why real estate investors need to perform a thorough investigation of an area where an investment is being considered (as we discuss in Chapter 10). But even after you buy a property, you can't simply sit back and let the investment ride as the area deteriorates around you. If the neighbourhood you're in starts to take a downward turn, be prepared to sell and reinvest in a more dynamic area that offers more upside potential.

Adding Value through Change in Use

The entrepreneurial spirit of real estate investors is also rewarded when they're able to increase the return from real estate by adding value through a change in use. A change in use is taking land that isn't currently being used optimally or, as valuers phrase it, for its highest and best use, and repositioning the property in a manner that results in the highest value. Several common ways to achieve this are possible, including

>> **Improving the land use:** The process of gaining the necessary approvals to put land to a more productive use can take time, but is an extremely powerful way to increase the value of real estate. In nearly every city or town in the country, some land uses, typically agricultural, become less productive (or inadequate) as the area is developed. Taking the steps to get this land approved as residential or commercially zoned property can dramatically enhance property value.

>> **Converting use:** The conversion of real estate to another use isn't a new idea, but real estate developers have increasingly practised the concept in recent years. Many other examples of change in use exist: the conversion of apartment blocks to *strata-titled* apartments or units that you can sell individually, or the modification of old warehouses to residential loft apartments and offices.

Improving Management

Management is the one aspect of owning real estate that offers owners an advantage over other types of investments. You can't call Bill Gates and tell him to change Microsoft's products or pricing, even if you do own shares in the company, but superior management of your own rental properties can have a direct impact on your results.

The ability to control and immediately implement different management strategies can lead to more satisfied tenants and longer term tenancies. Some owners are very hands-on with their properties (which we don't recommend for first-time investors or those who aren't prepared to stay on top of current laws — refer to Chapter 13 for more on property management). Most prefer to let a professional handle the day-to-day challenges. A savvy investor knows that the best returns on investment go to owners who have top management. Give your real estate agent a chance if they make an error (no-one's perfect), but be prepared to sack them and get another manager if you're having to manage the manager too much.

Chapter **18**

Ten Steps to a Real Estate Fortune (Or a Great Second Income)

M any real estate spruikers make it sound really easy for anyone to make a fortune in property investment overnight. Buying distressed properties can provide handsome returns, and acquiring real estate below its intrinsic value will no doubt enhance your chances of financial success.

This is simply the traditional sage advice (buy low, sell high) applied to real estate. And, if it can be done routinely and without problems with dreadful timing (buying just before a crash), devastating physical problems, or failing to cover your expenses, time and tax with a high enough profit, then it can be quite fruitful.

However, finding well-located, physically sound properties that are available at below-market prices isn't simple. Most sellers know the value of their property and don't simply give away a great property. We often think that the old saying, 'You get what you pay for' was coined by a real estate investor who just bought a bank's mortgagee sale property only to find it has a termite or drainage problem.

In our experience, successful real estate investors tend to be savvy, hard-working, conscientious individuals who enthusiastically perform comprehensive due diligence before buying a property and work with a team of experienced and professional experts. They don't reinvent the wheel with each deal, because they know what sort of property they're after. They have a vision and use their tried-and-true game plan for each property. If you develop these talents, you can uncover unique properties with value-added potential that are often missed by your competitors.

Sometimes the local market conditions *will* be conducive to acquiring properties that are distressed or on favourable terms. These can be great buying opportunities that shouldn't be missed. Just be sure that you've thoroughly checked out the property, you stay disciplined and don't overpay, and then implement your value-adding and sale plans.

Other times you'll encounter available properties that seem fully valued and offer only incremental opportunities to quickly make physical improvements or enhance cash flow. But these properties can still be great additions to your real estate portfolio, and should be acquired when they have a strategic location or are located in the path of progress and are poised for long-term stable growth in rental rates. These are the cornerstones of your real estate portfolio — the keepers.

The ultimate goal is to build a sustainable real estate portfolio through opportunistic buying. Sometimes a buy-and-flip opportunity will arise; however, most of the time, the best plan will be to buy and hold.

You look to raise the capital value of your investment through smart capital expenditure and look to build up that equity to cover your lender's requirements for the next property. You may, meanwhile, come across opportunities to make a quick profit through a buy-and-flip property. Don't forget, however, that you need to have held a property for a year before you qualify for the 50 per cent capital gains tax reduction.

General real estate cycles and the economic conditions in your local market area dictate which approach is appropriate at any given time. The key is to have a long-term plan to continually reinvest your gains, whether that's cash or equity growth, back into the acquisition of more properties, unless the market conditions are so unfavourable that all local properties are overvalued. Then you want to reinvest your proceeds into improvements of your current properties or seek real estate investments in other markets where the prices aren't unrealistic.

The ultimate goal is to use the steady appreciation strategies to build your real estate holdings into a larger portfolio of properties. Ultimately, you build your real estate holdings into a portfolio of quality properties and utilise the buy-and-hold-for-your-lifetime strategy to create a comfortable lifestyle.

We suggest that you begin investing in real estate with small residential properties, such as houses and units (but not necessarily apartments because they lack scarcity value). The initial capital requirements for residential properties are generally lower than for commercial properties. After you've mastered residential investment, you may want to consider investing in commercial properties, which can offer higher sustained returns.

The secrets to making money in real estate are really quite simple — buy right, add value, reinvest and take the opportunity to sell if the right offer rears its head. In this chapter, we give you ten methods to achieve a real estate portfolio that will substantially improve your wealth.

Building a Portfolio through the Power of Compounding

One investment property on its own is unlikely to allow you to reach your dream of wealth through owning real estate. For real wealth, you need to build a property portfolio. Unless you've got several million dollars up your sleeve (in which case, you're already there), you need to take a long-term view about real estate and aim to create your fortune through buying a number of properties over a period of several years.

No set number of properties will work for everyone. Some people invest in property because they want to be a little more comfortable in retirement. Others want to be very comfortable in retirement. And still others want to be rich. To achieve any of these aims in property, you need to have a plan in place (write it down and put it in a place where you can refer to it easily) that may outline how many properties you need to have in your portfolio in order to achieve your dream. These days, a number of property wealth advisory firms exist to help you unpack all of this but make sure they are experienced professionals with the relevant qualifications and industry memberships before choosing to work with them.

REMEMBER

Property's real power comes from time — the power of compounding. If an $800,000 property's value increases by 6 per cent a year, it will be worth about $1.07 million after five years or $1.432 million after ten years. But, if you buy other properties along the way, with each increase in property values you would quickly have a collection of assets (properties) that could have a value of a few million dollars. If $2 million increases in value by 6 per cent, you have an increase of $120,000. And getting that growth, on average, each year is a very powerful wealth builder.

Moving Debt from 'Bad' to 'Good'

Although the best investment strategy is to buy top-notch properties at low prices and hold them forever, occasionally the circumstances dictate that you should sell a property. At other times, selling an investment property is the right decision because it could help your overall financial position.

Selling a property may present an opportunity to rearrange your debt structure. Australian tax law creates two distinct forms of debt. 'Bad' debt is debt that you can't claim a tax deduction for, usually because it's for personal use. 'Good' debt gets its name because you can claim a tax deduction for the cost of the interest, thereby reducing the average cost. See Chapter 16 for more on these two debt types.

If you want to trade up your own home, for example, but lack the required equity in your existing home, or would have an uncomfortably large home mortgage, selling an investment property may help by minimising bad debt.

If you had a $400,000 debt on your home loan, it would cost you $20,000 a year in interest repayments (assuming a 5 per cent interest rate). If you also had a $400,000 debt on an investment property, the $20,000 annual interest payment would be a tax deduction and you would get as much as $9,000 back on your tax return (if you're paying the top marginal tax rate). In this situation, you have two debts. One of them costs you $20,000 a year, while the other could cost only $11,000 a year.

Reducing your bad debt is a good way of improving your overall cash position. You can do this in a number of ways:

>> **Pay down your bad debt.** If you have excess funds each month from your property investments, use those funds to pay down the personal, non-deductible debts on your own home, personal car or credit cards.

>> **Make interest-only repayments on your investment property.** When multiple property debts exist and one of them is a home loan, make your investment property loan repayments interest-only. Banks will usually be happy, as long as you're paying down the principal on at least one of your loans with them.

>> **Sell an investment property.** If you get a few years into your property portfolio strategy and you still have significant debt on your own home, you may find an opportunity to take some profits by selling a property and paying down your home mortgage, and then reborrowing for another investment property. Beware of the impact of stamp duties and sales costs on this process, however, as they'll eat into your profits.

Valuing Your Time

When you enter the world of real estate investment, you're effectively running your own small business. Whether you own one, two, three or more properties, you need to make some decisions about what you're going to do in terms of property management and what you're going to pay others to do on your behalf.

A good starting point is to put a value on your own time. What do you get paid for your ordinary work? If you're paid $120,000 a year, that's roughly $60 an hour for a 38-hour week. From this point, many people believe that your free time takes on a higher value because it's a scarcer resource. You might place a value on your free time of, say, $80 an hour.

How much time is it going to take you to do a particular job on one of your properties? Having a rental property off the market for three weeks while you spend evenings and weekends painting, in a misguided attempt to save the fee a contractor would charge for painting, makes no sense. It costs you $1,500 in materials, you've lost $2,000 in rent, and you've lost your free time for three weeks. The painter would take two days on the job, and likely do a much better job than you as well, and you'd have the place ready to be tenanted again in no time.

You need to make these decisions regularly. And don't forget to take into account that the money you spend on paying people to work on your rental property usually qualifies for a tax deduction or can be depreciated.

REMEMBER

The argument about the value of your time is probably most important when deciding whether you want to manage your property yourself. Our recommendation is that, particularly if you have only one or two properties, hiring professional property managers is best. Managing your own single property will save you, perhaps, $200 a month. How much extra work will you have to do for that? Perhaps none, if you have a great tenant, who never needs to be chased up for rent, living in a property that never requires you to spend your precious spare time dealing with contractors to fix annoying little problems. In that situation, saving the money may be worthwhile, but that scenario is rare.

You also need to factor in the cost of keeping current with tenancy laws, registering bonds with the local government authority, the occasional trip to the tenancy tribunal to deal with claims, the cost of time running reference checks on prospective tenants, advertising fees and so on.

You're the only person who can value your time properly and it's you who needs to make those decisions. Also, you need to be honest about whether you could do the job as well as a professional property manager.

Building Up Savings and Cleaning Up Credit

We disagree with anyone who implies that you can begin your real estate investment career without any cash. Our experience is that the best opportunities and the most options are available to those real estate investors who have both cash and good credit.

You can't escape certain out-of-pocket expenses or the opportunity cost of lost income as you expend your time and energy tracking down properties with desperate situations.

Because purchasing real estate virtually always requires you to borrow funds, make sure your credit report is as accurate and as favourable as possible. Your credit score is a key element in not only qualifying for real estate loans, but also getting the best terms to maximise your use of borrowed capital.

Get a copy of your credit report and correct any errors — today. Charges that were actually paid or a department store credit card account that shows late payments when the amounts were disputed can all contribute to a significant reduction in your credit report score. At the very least, ask the credit bureau to place a letter in your file with your version of any disputes. If legitimate delinquent balances appear, formulate payment plans and send the credit reporting bureau updates showing the balance was paid.

REMEMBER

Investing in real estate requires a long-term commitment and strategy, and initially may require some sacrifices — especially if the property is negatively geared and is eating into your personal bank balance.

The new real estate investor should try to buy properties with the opportunity to increase rents with simple spending initiatives and preferably even cutting current expenses. Most people generate wealth and achieve a higher standard of living through sacrifice and living below their means in the short term. Maybe you can live with your current car for a couple of years, or you can pass on the gym membership (that you'll stop using in three months anyway).

Sustained success in real estate requires you to have cash and good credit. So don't procrastinate — begin working on this step right now.

Renting Out Your Holiday Home

If the Great Australian Dream is to own your own home on a quarter-acre block, then the icing on that dream cake (to mix some metaphors) is probably to also purchase a 'holiday home'. That property might be coastal, lakeside, by the river, in the mountains or somewhere interstate.

A holiday home can be the greatest lifestyle asset you ever purchase. But it can also be a financial black hole. Too many people buy holiday homes with the aim of spending a couple of weekends a month and the school holidays there, only to find that they can't get away as easily as they thought they could, work commitments have become more pressing, or the kids have commitments in town and they don't want to go.

If you rent out your holiday home, the property becomes an unusual mix of 'home' and 'investment property'. Part of your expenditure on the house — interest, capital works, agents' fees, insurance and so on — can't be written off (because the house is a personal expense) and part of it can (because the house is also an investment).

If you crunch the numbers and decide that you'd like to make the purchase a mix of second home and investment property, here are some tips that could make it more financially viable:

>> **Live there first:** Spend a bit of time, early on in your ownership, living there so you can find out what the house needs. Don't forget that your occasional tenants will usually expect to have mod cons, such as a microwave and air con, plenty of spare cutlery and glassware, a Smart TV, wifi, streaming options, dishwasher and barbecue.

>> **Make your renovations after the first year:** If you're going to do major renovations to the place, do them after the first year of ownership, when the Tax Office is less likely to quibble about whether they were repairs or upgrades.

>> **Have a locked cupboard:** If you have special personal items (cutlery, wine, books, linen), build a special cupboard with a key-operated lock to house them, so you don't have to cart them to and from home every other weekend.

>> **Rent out during the holidays:** To maximise your income, make the house available for rent for the major holidays in the first few years (mid-December to the end of January, plus Easter, major long weekends and school holidays). These periods are peak season when you can command the greatest rental return. A few years into your property ownership, hopefully with some positive experiences, profits and a growing income stream in hand, you'll be able to afford to use the house during holidays yourself.

>> **Rent out the house as much as you can in the early years:** The first few years of owning any property tend to be the hardest financially. By renting out the property as regularly as possible in the early years, you can help make meeting the ongoing expenses easier.

>> **Apportion tax:** If you're ever audited, the Tax Office takes into account when you had the property 'available to rent'. If you use it personally during the peak times, the ATO may disallow some deductions based on that portion of the usage.

REMEMBER

You need to understand the difference between a home and an investment property. Don't push things with the Tax Office. Carefully work out with your accountant a fair proportion of your expenses to claim against your income and the proportion for personal use.

Buying Property in the Path of Progress

Locate properties that are in the path of progress — areas that will continue to improve through new investment and economic activity (refer to Chapter 10). You can't realistically move your property, so your analysis of the location and its future potential is critical. After you locate the best cities or suburbs, look for the two common types of underachieving real estate assets:

>> Those properties that are tired and worn and have extensive deferred maintenance

>> Those that are physically sound but poorly managed

Buying property in the path of progress requires plenty of research. It's about finding land, rundown real estate or reasonable properties that can benefit from an upcoming increase in the demand for space in the area.

Buying the Right Property at the Best Price Possible

Always buy property for the best possible price. This simple statement makes a lot of sense, but may be easier said than done. We suggest following certain guidelines. A savvy real estate investor usually doesn't buy a brand new or recently renovated property, unless it's in the path of progress or a prime location, because the value-adding or upside has already been taken (by the current owner or developer). These properties may be solid investments, but you'll be limited to the market increases in rent and value only.

However, buying a new or fully renovated property can be a good investment alternative, particularly when the investor can take advantage of depreciation benefits. Buying a residential rental property in the first phase of an oceanfront development or a development in another special location that's difficult to replicate could be a great investment in the long run. The pricing in the first phases of new developments is often very favourable because the developer must pre-sell a certain number of the units before their longer term financing kicks in.

Occasionally, you may have the opportunity to buy a property from someone who requires an immediate sale at significantly below market value. Life happens, and it can create many opportunities to pick up properties on a fire-sale basis. Having cash reserves and/or a line of credit can give you a real advantage when these opportunities arise. Don't miss these windfalls, but don't count on them either!

REMEMBER

For those who want to be involved full-time in their real estate investments, property acquisitions should be those that haven't received the love they deserve and could benefit from some carefully targeted spending. You want to buy properties that offer challenges that match your personal talents, or the expertise of your expert team, so you can use your combined skills and connections to upgrade them, enhance their value and increase the rental income.

Developing an accurate projection of income and expenses requires considerable research to determine what rents could be extracted after you've implemented your planned upgrades. This practice is the only way to know the investment value or what the property is worth to you.

TIP

Two important characteristics of successful real estate investors are discipline and the ability to predetermine the maximum price they'll pay for a property to ensure plenty of room for upside potential. You don't want to simply lower your purchase price by the cost of the repairs, because the value you add to the property should be significantly higher than your out-of-pocket expenses.

Renovating Property Right

If your strategy involves finding properties that are well located and then renovating them to increase cash flow and value, make sure you don't overspend on physical improvements. You only want to make those renovations or upgrades that increase the desirability of the property to your target market. Your property is a rental, not your own home. You may want to put premium countertops and appliances in your home, but you won't get a good return on your investment if you overcapitalise your rental property.

Improvements should allow you to increase the rent or add to the property value so that you receive a return of $2 to $3 for every $1 spent on the improvements. The best properties to renovate for most novice real estate investors are those requiring simple fixes: Painting, landscaping and minor repairs generally offer excellent results for only minor costs. These simple repairs are also either within the DIY skill set of most real estate investors — who may have developed and perfected their talents by maintaining and upgrading their own homes — or are something they could easily project manage.

If you use contractors, get three comparable quotes from licensed, competent professionals. However, if you already know you have a competitive quote, you can expedite the process by asking the contractor if lowering the price by 5 to 10 per cent is possible — that may save the need to get additional quotes.

Whether you do the work yourself or hire a contractor, make sure you obtain all required permits and that all improvements meet the applicable building and occupancy codes.

Keeping Abreast of Market Rents

One of the biggest challenges for most rental property owners is determining the proper rent to charge tenants for newly renovated units. This aspect of property ownership and management simply requires some homework and research — and your property manager will also be able to provide advice on this matter. Every property is unique, but your best indications of the market value of your renovated property can be found through a market survey of comparable properties, or by asking local real estate agents for their estimates.

After you've acquired and upgraded your new rental property, test the rental market by offering your vacant unit or space at the higher market rates you determined in your rental survey. The response you receive from prospects lets you know if you're asking too much or if you still have some upside on your rents.

We recommend that you keep the rent level slightly below the full market rent for existing long-term tenants to show your appreciation for their long-term tenancy and to encourage them to stay.

Increasing Income and Value through Superior Management

Superior management makes the difference between average and excellent returns in the long run. If you renovate and reposition a residential property or a commercial property with new tenants at higher rents, you need to retain the tenants and minimise turnover. You can also further enhance net income by effectively and efficiently controlling expenses.

Even if you've just acquired the property, you need to consistently work your long-term investment strategy by operating and managing the property effectively to achieve maximum value as if you were going to refinance or were preparing the property for sale.

Your target buyer is going to be someone who wants to buy a *turnkey* property (one that's operating optimally and doesn't require renovation or a change in tenants) for personal use or as a prime rental investment (offering a steady, highly predictable stream of income like fixed-interest/bond investors receive). Real estate valuers will determine a higher value for properties with a strong track record of solid rental income. Remember that, to achieve maximum value, you need to have consistent income with rents at market rates, stable tenancy and reasonable expenses. But don't go for lower expenses at the risk of decreasing kerb appeal due to deferred maintenance.

Index

collateral, 53

commercial real estate, 31, 70, 122–123, 181

commission, 57, 59–61, 101–102

community, 163, 170, 171, 172, 173–174

competition, 39, 41, 105

compounding return, 292, 293–294, 319

concessional contribution, 118–119, 132–133

condition, 202–203, 216–217

conditional offer, 50

conflict priority rule, 101

construction-cost depreciation, 272–273

contents insurance, 18, 257, 259–260. *See also* insurance

contingency, 197

contract note, 200

contract of sale, 198–204

contractor, for rental property renovation, 241–242

conveyancer/conveyancing, 52, 215, 216

co-ownership, 207–208

corporate trustee, 127

cost approach to valuation, 186–188

costs of entry, 69–72

council rate, 141

counteroffer, 198–199

credit card, 108

credit report/credit scores, 82, 111–112, 322

credit union, 75

cross collateralisation, 78

D

debt, 104, 105–107, 112, 299, 302, 320

deduction, 15, 27, 138, 268–271, 276

deferred maintenance, 182

demolition, 47

deposit

  banks and, 74

  insufficient income and, 112

  limitations regarding, 71–72

  paying, 200–201

  for property investing, 10

  for rental property, 247

  requirements for, 70

  for residential properties, 25

  standards for, 214

deposit bond, 201

depreciation, 12, 15, 32, 187, 271–275

deterioration, physical, 187

developers, buying from, 63–64

discount variable rate, 85–86

diversification, 29, 74, 125–126, 155, 302–305

due diligence, for accepted offer, 217–225

due-on-sale clause, 98

E

economic development incentive, 163

economies of scale, 103–104, 144

education, 73

emergency fund, 138

entry condition report, 247

environmental inspection, 223–224. *See also* inspection

equity, 77–80, 294–295, 298–301

excess liability (umbrella) insurance coverage, 257

exit fee, 106, 109–110

exit strategy, 285–289

expense statement, 218

expenses, 12, 13, 15, 26–27, 30, 229, 313–314

expressions of interest, 40

external obsolescence, 187

F

fee, 59–60, 65, 144–145, 179–180, 225, 237

financial feeding, 32

financial planning, 17–20

financing. *See* loans and financing

financing condition, 203

fixed-rate mortgage, 87–88, 91–92

fix-up cost, 196–197

flipping, residential property, 42–44

flood, storm and earthquake insurance, 258. *See also* insurance

foreclosure, 79

functional obsolescence, 187

About the Authors

Here are some good reasons we — Nicola McDougall and Bruce Brammall — believe we're an experienced team of successful real estate investors and property investment professionals who have the knowledge to lead you through the property-investment maze:

Nicola McDougall is an award-winning property and finance journalist, co-author of *The Female Investor: Creating Wealth, Security & Freedom Through Property*, business owner, editor, successful property investor, and the chair of the Property Investment Professionals of Australia (PIPA).

She is also the former editor of *Australian Property Investor* magazine and has been involved in property research, analysis and reporting since 2006.

Nicola co-founded Bricks & Mortar Media, a specialist property and finance communications and public relations firm, in 2018.

She has also been the executive manager of Corporate Affairs at the Real Estate Institute of Queensland and is considered one of Australia's most experienced and knowledgeable property journalists.

Nicola has a Bachelor of Journalism and a Master of Creative Industries (Creative Writing) from the Queensland University of Technology.

Bruce Brammall is a licensed financial adviser and mortgage broker, experienced business journalist and finance columnist, bestselling author and successful property investor. As a finance reporter and deputy business editor during his 15 years with Australia's largest selling daily newspaper, the *Herald Sun* — where he got to marry his head for numbers (somewhat rare for a journalist) with writing — Bruce covered the gamut when it came to business and economic issues. He continues to write extensively on property, superannuation, self-managed super funds, shares and the grease that oils property (mortgages and lending) for major media outlets, including News Limited's Australian newspapers (including the *Herald Sun*, the *Daily Telegraph*, *The Courier-Mail*, *The Advertiser*, the *Sunday Times* and *The Mercury*) and *The West Australian*.

In 2008, he wrote *Debt Man Walking: a 10-Step Investment and Gearing Guide for Generation X* (Wrightbooks). The book launched Castellan Financial Consulting (now Bruce Brammall Financial, www.brucebrammallfinancial.com.au), his financial advice business, and, later, Castellan Lending (now Bruce Brammall Lending), his mortgage broking business. Prior to that he wrote *The Power of Property: Securing Your Future Through Real Estate*. They were both bestselling titles. In 2015, Bruce wrote *Mortgages Made Easy: 8 Steps to Smart Borrowing for Homes and Investment Properties*.

His interest in property began in 1999 when, after reading his first real estate investment book, he decided he wanted to buy his own home. He was talked into delaying that ambition by his now wife, Genevieve, who instead 'let' him buy an investment property. She then 'let' him buy more, and more, one or two of which were homes.

Bruce has a Bachelor of Arts (Communication) with a journalism major (University of Canberra), an Advanced Diploma in Financial Services (Financial Planning) and a Certificate IV in Mortgage Broking. He works in Melbourne as the principal adviser and mortgage broker with, respectively, Bruce Brammall Financial and Bruce Brammall Lending.

Bruce and Genevieve live in Melbourne with their children, Ned and Millie.

This book has been adapted by Bruce from the original US edition of *Real Estate Investing For Dummies*, written by Robert Griswold and Eric Tyson. Although the basic principles of property investment are similar the world over, fundamental differences exist between Australia and the United States that affect investment strategies, the seeds of which are sown in the vastly different tax treatments meted out to property investments in each country. Those tax differentials have a cascading effect as they work through the property-investment process.

Dedication

Nicola: For my beloved whanau near and far — Dad and Vick, Josh and Nichole, as well as my siblings, Bruce, Linda and Craig, nieces and nephews, aunties, uncles, in-laws and cousins. And to some of the extraordinary women who are sharing this life journey with me — Julie, Kelly, Marina, Lavinia and Antonia. Love you long time, ladies.

Bruce: For the troika who allowed the second edition of this tome to happen: my wife, Genevieve, and our gorgeous tin lids, Ned and Millie. A more perfect bunch of people to hang out and spend down time with I couldn't have hoped would land in my lap. You are my reason to keep trying harder at everything. Thanks also to all of the wonderful clients and staff (Helen Savage, Ian Wood and Vikky Gallagher) of Bruce Brammall Financial and Bruce Brammall Lending. My businesses wouldn't exist if people didn't read books.

Authors' Acknowledgements

Nicola: My sincere thanks and gratitude go to my amazing editorial team at Wiley, especially my commissioning editor, Lucy Raymond, and publishing editor, Leigh McLennon, as well as many others for their help and guidance.

Updating the third edition was also made somewhat easier by having such a fine text to work from, so I acknowledge Bruce for his narrative prowess.

Much has changed in the property investment world since the second edition was published, so I would like to acknowledge the team at The Property Couch Podcast and Empower Wealth Advisory for their insights into some of the more intricate topics.

I would also like to offer my sincere thanks to my business partner, Kieran Clair, for not only holding the fort in our successful small business while I devoted every spare minute to this project, but also providing valuation expertise used in this edition. Likewise, my thanks go to my Bricks & Mortar Media clients for their continued support.

Gratitude also (again) goes to my husband, Josh, and my friends and family while I secreted myself away from them all to work on this edition.

Bruce: For there to be a second (and now third) edition of a book such as this, the first edition must have hit the mark. So ongoing thanks to those in the responsible roles at the time for making the first edition a success, including former John Wiley & Sons general manager Lesley Beaumont, acquisitions editor Charlotte Duff and editor Kerry Davies.

But fitting in time to write the second edition, around a hectic financial advice and mortgage broking business and family life, is only marginally easier than writing a first edition and not much less daunting. It simply wouldn't have occurred without subtle coaxing from acquisitions editor Clare Weber and project editor Dani Karvess.

Every writer needs editors and I've been fortunate enough to have worked with some very good ones over more than two decades in the craft. Charlotte Duff — back again as editor this time — fits squarely into that category. My sincere thanks go to Charlotte for not just making the editing process headache free, but also improving the book at every turn.

Thanks to co-authors Eric and Robert for providing the original basis for the first edition of this book (published in 2008) with the US edition *Real Estate Investing For Dummies* (Wiley, 2005). The book has been essentially rewritten because of the extensive differences between Australian and US tax laws that change many of the fundamentals of property investment strategies between the two countries.

Thanks to my gorgeous wife, Genevieve, for her never-ending encouragement. And for her ongoing permission to take on these projects — they wouldn't be possible without an understanding partner. To my children, Ned and Millie, thanks for making concentration difficult. It's unusually hard to focus with you two around. And you provide the perfect reason to have a break.

Thanks to my family (Mum, Dad and Dirk), friends, Bruce Brammall Financial and Bruce Brammall Lending clients, colleagues and contacts who, over the years, have extended my property knowledge through their own investment hits and misses.

And, lastly, to former colleague Craig Binnie for throwing me the book that first sparked my obsession with real estate investment. I thank you also for the memorable six-month-long property versus shares argument that followed (though our then colleagues probably don't).

Publisher's Acknowledgements

Some of the people who helped bring this book to market include the following:

Acquisitions, Editorial and Media Development

Project Editor: Tamilmani Varadharaj

Acquisitions Editor: Lucy Raymond

Editorial Manager: Ingrid Bond

Copy Editor: Charlotte Duff

Production

Proofreader: Susan Hobbs

Indexer: Estalita Slivoskey

Printed and bound by CPI Group (UK) Ltd, Croydon, CR0 4YY

22/02/2023

03194225-0001